TIMBERS of the WORLD
WORLD
Volume 2

TIMBERS of the WORLD

Volume 2

TRADA/The Construction Press

The Construction Press Ltd.,
Lancaster, England

A subsidiary company of Longman Group Ltd., London
Associated companies, branches and representatives
throughout the world.

Published in the United States of America by
Longman Inc., New York.

Originally issued as a series of separate publications by the
Timber Research and Development Association.

First published in this format, 1980.

ISBN 0 86095 837 X

Printed in Great Britain by the Pitman Press, Bath

CONTENTS

PREFACE

In 1945 the Timber Development Association, as it was then known, revised a Red Booklet entitled 'Timbers of British West Africa' and republished it as 'Timbers of West Africa'. At that time only a few African timbers were well known to the trade, mainly from the west coast, and the need for information regarding what were then lesser known timbers was great, and for many years the original content and geographical coverage of the booklet were considered adequate. It was revised in 1968 and again in 1972, by the Timber Research and Development Association, and together with its companion booklets, 'Timbers of South East Asia', and 'Timbers of South America', provided a useful service to trade and industry by detailing the practical characteristics of many commercial timber species from these areas.

Timber as a major raw material came to be in greater demand and, in consequence, there was a greater need for a wide knowledge of the world's timber resources. With this in mind, the Timber Research and Development Association decided to publish a series of booklets giving a wider and more adequate account of the commercial timbers of the world. This series of booklets is now brought together to form the present 2–Volume Timbers of the World.

DURABILITY OF TIMBERS

Durability, or resistance to decay, is important when woods are selected for certain uses where the conditions are favourable for decay to occur. Sapwood is nearly always perishable in these conditions, but generally more permeable than heartwood, consequently it should not be used in exposed situations without preservative treatment. Heartwood varies in its natural resistance to decay according to the species and the amount of decay inhibiting substances contained in the wood.

The various grades of durability mentioned in the text are those resulting from exposure tests carried out in the United Kingdom and, accordingly, are approximate values applicable to areas with similar climate.

The tests refer to all-heartwood stakes of 50mm x 50mm section driven in the ground. The five durability grades are defined as follows:

Perishable	Less than 5 years when in contact with the ground.
Non-durable	5—10 years when in contact with the ground.
Moderately durable	10—15 years when in contact with the ground.
Durable	15—25 years when in contact with the ground.
Very durable	More than 25 years when in contact with the ground.

AVAILABILITY OF TIMBERS

Before specifying, it is advisable to check on the availability of the timbers described in this book.

LAYOUT OF THE BOOK

For each geographical area (that is, in each chapter) the timbers are placed in two groups, ie hardwoods and softwoods, and are arranged in alphabetical order of their common names; these names are, wherever possible, the standardised ones given in BS 881 and 589: 1974: 'Nomenclature of commercial timbers, including sources of supply'.

Following the notes on individual timbers each chapter has a guide listing those timbers suitable for specific purposes and a section dealing with the amenability of heartwood to preservative treatment. The book ends with references and an index.

1
PHILIPPINES AND JAPAN

JAPAN

HOKKAIDO

SADO

OKI GUNTO

HONSHU

SHIKOKU

KYUSHU

OKINAWA

BATAAN

LUZON

PHILIPPINES

MINDORO

MASBAT

PALAWAN PANAU

SAMAR

LEYTE

NEGROS BOHOL

MINDANAO

JOLO

PALAU ISLANDS

INTRODUCTION

The geographical scope of this chapter is confined to that part of Asia that includes the islands of Japan and the extensive Philippine Islands.

Japan
Japan consists of a long, narrow, and continuous chain of volcanic islands in the north west of the Pacific Ocean. Its northern limit is the coast of Hokkaido, south of the Kuril Islands, and its southern extreme is at Tokuno Island, north of Okinawa. The islands are bounded on the west by the Korea Strait and the Sea of Japan, and on the east by the Pacific.

The principal islands forming Japan are Honshu, the mainland or main country; Kyushu; Shikoku; Oki Gunto; Osumi Gunto; Tsushima, in the Korea Strait; Awaji, lying between Shikoku and the main island, sacred in the eyes of all Japanese as the first spot on earth to be evolved out of chaos by the gods of heaven at the creation of the world, and to the north, beyond Honshu, Hokkaido, one of the largest islands of the whole archipelago.

Honshu is the largest, wealthiest, and most populous of the islands with an area of some 233 000 square kilometres, while Hokkaido, separated from Honshu by the narrow Tsugaru Straits, has an area a little less than that of Ireland as a whole.

Climate
Japan is subject to greater extremes of heat and cold than England, climatic conditions largely contributing to the comparatively slow growth of trees and the resulting mildness of much of their timber, for example oak and beech.

Hokkaido is usually buried in deep snow during the long winter of four or five months, and the same may be said of all the provinces of the west coast of the main island, which are further exposed to the bitter winds from the Sea of Japan. The east coast is comparatively mild, due to the influence of the Kuro Siwo or Black Stream, the 'Gulf Stream' of the Pacific, which, flowing north from the tropical seas south of the Philippines, strikes the coast of Kyushu in the south-east, and its main flow then skirts the whole of the east coast until finally it is lost in the waters of the northern Pacific. It brings with it warmth and moisture from the tropics and exercises an influence similar to that of the Gulf Stream on the shores of Britain.

In the southern islands the climate and the vegetation are both sub-tropical, and except on the mountain tops snow is unknown. The mean annual temperature in Tokyo is 14°C (57°F), the mean maximum is 30°C (86°F), and the mean minimum, minus 2°C (28°F). The highest temperature recorded on any one day is 36.5°C (98°F) in July, and the lowest, minus 9°C (15°F) in January.

The average rainfall is 3680mm and the average number of days on which either rain or snow falls is 140. The wettest months are June and September, the recognised two rainy seasons, during which torrential rain is often continuous without a break for several days. The first three months of the year are cold and damp, but April and May are generally delightful and seldom marred by high winds or heavy showers, but by far the pleasantest season is the Autumn from October to December, a period known as the Koharu, or Little Spring, when fine weather with bracing air and blue skies can be relied upon.

In few countries are tropical and temperate vegetation so mingled as in Japan, where trees of Europe and North America, such as elm, beech, oak and chestnut, grow almost side by side with bamboo, sugar cane, and tobacco of tropical Asia.

Commercial centres
The increase of manufactured goods since 1945 has produced a steady increase in the urban population, the tendency to migrate to the towns and cities being more marked than anywhere else in the world, and essential to sustain the vast industrial enterprises in the island of Honshu particularly. The great ports and harbours of Osaka, Tokyo, Kobe and Yokohama are principal areas for foreign trade, but as with America and the UK imports of timber form an essential ingredient of industry, and Japan today imports considerable amounts of timber, especially from the Philippines.

Philippine Islands
The Philippines are an extensive group of islands, more than 3000 in number, and with the Sulu Islands cover a land surface of about 300 000 square kilometres. The principal islands are Luzon, Mindanao, Paragua, Negros, Panay, Samar, Mindoro, Bohol, Cebu, Leyte and Masbate. Manila is the capital.

4

The northern extremity of the group is at Batan, South-east of Taiwan, the southernmost point is Jolo in the Celebes Sea, and the islands are bounded on the east by the Pacific, and on the west by the South China Sea.

Mainly of volcanic origin, the Philippines are traversed by irregular mountain ranges, well clothed in vegetation and separated by plains of great fertility, watered by innumerable lakes and rivers affording ample means of transport.

The climate is tropical; rain from south-west monsoon falls between June and September on the west coasts, and from October the north-east trade winds bring rain to the east coasts. The mean annual temperature throughout the islands is $27^{\circ}C$ $(80^{\circ}F)$.

The indigenous flora is generally similar to the Malaysian flora, with the addition of some more northern varieties and also a few Australian genera.

Although large forest areas still exist throughout the islands, much timber was destroyed in the fighting in the last war, and recovery is not only a slow process, but, since considerable efforts are being made to increase the food supply of the Philippines, land clearance schemes have reduced to a degree some previously well-forested areas. Exports of timber to a great extent are confined to the Dipterocarps, especially the lauans; other types are more generally absorbed in home consumption, often on an inter-island basis.

PART I HARDWOODS

AGARU

Dysoxylum decandrum Merr.   Family: Meliaceae

Other names
paluahan, bagulibas, buntugon.

Distribution
Various species of *Dysoxylum* occur in tropical Asia and Australia, and a number are also found in the Philippines, although fairly scattered throughout their distribution.

General characteristics
D. decandrum is a medium-size tree, with a straight bole, and a diameter of about 0.6m.

The sapwood is light yellow in colour, 20mm to 30mm wide, and rather sharply, but irregularly marked off from the heartwood which is light yellow when freshly cut, turning to light yellowish-brown during drying, the colour shading gradually from the lighter inner edge to the darker outer edge of each growth ring. The grain is commonly wavy, giving a beautiful moiré silk effect to the wood. The texture is fine, dense, and smooth and, when fresh, the wood has a characteristic odour reminiscent of sandalwood; this disappears superficially on drying, but is restored if the wood is scraped or cut.

The timber is easy to dry without excessive degrade, easy to work and machine, and is classified as durable, when used in contact with the ground. Weight about 721 kg/m^3 when dried.

Uses
Agaru is similar in general appearance and mechanical properties to Indian satinwood (*Chloroxylon swietenia*), and therefore suitable for high-class furniture and cabinet-work, and to some extent is used in the Philippines for these purposes, but due to its scattered growth, it does not appear in regular quantities on the Manila market, and appears to find a more limited local use in building construction for posts, beams, joists and rafters, flooring, windows and sills, doors and as hewn railway ties.

AGOHO

Casuarina equisetifolia Forst.   Family: Casuarinaceae

Distribution
Occurs in the Philippines in almost pure stands on sandy shores, extending inland along streams and in sandy river beds of 800m elevation.

The tree
A small tree, it may reach a height of 50m but is usually smaller, with a diameter of 0.9m and a clear bole length of about 10m.

The timber
The sapwood is wide and buff-coloured but distinct from the heartwood which is light-red or dark reddish-brown, often with darker, narrow lines of parenchyma. The grain is straight, occasionally crossed, with a fine to moderately fine texture, while the wood is heavy to extremely heavy, weighing on average 1060 kg/m³ when dried.

Drying
Difficult to dry and prone to check and warp even under ordinary air drying. Partial air drying under cover is recommended prior to kiln drying.

Strength
The strength of agoho closely approximates to that of selangan batu merah (*Shorea guiso*) of Sabah.

Durability
Moderately durable.

Working qualities
Rather difficult to work, the wood adjacent to the large rays tending to crumble and tear in sawing and planing, but bearing in mind the uses for the timber, finishing quality may not be important.

Uses
Beams, joists, and foundation piling in buildings and house construction. Also for tool handles.

AILANTHUS

Ailanthus altissima Swingle   Family : Simarubaceae
syn. *A. glandulosa* Desf.

Other names
tree of heaven.

Distribution
Found in eastern Asia, northern Australia, and indigenous in China, in the northern provinces, and occurs in Japan.

General characteristics
A tall, straight tree, some 30m in height, with a diameter of 1.0m whose pinnate leaves give it a superficial appearance of ash (*Fraxinus* spp.) when seen growing in the UK where it was introduced, but in China and Japan, the leaves are longer, spreading palm-like from the ends of branches.

The timber is similar to ash in general appearance, and may be mistaken for it at first glance, but ailanthus is usually more white in colour, as opposed to the yellowish or brownish cast more typical of ash. Close examination of end grain however serves to distinguish the species since ash has its late-wood pores generally in pairs, while those in ailanthus are in clusters arranged tangentially, while the rays are larger in ailanthus. Both woods are ring porous.

Ailanthus is an elastic wood with a fine satiny sheen, but is of minor commercial importance, although used locally for joinery and for cabinets.

ALBIZIA SPECIES

Albizia spp.   Family : Leguminosae

Various species of the genus *Albizia* occur in the Philippines, all having a wide, whitish-coloured sapwood, and light to dark brown, durable heartwood, the colour varying with the species and growth conditions.

Albizia acle Merr. produces acle, otherwise known as akli. Acle is probably the most important species; a hard, moderately heavy to heavy timber, weighing from 608 kg/m³ to 660 kg/m³ when dried. The whitish sapwood is up to 50mm wide, sharply defined from the heartwood which is pale, dull brown to dark walnut-brown. The colouring matter is soluble in water and alcohol, and the wood has a strong peppery odour, the dust often causing unpleasant sneezing when worked, especially when very dry wood is machined.

The bole of the tree is often crooked, and this gives rise to grain which is sometimes very curly or crossed, and the texture is rather coarse but even.

Uses
General construction, sills, posts, sleepers, and from selected logs, furniture, cabinets and high-class interior joinery. The wood is very durable.

A. marginata Merr. produces a timber known as unik. This is a soft, light-weight wood, about 512 kg/m³ when dried, with a whitish sapwood gradually merging into the pale, pinkish-brown or reddish-brown heartwood, often with conspicuous broad growth rings. The grain is almost perfectly straight, and the texture fairly fine. The timber is moderately durable.

Uses
Since its distribution appears confined to Luzon, its commercial value is limited, but it is used locally for bancas (long seats or benches typical of the Philippines), interior trim and ceilings, and for cases for shipping cigarettes.

A. procera Benth. produces a timber known as acleng-parang. This is a hard, moderately heavy to heavy timber, weighing about 848 kg/m³ when dried, with a rich, dark chestnut-brown heartwood, generally with conspicuous irregular darker and lighter bands, with a straight grain, and fine, glossy texture. Said to be durable.

Uses
Acleng-parang is sometimes sold as an alternative to acle, and is used for similar purposes, but it has a rather wider use and this includes carving, gun stocks and agricultural implements.

A. retusa Benth. produces kasai, a timber very similar in appearance to acleng-parang, but a little lighter in colour, used for general construction and interior joinery.

A. saponaria Bl. produces salingkugi, very similar to kasai.

A. lebbeck Benth. which produces kokko of India and Burma, also occurs in the Philippines, and is cultivated in some of the islands, particularly in Luzon. This is a dark, walnut-brown wood, with darker markings, weighing about 650 kg/m^3 when dried, moderately durable, and used for general construction, furniture, and sliced for decorative veneer.

A. lebbekoiodes Benth. produces kariskis, a timber very similar to acleng-parang.

ALDER, JAPANESE

Alnus glutinosa Gaertn.   Family : Betulaceae

Other names
The Japanese name for alder is hannoki, and this should not be confused with hinoki (cypress), or honoki (magnolia).

Distribution
Widely distributed from Europe, North Africa, into Asia, and Japan.

The tree
Generally reaches a height of 15m to 27m and a diameter of about 0.5m when the conditions are favourable, but often with a clear bole of no more than 6m or 7m and a diameter of 0.3m.

The timber
There is no general difference in colour between sapwood and heartwood, the wood being a pale reddish-brown colour, and rather more red than the same species found in Europe. It is a dull, featureless wood, except for some darker-coloured lines or streaks appearing on longitudinal surfaces, due to the broad rays.
The timber weighs about 530 kg/m^3 when dried.

Drying
The timber dries fairly rapidly and without undue degrade.

Strength
A soft, weak timber, similar to poplar in general strength.

Durability
A relatively easy timber to convert and machine, although sharp, thin-edged cutters are required in order to ensure a regular smooth finish in planing and moulding. The wood turns reasonably well, and can be stained, polished, glued and nailed without difficulty.

Uses
Turnery, usually in the form of rollers, broom handles, brush parts, clog soles and for plywood. Gnarled pieces are frequently used in Japan as decorative media.

AMUGIS

Koordersiodendron pinnatum Merr.   Family: Anacardiaceae

Other names
ambugis, mugis, amugis perfecto. (See also *Palaquium* spp.)

Distribution
A tall, straight tree, up to 1.0m in diameter, widely, but sparsely distributed throughout the Philippines.

General characteristics
The sapwood is up to 50mm wide, pale, dull red in colour, rather sharply defined from the heartwood which is a dull, coppery red. The grain is usually straight, but sometimes with short, regular waves, and often with numerous, very small knots. The wood is moderately hard to hard, and fairly heavy, weighing 800 kg/m^3 to 881 kg/m^3 when dried.

Uses
The timber is moderately durable and is used for beams, joists and rafters, and for vehicle bodies, flooring, furniture and cabinets.

Note : several other reddish coloured woods are often loosely called amugis as follows,

Bassia ramiflora Merr. or baniti or amugis. Sapotaceae family.

Buchaniana arborescens Bl. or balinghasay or amugis. Anacardiaceae family.

Garuga spp. or bogo or amugis. Burseraceae family.

APITONG

Dipterocarpus spp.   Family : Dipterocarpaceae

Other names
bagac, Philippine gurjun.

Distribution
Widely distributed throughout the Philippines, especially in regions where the dry season is pronounced.

The tree
A lightly buttressed tree reaching a height of 30m to 40m and a diameter of 1.8m with a straight, cylindrical bole of about 25m to 30m.

The timber
The sapwood is 40mm to 60mm wide, pale brown in colour, and not sharply defined from the heartwood which is reddish to light brown. The grain is occasionally wavy and slightly crossed, and the texture, variable in different regions, ranges from moderately fine to moderately coarse. The wood contains a sticky resin which sometimes exudes on the surface of sawn material.
Three species principally supply apitong, ie *Dipterocarpus gracilis* Bl., *D. grandiflorus* Blanco. and *D. lasiopodus* Perkins,

and the weight of the wood varies according to species and to growth conditions, but an average is about 740 kg/m³ when dried.

Drying
Apitong is difficult to dry because it checks and warps even in ordinary air drying under Philippine air conditions, and it is susceptible to collapse when kiln dried from the green. Slow, partial air drying prior to kiln drying is recommended, and in experimental drying tests it was found that pre-steaming the green timber from the saw at 212°F in saturated condition for about two hours before the air drying and kiln drying processes, facilitated drying and minimized excessive degrade.

Strength
Compared with teak, air dry apitong is about 25 per cent stiffer, and 40 per cent more resistant to shock loads; in other strength categories, apitong is about equal to teak.

Durability
Moderately durable.

Working qualities
The timber is variable in its working properties. Resin may be troublesome in some cases, and negligible in others, while cutter wear may be rapid at times and less so in other parcels. In general, apitong planes and moulds to a clean, slightly fibrous finish, but there is an inclination for the grain to pick up in quarter-sawn material unless a cutting angle of not more than 20° is used. It takes nails and screws well, and can be stained without difficulty but the presence of resin may call for care in varnishing and polishing.
Cold logs of apitong are fairly easy to peel on the veneer lathe, but pre-heating logs in hot water promotes exudation of resin, thereby improving peeling quality.

Uses
The standard wood for all types of piling in the Philippines, it is also commonly used for building construction, posts, framing and flooring. Creosoted apitong is the premier wood for transmission poles and railway ties.

ARANGA

Homalium spp.   Family: Flacourtiaceae

About ten species of *Homalium* occur in the Philippines, most of them producing commercial timber, the largest trees having a diameter of about 1.0m.
The most important species are as follows,
H. luzoniense F.-Vill. produces typical aranga, or arangan.
H. bracteatum Benth. produces arangan.
H. oblongifolium Merr. produces aranga.
H. villarianum Vid. produces adanga, or matobato.

General characteristics
The general appearance, mechanical properties, and structure of these various species are very much alike except for slight variations in colour and density, which appear to be related more to local growth conditions rather than to species differences.
The wood of all species is hard and heavy, varying from 864 kg/m^3 to 881 kg/m^3 when dried. The sapwood, up to 50mm wide, is yellowish or pinkish, in some species sharply defined, in others merging gradually into the heartwood, which is very variable, ranging from yellowish, pinkish, to pale red, sometimes quite plain, in others containing irregular streaks of darker colour. The grain is usually straight, but may be shallowly interlocked, and the texture of all types is very fine, dense and smooth.
The timber dries well, is fairly hard to saw, but not difficult to shape and plane. It is classified as being very durable.

Uses
All species have similar uses, piling (not very resistant to *Teredo*), wharf and bridge building, posts, poles, sills, floors, interior finish, window frames, and for furniture and cabinets

ASH, JAPANESE

Fraxinus mandshurica Rupr.   Family: Oleaceae

Other names
tamo.

14

Distribution
Manchuria, Korea and Japan.

The tree
Attains a height of 18m to 30m and a diameter of 0.75m.

The timber
The sapwood is white, and the heartwood is light brown in colour, darker than European ash, and rather lighter in weight, being about 690 kg/m^3 when dried. The grain is straight, sometimes wavy, and the texture is coarse.

Drying
Dries fairly rapidly without much tendency to warp, split or check.

Strength
Although a strong timber for its weight it is generally less strong than European ash, and lacks the characteristic toughness of that timber.

Durability
Perishable.

Working qualities
Fairly easy to work, it has only a moderate dulling effect on cutting edges, and generally works to a good finish. It takes glue, stains, and polish satisfactorily.

Uses
Flooring, plywood, baseball bats, skis, furniture, etc. Selected material furnishes decorative veneer with mottle, fiddle-back and curly-grain features.

Note : This timber should not be confused with sen (*Kalopanax pictus* Nakai. syn. *Acanthopanax recinifolius* Seem.). Although similar in appearance to Japanese ash, it is lighter in weight, about 560 kg/m^3 when dried, and has none of the valuable attributes of ash. It is generally used for interior joinery and panelling.

BAMBOO

Although the Gramineae family of plants does not produce timber in the accepted sense, nevertheless, certain genera of this family produce bamboo, a material of extreme economic importance in the Philippines and elsewhere, used for construction or for the manufacture of furniture and implements, and for this reason a brief summary of the most important species is given here.

The erect bamboos are the most abundant and useful, and have cylindrical, hollow stems, with walls ranging from less than 5mm to 40mm or 50mm in thickness. In all species, the walls are thickest at the butt, and become gradually thinner towards the tip. In some species, the wall of the first few joints above the rootstock is so thick that the stems are almost, or quite solid. The erect bamboos have, as a rule, perfectly straight stems.

The following are a few of the most important species of the Philippines.

Bambusa blumeana Schultes f. produces the spiny bamboo, found in all settled areas at low and medium altitudes, and extensively planted. Considered to be the best structural bamboo in the Philippines. Used in house construction, temporary bridges and wharves, fish weirs, and for all purposes where the strongest and most durable bamboo is required.

Bambusa vulgaris Schrad. produces a tall straight bamboo known as kawayan-kiling. Whilst spiny bamboo is preferred for heavy work on account of its greater strength and durability, kawayan-kiling is favoured for furniture, floors, window and door frames.

Schizostachyum dielsianum Merr. produces bikal-babui a general purpose bamboo, used particularly for chairs.

Bamboo is used for a vast range of products, and particularly for the following,

House construction; posts, joists, studding, laths, rafters, purlins, door and window frames, shutters and eave troughs.

General construction; scaffolding and staging, centering for masonry culverts and arches, shade frames for nursery beds and for flag-poles.

Land transportation; yokes, vehicle shafts and rollers for mov-
ing heavy objects.
Furniture and household equipment; benches, chairs, tables,
beds and bookshelves.
Navigation; masts and spars for boats, oar shafts, boat poles,
seats and false bottoms, and ribs for boat awnings.

Because of the high yield of cellulose, much bamboo is used for
paper pulp.

BANUYO

Wallaceodendron celebicum Koord.   Family: Leguminosae

Other names
derham mahogany (USA).

Distribution
Philippines, mainly from Luzon and Masbate.

The tree
Although a fairly tall tree, the bole is short, and often crooked,
with a diameter of 1.5m.

The timber
The sapwood is whitish, up to 30mm wide, and generally
sharply defined from the heartwood which varies in colour
from light golden-brown to dark brown, sometimes with a
distinct reddish tint. The grain is usually straight, but may be
interlocked, curly, or wavy, while the texture is fine. The wood
has a glossy appearance when planed, and a thin, light-coloured
line of parenchyma marks each season's growth. The wood
weighs about 528 kg/m^3 when dried. It is said to dry easily and
well, to machine without difficulty, and to glue, stain and
polish satisfactorily. The wood is moderately durable.

Uses
Furniture, cabinets, doors, window frames, panelling, mouldings, ship cabins, and for musical instruments, particularly for
the backs and sides of guitars.

BATETE

Kingiodendron alternifoliium Merr.   Family : Leguminosae

Other names
bagbalogo, bahai, bitangol, palomaria.

Distribution
Found from central Luzon to Mindanao; large trees up to 1.0m in diameter, fairly numerous in parts of Masbate, elsewhere scattered.

General characteristics
The sapwood which varies in width from 15mm to 50mm is pale red at first, turning dull brown in drying, and not very well distinguished from the heartwood which is light to dark reddish-brown, with blackish streaks due to oil which exudes and stains all surfaces. The grain is fairly straight and the texture fine. The wood is soft to moderately hard, weighs about 704 kg/m^3 and is moderately durable.
Batete needs care in drying in order to avoid warping, but it does not tend to check unduly.

Uses
Beams, joists, rafters, flooring, doors, interior joinery.

BATICULIN

Litsea obtusata F.-Vill.   Family : Lauraceae

Other names
batikuling.

A particular feature of sculpture in the Philippines is the making of sacred images. Some of these are permanently set up outdoors, and first choice of timber for this purpose are woods like molave and merbau. Soft, less durable woods are also used, but these require annual painting, and preservative treatment initially, or ultimately, and wood of this type is less favoured. The principal type used for soft, easy carving, are the yellow baticulins, of which *Litsea obtusata* appears to be more regularly used and considered best.

The wood of *L. obtusata* has a pale yellow sapwood, up to 30mm wide, not clearly demarcated from the heartwood which is bright golden-yellow when freshly cut, turning darker on exposure. The wood has a faint odour reminiscent of both cedar and camphor. The grain is straight, and the texture fine, and the wood has a smooth, waxy feel, taking a glossy surface under sharp tools. It dries easily and well, and is very easy to work, and weighs about 400 kg/m³ when dried. It is classified as being moderately durable.

Uses
Apart from the carving and sculpture of sacred images, the wood is also used for panelling for altars, doors, musical instruments and cabinets.

BEECH, JAPANESE

Fagus crenata Bl.   Family: Fagaceae
and allied species

Other names
Siebold's beech, buna.

Distribution
Japan.

General characteristics
Very similar in appearance and characteristics to European beech, the sapwood is cream-coloured, the heartwood brown in colour. The grain is straight, and the texture fine, more nearly approaching that of central European beech, than of English. It weighs about 640 kg/m³ when dried, and is therefore lighter than European and American beech.
It is perishable, but accepts preservatives readily, and is used for furniture, flooring, joinery, turnery, plywood, tool handles, and for constructional work, sleepers (treated), and pulp.

BINGGAS

Terminalia citrina (Gaertn.) Roxb.   Family: Combretaceae
syn *T. comintana* Merr.

Distribution
Scattered in the Dipterocarp forests of Luzon, Mindoro, Leyte,

Negros, Mindanao, and elsewhere in the Philippines, and therefore limited in supply.

The tree
Although a large tree with only a moderate buttress, the bole is generally only about 12m to 18m in length, and may be irregular in form. Its diameter is usually about 0.9m.

The timber
The sapwood is light-yellow in colour and between 40mm and 100mm wide, and slightly distinct from the light reddish-yellow heartwood. Timber from large trees frequently contains either dark streaks, or has a violet tint. The grain is shallowly inter-locked or slightly crossed, and the texture is moderately fine with a rather glossy appearance. It is a heavy wood, weighing about 910 kg/m^3 when dried.

Drying
Difficult to dry from the green, being prone to checking and warping, and therefore requires great care.

Strength
A strong, hard wood, comparing favourably with hickory in toughness and with many of the Australian *Eucalypts* in general strength.

Durability
Durable.

Working qualities
Fairly difficult to work due to its hard, tough nature, but with care capable of a good smooth finish.

Uses
Frame construction in buildings, and for vehicle bodies. It is favoured locally for tool handles as an alternative to hickory, and in limited tests showed promise as a material for picker sticks in the textile industry.

BIRCH, JAPANESE

Betula maximowicziana Regel   Family : Betuliaceae

Other names
shira-kamba (Japan).

Distribution
The birches are found from the arctic circle to southern France, and throughout North America, Asia, China and Japan. *B. maximowicziana*, and possibly other species, provide Japanese birch.

The tree
Grows to a height of 18m to 21m and a diameter of 0.5m or a little more on good sites.

The timber
There is no clear distinction by colour between sapwood and heartwood, the wood generally being a bright yellowish-red, with a fairly straight grain, and a fine texture. It weighs about 670 kg/m^3 when dried.

Drying
Air dries rapidly, with a tendency to warp, and is particularly susceptible to fungus attack unless the piles are well ventilated.

Strength
A hard, tough wood, with strength properties rather better than those of European oak.

Durability
Perishable.

Working qualities
Works and machines well, although there is a tendency for the wood to bind on the saw, and is sometimes difficult to plane to a smooth finish when knots are present. The wood turns well, and can be glued, stained, and polished satisfactorily. It peels well for veneer.

Uses

Furniture, interior joinery, decorative veneer. Birch twigs are used for brooms, and for descaling in steel rolling mills. Timber that contains incipient decay (dote), is often used in Japan for fancy articles, the black zone marks providing a decorative medium.

BOXWOOD, JAPANESE

Buxus sempervirens L.   Family : Buxaceae

Other names
asame-tsuge (Japan).

Distribution
The tree is widely distributed from the Far East throughout Asia, Europe and the Mediterranean countries.

The tree
A small tree, some 6m to 9m in height, and a diameter of about 150mm.

The timber
A fine, compact wood of light yellow colour, with a grain that is sometimes straight, but more often irregular, and a fine, even texture. The wood weighs about 930 kg/m^3 when dried.

Drying
Dries very slowly with a pronounced tendency to surface check. Requires care in drying, since the billets also tend to split rather badly. Splitting these down to half-rounds, and careful piling helps avoid degrade, as does soaking the billets in a saturated solution of common salt, but this can only be done if the effect of the salt on saws, cutters, and machine tables is recognised, and allowed for.

Strength
A heavy, hard timber, twice as hard as oak, and 50 per cent stronger in compression along the grain.

Durability
Durable.

Working qualities

Although resistant to sawing it cuts cleanly, and after drying is rather hard to work. A reduction of cutting angle to 20° will reduce the tendency for irregular grain to tear. The wood turns beautifully, and takes stain and polish well.

Uses

Rollers and shuttles in the silk industry, tool handles, pulley-blocks, fancy turnery, chessmen, and engraving blocks, although cherry is generally preferred for this purpose in Japan today since it is cheaper, and more plentiful.

CALAMANSANAY

Neonauclea spp.   Family: Rubiaceae

Some twenty species of the genus *Neonauclea* occur in the Philippines, mostly small to medium-sized trees, and with the exception of slight differences in colour and texture, the wood is very much alike in general character, and is usually sold as calamansanay irrespective of species, although in certain of the islands, local names may also be applied to a given species. The following are some of the best and commonest species used.

Neonauclea calycina Merr. (syn. *Nauclea calycina* Bartl.) produces typical calamansanay of the trade, and is probably the principal source of the commercial classification.
The tree has a diameter of about 0.8m and the wood is a brilliant rose colour when freshly cut, fading to a dull orange colour after drying. The grain is shallowly interlocked, and the texture fine, the wood sometimes being mottled with irregular darker yellowish-brown or orange markings. The wood is durable.

Neonauclea bartlingii Merr. (syn. *Nauclea bartlingii* D.C.) produces lisak, otherwise known as calamansanay.
The wood is almost entirely yellow in colour, with a fine texture.

Neonauclea bernardoi Merr. (syn. *Nauclea bernardoi* Merr.) produces alintatau or bangkal. This has a pale red-coloured wood, with rather larger pores than the usual species, and therefore of coarser texture. While it is found in several of the islands, it does not generally appear in parcels of calamansanay on the Manila market.

Neonauclea media Merr. (syn. *Nauclea media* Havil) produces a wood very similar to that of *N. calycina*, but it is a little lighter in colour, and coarser in texture.

Neonauclea philippinensis Merr. (syn. *Nauclea philippinensis* Vid.) produces tiroron, or calamansanay. This has wood more distinctly brownish in colour than other species, and has a fine texture.

Neonauclea reticulata Merr. (syn. *Nauclea reticulata* Havil.) produces hambabalud, or calamansanay. This species comes from a medium-sized tree of some 0.4m diameter. The wood is light brown in colour with a slight reddish cast, and more streaked with orange or brown markings than most other species.

Neonauclea vidalii Merr. (syn. *Nauclea vidalii* Elm.) produces tikim or calamansanay. This is a fine textured, light reddish-coloured wood, very similar to typical calamansanay.

Weight
The wood of all species is similar in weight, from 640 kg/m³ to 672 kg/m³ when dried.

Drying
Rather slow to dry, and plain-sawn material has a tendency to warp rather badly and to develop surface checks.

Working qualities
All species are said to be rather difficult to work and machine, quarter-sawn stock in particular tending to pick up in planing and moulding. A cutting angle of 10° is helpful, and can assist in producing a reasonable finish. The timber tends to split in nailing, but holds screws quite well. It can be stained and polished after suitable preparation.

Uses
Structural applications for posts, beams, rafters, bridge and wharf construction, and for flooring, sills, tool handles, furniture and cabinets.

CALANTAS

Cedrela calantas Merr. & Rolfe.   Family : Meliaceae

Distribution
In the Philippines, two species of *Cedrela*, ie *C. febrifuga* and *C. paucijuga*, are confined to relatively small areas of Mindoro and Leyte, and the principal species, *C. calantas* appears to be widely distributed throughout the islands.

The tree
The trees vary in height from 21m to 30m with a diameter of 1.8m.

The timber
The sapwood is small, pale red in colour, and sharply defined from the light to dark red heartwood. The grain is straight or shallowly interlocked, and the texture is moderately coarse. The wood has a characteristic cedar odour due to an essential oil which sometimes exudes on the surface of the wood as a sticky resin. Soft, and light in weight, it weighs about 448 kg/m³ when dried.

Drying
Dries fairly rapidly and well but care is needed when drying thick material to avoid internal checking and collapse.

Strength
Variable, but roughly equal to American mahogany except in hardness and shear resistance.

Durability
Durable.

Working qualities
Works and machines readily, but sharp cutting edges must be maintained in order to obtain the best finish because of the soft, and sometimes woolly nature of the timber. Gum is sometimes a problem, but with care, and suitably filled, the wood stains and polishes excellently.

Uses
Cigar boxes, pianos, paddles and light oars, boats and ship's cabin finish, joinery, carving, furniture.

Curly, or bird's-eye calantas, otherwise known as maranggo in the Philippines, is the product of an associated species, ie *Azadirachta integrifolia* Merr. The wood is slightly harder and heavier than calantas, and has the same uses, except for cigar boxes, for which purposes, maranggo is considered to be too dark in colour.

CHERRY, JAPANESE

Prunus spp.   Family: Rosaceae

Other names
yama- zakura (Japan).

General characteristics
The wood is pale pinkish-brown in colour, turning a pleasant mahogany-red on exposure or with polishing. The grain is usually straight, and the texture fine and even. weight about 630 kg/m^3 when dried. The wood dries readily, but is inclined to warp. The wood turns well, but a cutting angle of 20° gives the best results in planing. It can be glued and stained, and takes an excellent polish.

Uses
Cabinets, turnery, domestic ware, engraving blocks.

DIOSPYROS SPECIES

The Ebenaceae family includes some thirty or more species of the genus *Diospyros*, providing commercial ebony and persimmon timber. A number of these species occur in the Philippines, where the timber can be roughly grouped into five types, but with two of the groups being the most favoured for high-class work such as furniture and cabinet making and known under the names ebony and camagon respectively.
Segregation of the species into groups is made according to the colour and character of the sapwood, which is generally

very wide, the heartwood of all types varying from jet black to blackish, frequently with lighter-coloured streaks. The grouping is as follows,

1 sapwood pinkish or pale red :— camagon group.
2 sapwood with distinct yellowish tint, becoming light yellowish-brown in drying :— heartwood good commercial camagon.
3 Sapwood whitish or dull light grey :— ebony or batulinau group.
4 Sapwood almost white, turning yellowish in drying :— ata-ata group.
5 Sapwood almost white or with a faint reddish tinge, but almost invariably changing shortly after felling to an even bluish-grey :— kanomoi group.

CAMAGON GROUP

The best known and one of the largest trees of the genus is *Diospyros discolor* Willd. the principal species providing camagon. The tree is generally about 0.6m in diameter, the sapwood is up to 200mm wide, generally retaining its pinkish or reddish colour, although fungal staining may introduce a dull grey appearance. The heartwood is sometimes almost dead black, but may be streaked with pink, yellow, brown or greyish colour.

Other species in this group are,
D. copelandii Merr. also known as talang-gubat. This has a diameter of about 0.3m and timber similar to camagon.
D. pilosanthera Blco. also known as bolong-eta. This has a diameter of 0.4m and a wider sapwood than *D. discolor*, but the small heartwood core is identical to that of camagon.
D. plicata Merr. and *D. whitfordii* Merr. produce tamil or palo negro ; both are about 0.3m in diameter, with a small heartwood core similar to camagon.

The principal species forming Group 2 are, *D. philippinensis* A.DC. and *D. velascoi* Merr. The former species is known locally as bolong-eta, or kanumai, and both are fairly small trees with a diameter of about 0.3m.
Apart from the difference in colour of the sapwood, the heartwood core in both species is very similar to camagon.

BATULINAU GROUP

The commonest Philippine name for many of the *Diospyros* species is batulinau, batlatinau, or bulatinau, in the same way that the Spanish name ebano is similarly, and loosely applied. More properly, batulinau or ebony is the product of a single species, *D. buxifolia* Pers. syn. *Maba buxifolia* Pers. This tree is widely distributed throughout the Philippines, but is scattered, with the majority being small trees. Good specimens have a diameter of about 0.4m.

The heartwood is jet black, sometimes with whitish or greyish streaks, and the wood is very hard, very dense and rather brittle.

ATA-ATA GROUP

D. mindanaensis Merr. is one of the largest and most widely distributed, and probably the best known of this group, so that the wood of other species, when its origin is unknown, is generally called ata-ata.

D. mindanaensis; ata-ata, anang, bolong-eta, or tamil-lalaki; has a diameter up to 0.5m and a dark, blackish heartwood generally streaked or mottled with lighter-coloured zones.

D. ahernii Merr. produces anang or ata-ata.
D. alvarezii Merr. produces bantulinau.
D. curranii Merr. produces malagaitmon.
D. foveo-reticulata Merr. produces kulitom or palo negro.
All have similar heartwood.

KANOMOI GROUP

D.multiflora Blco. syn. *D. canomoi* A.DC. is a tree up to 0.6m in diameter, and is the principal source of commercial kanomoi.
D. camarinensis Merr. produces kanumai.
D. maritima Bl. produces malatinta, or kanomoi.
D. nitida Merr. produces katilma or malatinta.

Weight

The weight of the various species differs according to the species and degree of sapwood present, but is generally within the range of 800 kg/m³ to 1040 kg/m³ after drying.

Uses

The segregation of the various species according to the character of the sapwood is relevant to certain uses. Musical instrument manufacturers favour the blue-grey sapwood of the kanomoi group, usually sold under the name malatinta, for backs, sides and finger boards of guitars, while camagon and bolong-eta sapwood, said to be fine, hard, smooth and tough, is used for tool handles.

Camagon sapwood is also used for small show-cases, mouldings, etc while that of all the *Diospyros* species is used in agricultural machinery and implements for parts subjected to severe wear, and for levers, connecting rods and long handles, where rather long or slender working parts require straight grained, fairly tough and springy wood.

The sapwood of bolong-eta (*D. pilosanthera*) is also used for butcher blocks and, along with ata-ata and camagon, for billiard cues. All types are used for shuttles, bobbins and golf-clubs.

The heartwood of all species, and sometimes sapwood and heartwood combined, has a variety of uses both in the high-class, and utility field, including furniture, veneer, cabinet making, turnery, inlaying, paper weights, gun stocks, bank fittings and musical instruments.

HOPEA SPECIES

The family Dipterocarpaceae includes some ten or more species of the genus *Hopea* which produce such timbers as merawan of Malaysia, thingan of Burma and Thailand, and selangan batu of Sabah. Certain species occurring in the Philippines fall into two groups and produce commercial yacal and mangachapuy, the yacals being harder, heavier, and stronger than the mangachapuys, and also more durable.

The following are the principal species forming the two groups.

YACAL

Hopea basilanica Foxw., *H. philippinensis* Dyer., and *H. plagata* Vid.

Other names
dalingdingan, gisok-gisok, banutan, siakal.

General characteristics
Sapwood 20mm to 80mm wide, pale yellow in colour when freshly sawn, but often greyish due to sap-stain, rather sharply distinguished from the heartwood which is light yellowish-brown, darkening rapidly on exposure; sometimes with narrow, irregular greenish streaks which in drying turn greenish-black. The grain is interlocked, making the wood difficult to split radially and producing a sharp ribbon-figure on quarter-sawn surfaces, and the texture is fine and dense, giving the wood a translucent appearance.

The timber is hard to very hard, tough and very stiff, and weighs about 880 kg/m^3 when dried. It is said to be very durable when used in contact with the ground.

Yacal needs careful drying; it is not prone to checking but tends to warp badly. It is rather hard to saw and machine, but is capable of a very clean surface off the saw.

Uses
All high-grade permanent construction, except salt water piling; posts, beams, joists, rafters, bridges, wharves, ship framing and decking, flooring, axe and cant-hook handles, sleepers, paving blocks, and wheelwright's work.

Note: a few species of *Vatica* and *Shorea*, principally *S. balangeran*, with similar characteristics are also included in commercial yacal.

MANGACHAPUY

Hopea acuminata Merr., *H. foxworthyi* Elm., and *H. pierrei* Hance.

Other names
bangoran, manggasinoro, barosingsing.

General characteristics
Sapwood 40mm to 80mm wide, lighter in colour than the heartwood which is pale straw colour turning rapidly to clear brown, often with irregular, narrow streaks, grass-green in colour when freshly sawn, but turns to dark greenish-brown or nearly black. The grain is interlocked, but never so strongly as in the yacals,

and there is a small, but attractive ray figure on quarter-sawn surfaces. The texture is fine to very fine, and the wood weighs from 590 kg/m³ to 725 kg/m³ when dried.

Mangachapuy is easy to dry without excessive degrade, easy to work and machine, and capable of a good, smooth finish in planing and moulding. The wood is moderately durable.

Uses
Posts, beams, rafters, flooring, sheathing, masts, spars, planking and decking for boats, doors, mouldings, pestle shafts in rice mills, furniture, cabinets, broom, rake and hoe handles.

HORSE CHESTNUT, JAPANESE

Aesculus turbinata Bl.   Family: Hippocastanaceae

Other names
tochi, tochi-noki (Japan).

Distribution
Found in Japan principally in the Chuenji district.

The tree
Grows to a height of 30m or more, and a diameter of 1.5m. The bole length is generally short, about 6m to 8m in length.

The timber
There is little distinction by colour between sapwood and heartwood, the wood generally being a golden-brown colour, darker than European horse chestnut. The grain is wavy or crossed, and the texture fine and uniform, and the wood is a little heavier than the European variety, weighing about 590 kg/m³ when dried.

Drying
Dries readily and without excessive degrade.

Strength
No information.

Durability
Perishable.

Working qualities
Works and machines without undue difficulty, although inclined to woolliness. Thin-edged, sharp cutters produce a very good finish, and the wood can be glued, stained and polished without difficulty. It is a good turnery timber.

Uses
Selected logs containing mottle figure, and especially those containing incipient decay, ie with yellowish patches of discoloured wood enclosed by black zone markings, are prized in Japan for decorative work. Normal stock is used for domestic utensils, food containers and fruit storage trays.

KAKI

Diospyros kaki L.f.   Family: Ebenaceae

Other names
Chinese persimmon.

Distribution
The genus *Diospyros* produces the true ebonies, and also includes a few species which are fruit-bearing, and unlike the ebonies, usually have a very wide, straw-coloured and commercial sapwood, and a comparatively small black core of heartwood. These are the persimmons, of which *D. virginiana* produces persimmon of North America, and *D. kaki* produces very similar wood, mainly from Japan. *D. lotus* L. produces the date plum of temperate Asia, but this is known more for its fruit rather than for its timber.

General characteristics
Anatomically, there is very little difference between kaki and American persimmon, but in many of the Japanese trees, the dark heartwood is often much wider than that found in the American species. The heartwood is basically dense black, but usually streaked with orange-yellow, brown, grey or salmon-pink, separately, or in combination, giving a highly decorative appearance to the wood, which has a cold, marble-like feel on planed surfaces. It is lighter in weight than ebony, weighing 768 kg/m³ when dried.

Uses

Highly-prized in Japan for ornamental work and small tables, the straw-coloured sapwood is used for golf-club heads, turnery, textile shuttles, and any work demanding a close, compact wood with an ability to wear smooth.

KATSURA

Cercidiphyllum japonicum   Family : Trochodendraceae
Sieb. & Zucc.

Distribution
Japan.

General characteristics
A deciduous hardwood tree, it tends to form several furrowed trunks, often spirally twisted.
The timber is of a light nut-brown colour, rather plain in appearance but with an occasional narrow, light-coloured line due to growth rings which are marked by a narrow band of parenchyma. The wood somewhat resembles American white-wood (*Liriodendron*), with its rather crowded, small pores and parenchyma, but katsura is a little more brown in colour.
Logs selected for timber are usually straight-grained, and the texture is fine and even. The wood is soft but compact, and light in weight, about 470 kg/m^3 when dried.
The timber dries easily and well, and is very easy to work and machine, its soft, yet compact nature lending itself to moulding and carving where there is a need for sharp arrises to remain intact and not chip out.

Uses
Furniture, cabinets, panelling, high-class joinery, mouldings, carving, engraving.

KEYAKI

Zelkova serrata Makino.   Family : Ulmaceae
syn. *Z. acuminata* Planch.

Distribution
Of several species of *Zelkova*, two are important, *Z. carpinifolia*

syn. *Z. crenata*, found in Iran and the Caucasus, and *Z. serrata*, syn. *Z. acuminata*. a native of China and Japan. Both species have been introduced into the UK.

The tree
Z. serrata attains a height of 36m and a diameter of 1.2m. The bole is smooth and straight in young trees, but progressively becomes deeply fissured, and in old trees has the appearance of a number of boles, fused together.

The timber
Zelkova is closely related to the elms, and the timber is not unlike elm in appearance. The wood is yellowish-brown in colour when freshly cut, turning a lustrous golden colour after drying, but lighter in colour than elm. The wood is ring porous, with a similar undulating arrangement of late-wood pores as in elm. The timber is a little heavier than elm and weighs about 625 kg/m^3 when dried, and is said to be very resistant to decay.

Uses
A strong, tough, and elastic wood, it is used in China and Japan at the present time mainly for the building and maintenance of temples, and is largely a protected tree, reserved for this purpose. The tree is capable of great age, and due to the particular form, and also to its capacity to produce very large burrs, highly decorative wood can be obtained, but while for centuries the wood was used for lacquer work, cabinets, carving, and highly polished columns in temples, very old trees, 1000 years old, it is said, became scarce, and for a long time now its use has been restricted, at least in Japan.

KIRI

Paulownia tomentosa C. Koch.   Family: Scrophulariaceae
syn *P. imperialis* Sieb. & Zucc.

Other name
foxglove tree (UK).

Distribution
Two species of *Paulownia* are of relative economic importance

ie *P. fargesii* which occurs in China, and *P. tomentosa*, which is found in Japan, and which was introduced into the UK from Japan in 1838.

The tree
Kiri is a fairly small tree some 15m to 18m in height, with a diameter of 0.6m or a little more.

General characteristics
The wood varies in colour, from silver-grey, to light brown, sometimes with a reddish cast. It is very light in weight, about 320 kg/m^3 when dried. The wood is very highly prized in Japan for a wide range of products, from cabinets and drawer linings, to musical instruments, clogs, and floats for fishing nets. It is also used to produce scale-veneer, which is of extreme thinness, and this is often mounted on paper to produce special visiting cards, particularly from the silver-grey coloured wood.

LANIPAU

Terminalia copelandi Elm.   Family : Combretaceae
syn. *T. crassiramea* Merr.

Distribution
This species appears to be confined to Leyte and Mindanao, especially in Agusan and Davao.

The tree
A medium-sized tree with a clear cylindrical bole of 8m to 10m and a diameter of 0.6m to 0.8m.

The timber
The sapwood is yellowish-brown, not much differentiated from the heartwood, which is reddish-brown, or pinkish-brown in colour. The grain is interlocked and sometimes wavy, and the texture is moderately coarse. The timber weighs about 561 kg/m^3 when dried.

Drying
Moderately difficult to dry, with similar drying characteristics to those of bagtikan, mayapis and tangile.

Strength
Moderately strong, and similar to almon in general strength, but this would seem of little consequence since the timber is seldom used for structural purposes.

Durability
Non-durable.

Working qualities
Works and machines fairly well, but its coarse nature tends to promote a rather poor finish in planing. It peels quite well, producing a core-stock veneer.

Uses
General construction and roofing shingles.

LAUAN

Shorea, Parashorea and   Family : Dipterocarpaceae
Pentacme species

The Dipterocarpaceae is by far the most important botanical family in the Philippines, at least half of the standing timber belonging to it. The trees are almost without exception tall and straight, and their timber is utilized for a wider range of uses than those of any other family.

While there is a very wide range of weight, hardness, colour, and mechanical properties, as well as durability, there are certain features of structure that are fairly uniform throughout the whole family, from the softest of the lauans to the hardest of the yacals. Growth rings are rare, except in the first years of growth, ripple marks are rarer still,. and when present, rather indistinct. The most characteristic feature of the timbers of this family is the presence of numerous resin ducts, partly scattered, but more often arranged in conspicuous narrow concentric lines, giving the appearance of growth rings.

The lauans consist of various species of *Shorea, Parashorea*, and *Pentacme*, and correspond roughly to the merantis of Malaysia and seraya of Sabah. In the Philippines it is the usual practice to

36

classify the timbers into two groups on the basis of colour, ie the darker coloured timbers as red or dark red lauan, and the whitish or pale-coloured timbers as light red or white lauan.

In some cases, an individual species is sold under a separate trade name, for example, *Shorea polysperma* may be marketed as tangile, but may also be included in parcels of red lauan. Furthermore, some species vary in colour, and may provide timber for both groups.

The principal species providing lauan are as follows,
Red lauan; *Shorea negrosensis* Foxw. (red lauan proper),
Dark red lauan; *S. negrosensis* Foxw; *S. polysperma* Merr.; *S. squamata* Dyer syn *S. palosapis* Merr. (in part); *S. agsaboensis* Stern. Some, or all of these species may be included as red lauan.
White lauan or light red lauan includes *Parashorea malaanonan* (Blco.) Merr.; *Shorea almon* Foxw., selected material of *S. squamata*, and species of *Pentacme*, of which *P. contorta* Merr. provides white lauan proper, and *P. mindanensis* Foxw, produces Mindanao white lauan.

The following are descriptions of the various species making up the lauans, with particular reference to those sold under separate trade names.

RED LAUAN

Shorea negrosensis Foxw.

Other name
Philippine mahogany (UK). This name is confusing and its use should be discontinued.

Distribution
Occurs widely in the Philippines, especially in Cagayan, Isabela, Laguna, Quezon, Negros provinces, Northern Mindanao and Bucas Grande Island.

The tree
A large tree, some 50m tall with a diameter of 2m. It is strongly buttressed, with a straight, cylindrical bole, slightly tapered.

Clear boles of 20m are common, and on good sites can reach 30m.

The timber
The sapwood is about 50mm wide, creamy or light grey in colour, and sharply defined from the reddish to dark red heartwood. It has a crossed or interlocked grain, showing a distinct ribbon-grain pattern on quarter-sawn surfaces. Weight about 630 kg/m^3 when dried.

Drying
Dries easily and with little degrade.

Strength
Generally the strength of red lauan compares closely with that of American mahogany, but it is less hard, and rather weaker in compression strength parallel to the grain.

Durability
Moderately durable.

Working qualities
Works easily with both hand and machine tools, and is capable of a good finish in planing and moulding, although it is sometimes essential to reduce cutting angles to 20° to avoid grain tearing. Takes stains and polish well and glues satisfactorily. Peels well for veneer.

Uses
Red lauan, as with other lauan types, is a general utility wood. It is however, widely used as peeler and veneer log; furniture, interior finish and panelling, planking and decking of boats, and for cabinets and cases of musical and scientific instruments.

WHITE LAUAN

Pentacme contorta Merr.

Distribution
Widely distributed in the Philippine Islands, in association with other white lauans and apitong.

The tree
A large tree attaining a height of 45m to 50m and a diameter of 1.8m.

The timber
The sapwood is 50mm to 90mm wide, light grey in colour, while the heartwood is also greyish with a reddish tinge, or light pink. The grain is interlocked, sometimes crossed, and the texture is moderately coarse. The resin ducts are in concentric arcs, and are filled with white resin. Weight about 530 kg/m^3 when dried.

Drying
Dries easily and well. Shrinkage, from green to 12 per cent moisture content 4.3 per cent tangentially, 1.8 per cent radially.

Strength
Comparable, or a little superior, to the general strength properties of American mahogany (*Swietenia* spp.), but slightly inferior in hardness and impact resistance.

Durability
Moderately durable.

Working qualities
White lauan works and machines easily and finishes quite well in planing and moulding. There is a tendency for the wood to tear in boring and mortising. It peels well, and takes glue, stains and polish satisfactorily.

Uses
Veneer, plywood, furniture, cabinets, interior joinery, boat planking.

ALMON

Shorea almon Foxw.

Distribution
Widely distributed in the Philippines in primary forests where there is no pronounced dry season, usually in association with other white lauans and apitong.

The tree
A large tree, reaching a height of 70m and a diameter of 1.6m. The bole is almost cylindrical and evenly tapered and is usually clear for 25m to 30m.

The timber
The sapwood is cream to light brown in colour, not sharply demarcated from the reddish to light brown heartwood. It is intermediate in colour between the red and white lauans, although in some regions it could pass for red lauan. The resin ducts are filled with white resin and it is comparatively light in weight, about 580 kg/m^3 when dried.

Drying
Said to be the easiest to dry of all the species in the lauan groups. Shrinkage from green to 12 per cent moisture content is 5.6 per cent tangentially and 2.8 per cent radially.

Strength
The strength properties of this timber compare closely with those of bagtikan; by comparison with American mahogany its strength in bending, compression and stiffness is superior to mahogany, but it is slightly inferior to that timber in hardness and impact resistance.

Durability
Moderately durable.

Working qualities
Works quite well in most machine operations but the grain tends to tear in shaping, turning, and boring It can be planed to a smooth finish and takes glue, stains and polish, satisfactorily, It peels well for veneer.

Uses
Veneer, plywood, furniture, interior finish and panelling, boat planking and decking and as structural members in light frame construction.

BAGTIKAN

Parashorea malaanonan (Bclo) Merr. Syn. *P. plicata* Brandis

Distribution
Occurs in the Philippines in some parts of Luzon, in Polilio, Mindanao, Biliran, Catanduanes, Negros, Masbate.

The tree
Attains a height of 50m to 60m and a diameter of 1.0m. The cylindrical bole is usually about 20m to 25m in length.

The timber
Bagtikan is of the light red lauan type; the sapwood is 20mm to 30mm wide, light grey in colour and not sharply defined from the heartwood which is greyish-brown and often with light-brown concentric bands which are spaced some 50mm to 100mm apart. The grain is usually crossed and the texture is moderately coarse. The wood is moderately heavy, weighing about 530 kg/m^3 when dried.

Drying
Rather difficult to dry, it has a marked tendency to check and warp and is susceptible to collapse. Air drying to 25 per cent moisture content prior to kiln drying is recommended. Shrinkage from the green to 12 per cent moisture content is 5.7 per cent tangentially, and 3.5 per cent radially.

Strength
Among the lauans, bagtikan is the strongest timber, excelling them all in general strength properties. It is superior to American mahogany (*Swietenia*) in stiffness (modulus of elasticity), impact resistance and toughness and compares very closely to mahogany in all other strength properties.

Durability
Moderately durable.

Working qualities
Rather hard to work and rather difficult to shape, but it planes well and takes glue, stains and polish satisfactorily. It also peels well for veneer.

Uses
For domestic consumption bagtikan is usually mixed with white lauan, almon and mayapis and used for house construction,

veneer, plywood, furniture and interior joinery. Bagtikan is usually included in shipments of light red lauan.

GUIJO

Shorea guiso Bl.   Family : Dipterocarpaceae

Other names
red balau (Malaysia) ; red selangan batu (Sabah).

Distribution
Found throughout S E Asia and throughout the Philippines.

General characteristics
The tree is large, up to 1.8m in diameter, and the timber is moderately heavy to heavy, weighing from 817 kg/m³ to 880 kg/m³ when dried.

The sapwood is up to 50mm wide, light greyish-brown in colour, not sharply defined from the heartwood which is light greyish brown to brown, sometimes with a distinct reddish tint. The grain is interlocked, and the texture coarse, but even. The wood dries slowly, and needs care if warping and splitting is to be avoided. Resin ducts appear as frequent narrow rings.
The wood saws easily, but is rather difficult to shape and plane to a good finish.

Uses
Beams, joists, rafters, flooring, windows, doors, keels, planking and decking for boats, piling, except salt water, vehicle parts, bridge and wharf construction.

MAYAPIS

Shorea squamata Dyer.

Distribution
Abundant in primary forests of the Philippines at low and medium altitudes, particularly in Luzon, Polilio, Leyte, Mindanao and Basilan island.

The tree
A medium-size tree with a large buttress, it reaches a height of

40m or a little more, and a diameter of 1.5m with a clear bole 20m to 30m in length.

The timber
A light-red lauan type, the sapwood is 25mm to 50mm wide, pinkish in colour, and gradually merging into the reddish heartwood. The colour of the heartwood is variable; from some localities it is sufficiently red to pass as tangile or red lauan, while in other areas it is light-red, and is marketed as white lauan. The grain is crossed or interlocked, and the texture is moderately coarse to coarse. The resin ducts are usually empty. The wood is comparatively light in weight, about 530 kg/m^3 when dried.

Drying
Variable in drying properties according to locality of growth. Timber from N and S E Luzon is moderately slow drying, with minor degrade developing in the form of checking and warping. Timber from N E Mindanao is said to dry much more slowly, especially from sinker logs which have a high green moisture content. This type of timber needs very careful drying if severe checking, warping and collapse is to be avoided.
Air drying to 25 per cent moisture content prior to kiln drying is recommended, otherwise a very mild kiln schedule should be employed when drying from the green. Shrinkage, green to 12 per cent moisture content is said to be 6.4 per cent tangentially, and 4.4 per cent radially.

Strength
Similar to almon in all strength categories.

Durability
Moderately durable.

Working qualities
Works readily, planes very well, but is poor in shaping, turning, boring and mortising. Peeling and gluing properties are good, but veneers are sometimes difficult to dry.

Uses
Furniture, cabinets, cigar boxes, veneer and plywood, boat planking and general construction.

TANGILE

Shorea polysperma Merr.

Distribution
The tree is widely distributed in high-altitude forest regions of the Philippines.

The tree
A large tree, reaching a height of 45m to 50m and a diameter of 2m and with a bole length of 25m to 33m.

The timber
The sapwood is 40mm to 50mm wide, creamy in colour and sharply defined from the red to dark brownish-red heartwood. The grain is crossed or interlocked, showing a distinct ribbon-grain figure on quarter-sawn surfaces. The texture is somewhat fine, and the wood has a slight lustre, is moderately hard, and comparatively light, weighing about 630 kg/m^3 when dried.

Drying
Moderately slow drying, it has a tendency to warp, and for wide, plain-sawn boards to cup, and accordingly, proper attention must be given to the spacing of sticks, which should be fairly close, while weighting down of stacks is recommended.

Strength
Very similar in all strength properties to red lauan (*S. negrosensis*).

Durability
Moderately durable.

Working qualities
Works well with all hand tools, but requires care in planing and moulding, particularly when planing quarter-sawn material, to avoid grain tearing. It turns, peels, glues, stains and polishes satisfactorily.

Uses
Tangile to some extent resembles true mahogany and for that reason has similar uses for furniture, cabinet making, joinery

such as sash-frames, doors and interior finish. It is used widely for boat planking, veneer, plywood, and for general construction.

TIAONG

Shorea agsaboensis Stern

Distribution
Found in abundance in Laguna and Quezon in the Philippines and also in low-altitude primary forests where there is abundant rainfall.

The tree
Tiaong reaches a height of 20m and a diameter of 1.75m.

The timber
Very similar to tangile in general appearance, but generally lighter in colour. It has few resin ducts which look like numerous broken lines on end-grain surfaces, whereas in tangile they appear as definite solid lines. Tiaong weighs about 630 kg/m^3 when dried.

Drying
No work has been carried out on this species, but it is believed to have similar drying characteristics to almon.

Strength
Similar to tangile and red lauan in general strength properties, but lower in stiffness.

Durability
Perishable.

Uses
General house construction locally, and for furniture, veneer and plywood.

LIUSIN

Parinarium corymbosum Miq.   Family : Rosaceae

Distribution
Widely, but sparsely distributed throughout the Philippines.

General characteristics

The tree has a diameter of 0.6m although larger specimens are found occasionally. The wood is hard and heavy, weighing about 1120 kg/m^3 when dried.

The wood is pale red in colour, sometimes streaked with very narrow, widely separated, dark belts of colour which do not generally follow the growth rings. The grain is straight, or slightly crossed, often with a characteristic regular wave, while the texture is fine; the wood has a faint acid odour.

The timber dries slowly and without much checking, but it is said to warp rather badly.

Difficult to work, blunting cutting edges rapidly, but with suitable techniques can be finished quite well.

Uses

Although said to be only moderately durable in respect of timber in contact with the ground, it has a high reputation for resistance to *Teredo*, and is favoured for piling in salt water. It is used for boat keels, railway ties (preservative treated), and when planing difficulties are overcome makes splendid flooring.

There is a further species, *P. laurinum* A. Gray occurring in the islands, known as tabon-tabon. This wood is practically identical to liusin, but the tree is smaller, up to 0.4m in diameter.

MALABAYABAS

Tristania decorticata Merr.   Family : Myrtaceae

Other names

Similar timber is produced by *T. littoralis* Merr. and is known as taba, while a few unclassified species produce tiga.

General characteristics

The wood of all the species is very hard and heavy, weighing around 1200 kg/m^3 when dried. The sapwood is up to 30mm wide, light brown in colour, merging gradually into the heartwood which is dark brown, turning almost black after long exposure. The grain is shallowly interlocked, and the texture fine and glossy. White deposits occur in many of the pores.

With care, the wood dries quite well, but there is a tendency for warping and checking to develop. Fairly hard to work, but it can be planed to a good finish with care.

46

Uses

Very durable, the three species mentioned are used for piling, bridge and wharf construction, posts, sills, joists and rafters. Taba and tiga appear to be used under their own names but malabayabas, while also used for these purposes often as a substitute for mancono, although for specialist uses it is inferior to mancono.

MALAGAI

Pometia pinnata Forst.   Family : Sapindaceae

Other names

malugay, agupanga (Philippines) ; taun (Papua New Guinea) ; kasai (Solomons).

Distribution

A single species, widely distributed throughout the South Pacific.

The tree

The tree reaches a height of 36m to 45m with a diameter of 1.0m above the buttress.

The timber

The sapwood is 30mm to 50mm wide, pale reddish in colour, and not clearly distinguished from the heartwood which is pale pinkish-brown darkening with age. There appears to be some variation in colour in the timber from different localities in the Philippines, some having a light red heartwood, while much grown in Mindanao is dark reddish-brown. The grain may be straight, but more usually it is interlocked, with a characteristic regular wave, while the texture is fine and smooth, although this may not apply to timber from all localities since the wood grown in Papua New Guinea is said to have a coarse and uneven texture. Weight about 750 kg/m^3 when dried.

Drying

Dries reasonably well, but care must be taken to avoid warping and checking.

Strength

The strength properties are similar to those of European beech.

Durability
Moderately durable.

Working qualities
Works and machines fairly well, with only a moderate blunting effect on cutting edges. With attention to techniques a good finish can be obtained in planing and moulding. The wood takes glue and the normal finishing treatments satisfactorily.

Uses
Where fairly abundant in the Philippines the wood is well-known and favoured for beams, joists, rafters, flooring, ceilings and interior trim, furniture, cabinets, levers, capstan bars, minor tool handles, and masts and spars in boat building. Australian tests on taun, the Papua New Guinea equivalent, indicate good peeling properties for veneer. Mindoro appears to have the most abundant supply.

MANCONO

Xanthostemon verdugonianus Naves.   Family : Myrtaceae

Other names
palo de hierro, Philippine ironwood, Philippine lignum vitae.

Distribution
The tree is generally scarce in the Philippines, except in Surigao in the north of Mindanao.

The tree
The tree attains a fair height, but the bole is generally very short, branches often starting 1m or 2m from the ground, although in exceptionally good trees the bole may be up to 10m clear of branches. Diameters vary from 0.3m to 1m.

The timber
The local names of ironwood and lignum vitae are more descriptive of the character of the wood rather than on a botanical relationship, although mancono is related to ironbark of Australia.
Despite the relatively small saw-logs, the timber is a valuable

local material, substituting for lignum vitae in many traditional uses. Mancono wood is very hard, and very heavy, weighing about 1280 kg/m³ when dried, a little heavier than lignum vitae.

The sapwood is from 10mm to 20mm wide, pale red in colour, sharply defined from the heartwood which is yellowish-brown when freshly cut, turning to a dark bronze after drying, and almost black with age. The grain is always crossed, frequently curly and twisted, but the texture is extremely fine and dense, to the extent that bare wood can be burnished almost like metal, due to the few, and very small pores scattered in the wood, the very fine rays, and the fact that soft parenchyma tissue is practically absent.

Drying
Large logs often contain radial heart cracks, but sawn material although drying extremely slowly, tends only to check superficially and not deeply.

Durability
Very durable. It is said that small logs used as posts have only about 10mm of decayed sapwood after 40 years in the ground, and similar stock used for salt water piling is only similarly degraded due to teredo attack after 20 years.

Uses
The wood is extremely difficult to work, but it is used locally for pulleys, rollers, bowling balls, dumb-bells, bearings, saw-guide blocks, tool handles, novelties, paper weights, posts and piles.

MAPLE, JAPANESE

Acer mono Maxim. et al.   Family: Aceraceae

A number of species of *Acer* produce maple, and it is probable that more than one provides commercial maple timber of Japan, but since this is generally of uniform character, it is also probable that some distinctions are made in the selection from the many species found in Japan. *A. mono* appears to be a principal species, along with *A. palmatum*.

General characteristics
A light-coloured wood, with grain usually straight, but occasion-ally wavy. The creamy white sapwood is not sharply defined from the heartwood, which however, generally has a reddish tinge. The texture is fine and even, and the growth rings produce fine brown lines on longitudinal surfaces. The wood is very similar in appearance to rock maple (*A. saccharum*), but is a little lighter in weight, about 670 kg/m³ when dried.

Uses
Used as an alternative to rock maple for furniture, panelling, cabinets, flooring, for bowling alleys, dance-halls, ware-houses, squash courts, and for decorative veneer.

MENGKULANG

Heritiera javanica Bl.   Family : Sterculiaceae

Other names
lumbayao, gisang.

Distribution
A number of species of *Heritiera* occur in the tropics, including niangon of West Africa, and chumprak of Thailand. *H. javanica* is the principal species found in the Philippines.

The tree
A fairly large tree, some 36m tall, with a diameter of 0.6m and a generally straight and cylindrical bole above the buttress.

The timber
The sapwood is pale yellowish-red in colour, merging gradually into the light red to reddish-brown heartwood, the wood from medium-sized trees resembling cigar-box cedar, and the darker-coloured wood being more like African mahogany in appear-ance. The grain is straight or interlocked, sometimes wavy, producing a stripe figure on quarter-sawn surfaces, while a fine fleck figure is also present, due to the rather large rays. The texture is open and rather coarse, and the wood has a greasy feel. It weighs about 720 kg/m³ when dried, and is moderately durable.

Drying
The timber dries fairly rapidly, without excessive degrade, there being only a mild tendency to splitting, warping and checking.

Strength
Similar to teak, but large trees often contain brittleheart.

Working qualities
Works and machines with moderate ease, but tends to blunt tools, especially saw teeth, fairly quickly. Quarter-sawn stock tends to pick up in planing and moulding and a reduction of cutting angle to 15° is helpful in obtaining a good finish. The pores contain a red gum which sometimes tends to interfere with polishing, but this can be overcome with care.

Uses
Used locally for furniture, cabinets, flooring, doors, interior finish, boat ribs and planking.

A wood known as lumbayao batu also occurs in the Philippines, but this is very hard, heavy, and darker in colour, and is less favoured. Generally used for constructional purposes, its botanical origin is obscure.

MERBAU

Intsia bijuga O. Ktze.   Family : Leguminosae

Other names
ipil (Philippines) ; kwila (Papua New Guinea) ; hintzy (Madagascar).

Distribution
Intsia bijuga occurs throughout the South-west Pacific Islands, Madagascar, and the Philippines, while *I. palembanica* is found in Malaysia and Indonesia.

The tree
Merbau is a tall, straight tree, up to 1.8m in diameter.

The timber

The sapwood is 40mm to 80mm wide, whitish, and sharply distinguished from the heartwood, which when fresh, is bright yellow, turning dark brown on exposure. Lighter-coloured parenchyma usually gives an ornamental figure on tangential surfaces. The wood has an oily odour, and small quantities of oil exuding from the surface cause characteristic small, dull black spots to occur on planed surfaces.

The grain is straight, but may be interlocked, and the texture coarse but even. The wood weighs about 900 kg/m^3 when dried.

Drying

The timber dries slowly, and requires care in order to avoid surface checking, particularly in thick dimensions.

Strength

No information, but it is reputed to be a good, strong wood.

Durability

Durable.

Working qualities

Rather hard to saw, the gum clogging saw teeth quite rapidly. A reduction of cutting angle to 20° in planing and moulding helps to reduce the tendency for grain to tear, especially in quarter-sawn material. The wood tends to split in nailing, but it holds screws well, and with care, can be stained and polished.

Uses

All high-class general construction, posts, beams, joists, rafters, transmission poles, sills, ties, flooring, siding, sheathing, doors and windows, ship, wharf, and bridge building, except salt water piling, agricultural implements.

The sulphur-yellow deposits in the pores are soluble in water and the dye thus produced can have a lasting effect on textiles or fair faced concrete, where these are used in contact with wet wood.

MOLAVE

Vitex parviflora Juss.   Family: Verbenaceae

Distribution

About nine species of the genus *Vitex* occur in the Philippines, but only about two are widely distributed or well-known, one of these, *V. aherniana* Merr. produces a timber known as sasalit, a very durable species with a high resistance to marine borer attack, but of limited availability, and the best known is *V. parviflora*, or molave.

The tree
A large tree with a diameter of 2m or more, but with a short, fluted bole.

The timber
The sapwood is small and not clearly distinct from the heartwood, which is pale straw-colour to light brown, sometimes with greenish tints. The grain varies from straight in well-grown trees, to wavy or curly, and the texture is fine, giving a smooth surface under sharp tools. The wood is hard, stiff, but inclined to be brittle, and weighs about 768 kg/m^3 on average when dried.

Drying
Rather difficult to dry and requires care since it is liable to develop large, deep, and irregular checks. It is not liable to serious warping.

Strength
No information.

Durability
Very durable.

Working qualities
Although hard and dense, the wood is said to work and machine with moderate ease, and to be capable of a very smooth surface in planing and moulding.

Uses
Piling, posts, bridges, wharves, particularly where *Teredo* is a hazard, sills, doors, windows, stairs, (treads, risers, balusters, and hand-rails), siding, sheathing, framing of hemp presses and sugar mills, cog-wheels, agricultural implements, and carving and sculpture of sacred images.

NARRA

Pterocarpus indicus Willd.   Family: Leguminosae

Distribution
This species is widely distributed throughout southern and south east Asia, producing Solomons padauk and Papua New Guinea rosewood. It is found throughout the Philippines, and is abundant in Cagayan, Mindoro, Palawan and Cotabato.

The tree
A large tree with an irregular fluted trunk, attaining a height of 40m and a diameter up to 2m above the broad, flat buttress which extends some 10m to 12m up the trunk.

The timber
The sapwood is 40mm to 60mm wide, light-coloured and distinct from the heartwood which may be light yellow or brick-red in colour. Red narra is generally associated with slow-growing, and ill-formed trees, and it is said that timber from trees in Cagayan is generally harder and heavier than that from other provinces, and is blood-red in colour. The wood is often prominently figured, due to a combination of storied elements, terminal parenchyma, and grain irregularities giving rise to mottle, fiddle-back, ripple and curl effects.
The well-known name amboyna, is restricted to the highly-decorative wood produced from burrs.
The grain is interlocked, wavy, or crossed, and the texture is moderately fine. The wood varies in weight, and generally speaking the darker the wood the heavier the weight, but on average it is about 660 kg/m^3 when dried.

Drying
The timber dries rather slowly, but reasonably well, the red-coloured wood requiring more care than the yellow variety.

Strength
Strength is not a general requirement in the normal uses to which narra is put, but straight-grained material is only slightly inferior in general strength properties to European beech.

Durability
Very durable.

Working qualities

Fairly easy to work and machine, with only a slight dulling effect on cutting edges. A good finish is obtained when planing or moulding straight-grained material, but otherwise, the cutting angle should be reduced to 20° in order to obtain the best results. The timber can be nailed, screwed, and glued satisfactorily, and takes an excellent polish.

Uses

Furniture, high-class joinery, panelling, interior trim for houses and boats, decorative veneer, and as cases for scientific instruments.

OAK, JAPANESE

Quercus spp. principally   Family : Fagaceae
Q. mongolica var. *grosseserrata*

Other names

ohnara is the Japanese name for *Q. mongolica* Turcz. var. *grosseserrata* Bl. the timber of which is normally exported to Europe. Other species are usually referred to as follows, konara (*Q. glandulifera*) ; kashiwa (*Q. dentata*) ; shira-kashi (*Q. myrsinaefolia*) ; ichii-gashi (*Q. gilva*) ; aka-gashi (*Q. acuta*) ; ubame-gashi (*Q. phillyraeoides*).

Distribution

Ohnara, or Japanese oak, generally comes from the north island of Hokkaido, but it also occurs in the central district of the main island.

The timber

The timber is a uniform yellowish-brown, a little paler in colour than that of European or American white oak, and much milder in character, due to the slow, even growth. It weighs about 670 kg/m^3 when dried. Timber from trees grown in the main island generally has a pinkish shade.

Durability

Moderately durable.

Uses

Furniture, cabinets, joinery, panelling.

PALAQUIUM SPECIES

The Sapotaceae family includes some twenty-five species of the genus *Palaquium*, of which one or more occur in practically every island and province in the Philippines.

The trees are medium-sized to large, with tall, straight trunks, and diameters up to 1.5m.

Although not as abundant as the lauans, the logs are invariably present in Manila yards, the timber sometimes being mixed with lauans and other miscellaneous red woods for local markets.

The wood of all species, except for some differences in colour, weight, and hardness, is practically identical, and local names in various regions are applied to all species almost indifferently. The following are some of the principal species, along with their local names.

P. ahernianum Merr.	kalipaya.
P. cuneatum Vid.	malikmik.
P. foxworthyi Merr.	tagatoi.
P. gigantifolium Merr.	alakaak.
P. luzoniensis Vid.	nato.
P. merrillii Dubard.	dulitan.
P. philippense C. B. Rob.	malacmalac.
P. tenuipetiolatum Merr.	manicnic.

The timber is favoured among Filipino and Chinese cabinet-makers for furniture, particularly for drawer sides and backs, shelves, etc. because of its ease of working and freedom from warping, and timber for this type of use is generally called amugis corriente, which roughly means, normal, or usual amugis, which firstly, identifies selected wood, not necessarily of one species, and secondly, serves to distinguish it from amugis perfecto, or true amugis, which name is more properly applied to the timber of *Koordersiodendron pinnatum* Merr. a member of the Anacardiaceae family, similar in appearance to *Palaquium* species.

The various species of *Palaquium* vary from soft to moderately hard and light to moderately heavy, the wood weighing from 640 kg/m^3 to 720 kg/m^3 when dried. The sapwood is 20mm to 50mm wide, and in large trees sharply marked off from the heartwood which varies from light red to dull reddish-brown. The grain is straight or slightly interlocked, sometimes with a regular wave forming a diagonal ribbon figure on quarter-sawn

surfaces. The texture is fine, and promotes a smooth, almost glossy finish when the wood is planed.
The timber dries easily and well, and is easy to work.

Uses
Said to be non-durable when used in contact with the ground, all the species are used for general utility purposes, often as an alternative to lauan, and is often favoured, because, despite its low resistance to decay, it is said to be rarely attacked by beetles. A good joinery, and general purpose timber for interior use.

PALDAO

Dracontomelum dao Merr. & Rolfe.   Family : Anacardiaceae

Other names
dao (Philippines).

Distribution
Various species of *Dracontomelum* occur in Papua New Guinea and neighbouring islands, producing the timber, known as Papua New Guinea walnut, but the principal species found in the Philippines is *D. dao* the source of commercial paldao or dao.

The tree
A tall, straight tree with a diameter of about 0.6m to 1.0m. In open situations the bole is often crooked, but under forest conditions this is usually straight, but always with very long, thin buttresses extending some 6m or 8m up the trunk.

The timber
The sapwood is very large, light pinkish or brownish in colour, rather sharply distinguished from the heartwood which is brownish or greenish-grey, with irregular dark brown or almost black streaks. The grain may be straight or interlocked and sometimes wavy, and a broken ribbon-grain figure often occurs on quarter-sawn faces. The texture is medium and even. The wood weighs about 740 kg/m^3 when dried.

Drying
Dries well with care, but there is a tendency for the wood to warp badly.

Strength
No information.

Durability
Moderately durable.

Working qualities
Works and machines readily, with only a moderate blunting effect on cutting edges. Interlocked grain tends to pick up in planing and moulding and a reduction of cutting angle to 20° is beneficial. The wood takes an excellent polish.

Uses
Carpentry and joinery, flooring, furniture and cabinets, etc. Locally, the buttress timber is used for decorative table tops. Good decorative veneer is produced from selected logs.

PALOSAPIS

Anisoptera thurifera Bl.   Family: Dipterocarpaceae

Distribution
Various species of *Anisoptera* produce mersawa of Malaysia, krabak of Thailand, and palosapis of the Philippines, where the principal species, *A. thurifera* occurs in primary forests, in heavy stands in most of the islands.

The tree
A large tree, reaching a height of 40m to 45m and a diameter of 1.2m to 1.8m with a straight, unbuttressed regular bole 20m to 30m in length.

The timber
The light-coloured sapwood is 50mm to 80mm wide, not very distinct from the heartwood which is buff coloured initially, turning yellowish or yellow after drying. The grain is straight, sometimes crossed or wavy, with a slight ribbon figure on quarter-sawn surfaces, and the texture is moderately fine to coarse. The wood weighs about 720 kg/m³ when dried.

Drying
Dries slowly, with a reluctance to give up its moisture from the centre of thick material. Thin sizes are susceptible to warping, and care must be taken to ensure good sticking practice. Shrinkage, green to 12 per cent moisture content is 6 per cent tangentially, and 2 per cent radially.

Strength
By comparison with tangile, the timber is about 20 per cent stiffer, slightly stronger in compression parallel to the grain, and about 40 per cent more tough.

Durability
Moderately durable.

Working qualities
Machines readily, but with a severe blunting effect on cutting edges. The rather fibrous finish obtained in planing and moulding can be improved by a reduction of cutting angle to 20°. The wood can be peeled satisfactorily for veneer.

Uses
Boat planking, plywood, interior finish, general construction, vehicle bodies.

SOPHORA

Sophora japonica L. Family : Leguminosae

Other names
pagoda tree (UK) ; yen-ju, en-ju (Japan).

Distribution
S. japonica occurs in China and Japan, and a further species, *S. tetraptera*, is found in New Zealand. *S. japonica* was introduced into Britain in 1753 as an ornamental tree, its long, pinnate leaves, and graceful, bushy crown, together with its cylindrical seed pods, constricted between the seeds like a string of beads, presenting a very pleasing appearance.

General characteristics

Sophora is closely related to *Laburnum, Wistaria,* and *Acacia,* and the wood is of a golden-brown colour with a greenish tint, and somewhat resembling laburnum wood. It possesses a lustrous sheen, and fairly fine texture, and weighs about 673 kg/m³ when dried.

Uses

Under open growth conditions, the form of the tree generally precludes long, wide, boards, and it is unlikely that sophora will be seen on world timber markets. It is however, considered a valuable material in Japan where the strong, tough timber is used largely for pillars and house framing. It is said to be durable.

TINDALO

Pahudia rhomboidea Prain. Family: Leguminosae

Distribution

Fairly widely distributed throughout the Philippines, but not as abundant as narra.

General characteristics

A straight, but not tall tree, with a diameter of 1.2m. The wood is hard and heavy, weighing from 772 kg/m³ to 805 kg/m³ when dried. The sapwood is whitish, 20mm to 40mm wide, and sharply distinguished from the heartwood which is saffron coloured, or pale orange, turning to a deep, rich red colour with age, sometimes with irregular blackish streaks, and occasionally with scattered bird's-eye knots. The wood has a slight odour when freshly sawn, reminiscent of peanuts.

The grain is usually straight but may be shallowly interlocked, and the texture is fine. The wood is said to dry easily and well, with only a slight tendency to warping and checking, and is fairly easy to machine, the dense, compact nature of the wood producing a smooth, almost glossy finish in planing and moulding when cutters are maintained in sharp condition.

It is moderately durable, and is considered one of the finest Philippine cabinet woods.

Uses
Interior finish, flooring, doors, windows, sills, stair treads, hand rails on account of its good colour and smooth hardness, musical instruments, cabinet making, and for all kinds of high-grade construction except posts set in the ground.

WILLOW

Salix spp.   Family: Salicaceae

Various species of willow occur throughout Europe, North Africa, Asia, etc including China and Japan, and generally provide basket-making and rough weaving material and timber. The principal Japanese species is *Salix jessoensis* Seem.

General characteristics
The Japanese name for this wood is tokachiyanigi. The sapwood is white to straw-coloured, gradually merging into the pinkish-yellow heartwood. The grain varies considerably according to the growth habit of the tree, ranging from straight to wavy, but with a fine, even texture. The wood is light in weight, about 433 kg/m^3 when dried.

Uses
Local uses include artificial limbs, clog soles, toys, lorry bottoms and for fibre board.

PART II SOFTWOODS

ALMACIGA

Agathis philippinensis Warb.   Family: Araucariaceae

Distribution
Although widely distributed throughout the Philippines, almaciga occurs rather sparsely in the higher altitudes above the Dipterocarp forests, and occasionally at sea level in a few places.

The tree
A large, tall tree, reaching a height of 60m and a diameter of 3m on good sites. The bole is straight and cylindrical, and clear of branches for 20m to 30m.

The timber
The wood is similar to kauri, being pinkish-buff in colour, with no distinction between sapwood and heartwood. The grain is straight, and the texture very fine, and the wood has neither odour nor taste. The weight is variable, depending on growth conditions and may be fairly light, or comparatively heavy, but on average it weighs about 550 kg/m^3 when dried.

Drying
Dries readily and without undue degrade.

Strength
By comparison with lauan, the timber is similar to almon in general strength properties, and compared with pitch pine, it has about the same strength, except in bending strength and stiffness, where it is rather inferior.

Durability
Perishable.

Working qualities
The wood works easily and well. It has good nailing and screwing properties, and stains and polishes excellently. It has fairly

good peeling properties, and produces a high proportion of face quality veneer.

Uses
Owing to the valuable resin (Manila copal) produced by the tree, and used in the manufacture of high-grade, glossy varnishes and lacquers, the felling of almaciga is discouraged by the Philippine government in order to protect the copal industry, but almaciga wood is suitable for artificial limb manufacture, instrument cases, pencil slats, joinery and veneer.

BENGUET PINE

Pinus insularis Endl.   Family : Pinaceae

Other names
saleng, bel-bel, parina, salit.

Distribution
Occurs in a long narrow belt in the mountain area of north-west Luzon in abundant quantities, and sparsely near the coast of Zambales.

The tree
A moderately tall tree with a diameter of about 1.4m.

The timber
A hard pine of the pitch pine type. The wood is moderately hard to hard, and the heartwood is very much heavier than the sapwood, in fact in some specimens the heartwood is heavier than water. The heartwood is very resinous, ranging from pale yellow to rich orange-brown, and that from overmature trees sometimes being almost completely impregnated with resin. There is a marked contrast between the lighter-coloured early-wood and the much darker zones of late-wood in each growth ring. The grain is generally straight, and the texture fine. The wood weighs from 673 kg/m³ to 880 kg/m³ or more depending on the resin content.

Drying
The timber is said to dry slowly but well.

Strength
No information.

Durability
Sapwood non-durable, heartwood durable in respect of decay, very durable in respect of insects. It is rarely if ever attacked by insects, even termites avoiding the heart and resinous knots.

Working qualities
Fairly easy to work and machine, but extreme gumminess slows most machine operations.

Uses
Used in the mountain districts for practically every utilitarian purpose. It seldom reaches the Manila market.

A further species, *Pinus merkusii* Jungh & de Vr. occurs in the interior of Mindoro and Zambales. Known as Mindoro pine, or tapulau, it is similar to benguet pine, and often even more resinous.

FIR, JAPANESE

Abies mariesii Mast.   Family: Pinaceae

Other names
todo matsu (Japan).

General characteristics
This species belongs to the same group that produces amabilis fir of North America. The wood is a little darker in colour than most species of *Abies*, due to the darker late-wood bands, and a little coarser in texture than spruce. It weighs about 416 kg/m^3 when dried.

Uses
Used separately or mixed with spruce for general utility purposes.

HEMLOCK

Tsuga spp.   Family: Pinaceae

A few species of the genus *Tsuga* occur in China and Japan, *T. chinensis* and *T. yunnanensis* growing in China, and *T.*

diversifolia and *T. sieboldii* in Japan. All these yield timber for local use, and it is doubtful if any will generally be exported.

General characteristics
The well-known western and eastern hemlock of North America belong to a group of species of *Tsuga* in which the leaves are minutely toothed, whereas the Chinese and Japanese species have entire leaves, but apart from this the timber is to all intents and purposes the same in general appearance in both groups, being non-resinous, and pale brown in colour with the darker late-wood bands having a reddish or purplish cast.
Probably the most important species is *T. sieboldii* Carr. of Japan, which weighs about 465 kg/m^3 when dried, has a straight to crossed grain and a fairly coarse texture, and lacks the lustre typical in western hemlock.

Uses
General construction, carpentry and joinery, and to a minor extent for veneer.

LARCH, JAPANESE

L. kaempferi Sarg. syn.   Family : Pinaceae
L. leptolepis Gord.

Distribution
Japan, principally in Shinano Province.

The tree
Attains a height of 18m to 30m and a diameter of 0.75m.

The timber
The sapwood is light-brown in colour, sharply defined from the reddish-brown heartwood. The growth rings are clearly marked, with well-defined latewood bands. The wood is resinous, with a straight grain, and medium fine texture. It weighs about 560 kg/m^3 when dried.

Drying
Dries fairly rapidly with some tendency to warp, split and check.

Strength
Although about 30 per cent softer than European larch, the timber is practically as strong.

Durability
Moderately durable.

Working qualities
The timber works readily, but since the soft, earlywood tends to crumble when planed, sharp cutting edges are needed to ensure a good finish. Knots are hard, and can be troublesome in the lower commercial grades. The wood can be painted or varnished without difficulty, but it tends to split when nailed.

Uses
General construction, furniture, flooring, bridge construction and boat building.

RED PINE, JAPANESE

Pinus densiflora   Family : Pinaceae

Other names
akamatsu

Distribution
Widely distributed from Kyushu to Hokkaido in Japan.

General characteristics
The sapwood is whitish in colour, and the heartwood is light reddish-brown, of the soft pine type, similar in strength properties to European redwood, with a straight grain, and fine texture, weighing about 400 kg/m^3. Non-durable, it is used locally for building construction, joinery, panelling and boat building. The timber is inclined to be knotty, and is difficult to obtain in relatively clear stock.

SPRUCE JAPANESE

Picea jezoensis Carr.   Family : Pinaceae
syn. *P. ajanensis* Fisch.

Other names
yeddo spruce (UK) ; yezo matsu (Japan).

General characteristics
The spruces can be divided into two basic groups, ie those in which the leaves are flattened or distinctly 2-edged, with grey lines on one side only, and those with quadrangular section leaves with grey line on both sides. Norway and Canadian spruce belong to this latter group, while Sitka spruce, and yeddo spruce belong to the former, accordingly, Japanese, or yeddo spruce has more of the characteristics of Sitka spruce, than of European spruce or whitewood.

The timber is non-resinous, without odour, and non-tainting, whitish in colour, often with a pinkish cast, mainly straight-grained, but sometimes with spiral grain, and weighing about 432 kg/m³ when dried.

Uses
The timber is non-durable, and is used locally for utilitarian purposes in building and joinery, and is often mixed with fir.

SUGI

Cryptomeria japonica D. Don.   Family : Taxodiaceae

Other name
Japanese cedar.

Distribution
Japan and Taiwan.

The tree
Under favourable conditions the tree attains a height of 45m or more, and a diameter of 2m and occasionally much more.

The timber
Sugi is related to sequoia and swamp cypress, and in appearance is similar to the latter, being a warm brown colour with yellow or dark brown streaks forming a somewhat wavy pattern, but it is harder, and firmer textured than cypress.

A feature of sugi is the resin which occurs mainly in vertical parenchyma cells, and is black in colour. This tends to glisten on longitudinal surfaces, and imparts a slight lustre to the wood, which is straight-grained, and weighs about 400 kg/m³ when dried.

Drying
Requires care, particularly in thick sizes, since there is a definite tendency for the wood to split and check.

Strength
No information.

Durability
Durable.

Working qualities
Saws and machines with only a moderate blunting effect on cutting edges, due mainly to the resin, but knots can be troublesome in planing and moulding since the tendency for the grain to tear is increased in the vicinity of knots. With care, the wood can be finished smoothly, and it takes the usual finishing treatments quite well. It tends to split in nailing, but holds screws well.

Uses
For centuries, the tree has been venerated by the Japanese, the mysticism and pious sentiment being restricted to the growing tree, not the timber, which has rarely been cultivated, with the result that this is usually rather knotty, although the tree is capable of producing much clear timber. It is used for house framing, gate-ways to temples, and for joinery and furniture frames.

USE GUIDE FOR PHILIPPINE AND JAPANESE TIMBERS

AGRICULTURAL IMPLEMENTS

agoho
almaciga
aranga
Diospyros spp. (sapwood)
guijo
larch
malabayabas

mangachapuy
mengkulang
merbau
molave
pine, benguet
yacal

BEARINGS, BUSHINGS, COGS AND PULLEYS

boxwood   malabayabas   mancono

BOAT AND SHIP CONSTRUCTION

Decking
apitong
guijo
larch
lauan, red

mangachapuy
mengkulang
palosapis
yacal

Framing
mengkulang   molave

Keels and stems
aranga
guijo
liusin

molave
yacal

Masts and spars
guijo (small spars)
lauan, red (small spars)

malagai
mangachapuy

Oars and paddles
almaciga (light sculls and paddles)
calantas   lauan, white   molave

Planking
guijo
larch
lauan, red
lauan, white

mangachapuy
mengkulang
palosapis
yacal

Superstructures
banuyo
calantas
lauan, red
mengkulang

narra
oak
Palaquium spp.
tindalo

BOXES AND CRATES

Cigar boxes
calantas (high-grade)

lauan, light red (cheap-grade)

Clothes chests

narra

chestnut, horse

hemlock

Packing cases
apitong
fir
guijo
hemlock
mengkulang

palosapis
pine, benguet
pine, red
spruce

Scientific instrument cases
lauan, red

narra.

CONSTRUCTION

Heavy
agoho
amugis
aranga
binggas

malabayabas
merbau
molave

Light
acle
agaru
almaciga

apitong
batete
beech

Light *(continued)*

birch
calamansanay
calantas
fir
hemlock
keyaki
larch

oak
Palaquium spp.
palosapis
pine, benguet
pine, red
spruce
suqi

DOORS

agaru
apitong
ash
banuyo
batete
baticulin, yellow
guijo
hemlock
lauan, red
mangachapuy

mengkulang
merbau
molave
narra
oak
Palaquium spp.
palosapis
tangile
tindalo

FANCY GOODS AND NOVELTIES

agaru
alder (gnarled pieces)
aranga
birch
bolong-eta (sapwood stained
    black)
boxwood
calamansanay
camagon (sapwood stained black)

cherry
Diospyros spp.
kaki
kiri
malabayabas
mancono
molave
narra
    tindalo

FLOORING

agaru
amugis
apitong
aranga
ash

batete
beech
binggas
calamansanay
fir

71

FLOORING *(continued)*

guijo
hemlock
larch
malagai
mangachapuy
maple
mengkulang
merbau
molave

narra
oak
Palaquium spp.
paldao
palosapis
tangile
tindalo
yacal

FURNITURE AND CABINETS

agaru
ash
batete
banuyo
baticulin, yellow
beech
calantas
cherry
Diospyros spp.
guijo
kaki

katsura
kiri
lauan
maple
mengkulang
merbau
narra
oak
paldao
tangile
tindalo

JOINERY

High-class
acle
agaru
ash
banuyo
calantas
cherry
katsura
keyaki

larch
lauan, red
maple
narra
oak
paldao
tindalo

Utility
almaciga
amugis
aranga

banuyo
batete
baticulin, yellow

JOINERY Utility *(continued)*

beech
birch
calamansanay
fir
hemlock
lanipau
larch

Palaquium spp.
palosapis
pine, benguet
pine, red
spruce
sugi

MARINE PILING AND CONSTRUCTION

Under water
a Teredo infested waters
agoho
liusin

mancono
molave

b Non-Teredo waters
in addition to above,
agaru
aranga

calamansanay
merbau
yacal

Above water
a Docks, wharves, bridges, etc.
agoho
aranga
apitong
binggas
calamansanay
larch

mengkulang
merbau
malabayabas
mangachapuy
palosapis
yacal

b Decking
aranga
apitong

calamansanay
yacal

MUSICAL INSTRUMENTS

apitong (harp bases)
banuyo
baticulin, yellow
bolong-eta
calamansanay

calantas
camagon
ebony
kiri
lauan

MUSICAL INSTRUMENTS *(continued)*

malatinta
merbau
narra
paldao

palosapis
tangile
tindalo
tiaong

SCULPTURE AND CARVING

a Sacred images and statues
baticulin, yellow
calantas
lauan, red

merbau
molave
tangile

b Andas (litter or bier on which saints or statues are carried)
acle
banuyo

lauan (low cost)
narra

c Permanent pedestals and platforms for images and statues
molave

d Altars and ornamental fixtures in churches
acle
narra

tindalo

e Carved feet, panels and finials for furniture
acle
baticulin, yellow
calantas
Diospyros spp.
katsura

keyaki
molave
narra
tangile
tindalo

SPORTS GOODS

agaru
agoho
almaciga
aranga
ash
ata-ata (sapwood)
bolong-eta (sapwood)

calamansanay
calantas
camagon (sapwood)
camagon (heartwood)
guijo
kaki
lauan

SPORTS GOODS *(continued)*

malabayabas
mangachapuy
mancono
maple
mengkulang

merbau
molave
narra
tindalo
yacal

STAIRS

a Balusters and handrails

apitong
aranga
batete
calamansanay
guijo
lauan
mangachapuy
maple

mengkulang
merbau
molave
narra
oak
Palaquium spp.
tindalo

b Treads and risers

maple
molave

tindalo

generally preferred, but any of a also used.

TURNERY

alder
beech
birch
boxwood
cherry

kaki
mancono
maple
oak
tindalo

VEHICLE BODIES

amugis
apitong
guijo
lauan
mangachapuy

merbau
narra
palosapis
willow (bottoms)
yacal

VENEER AND PLYWOOD

a Corestock
fir

hemlock

lauan, white

spruce

Decorative
agaru

ash

batete

birch

bolong-eta

camagon

ebony

keyaki

malatinta

maple

molave

narra (amboyna)

oak

paldao (selected)

tindalo

c Utility (plywood, chip-baskets, small laminted items, etc)
alder

almaciga

ash

beech

birch

hemlock

kiri

lauan

malagai

palosapis

spruce

TERMITE RESISTANCE

Termite activity represents a serious hazard to timber structures in the Philippines, particularly to house foundations. The use of timbers which offer some natural resistance to termite attack minimises the generally disastrous effect of termites, but chemical soil treatments at the time of building, and preservative and insecticidal pressure treatment of building timber, not only widens the range of suitable timbers, but offers greater protection to termite attack.

Physical barrier systems, such as termite caps, incorporated into the construction of buildings must be free from perforation and form a continuous barrier, but they cannot entirely be relied upon to offer suitable safeguards against termite attack.

The following list of timbers is grouped according to their natural resistance to termite attack, and is based primarily on local preferences and traditional use, and not necessarily on the results of field tests. The classification is based on the resistance of heartwood, unless otherwise stated.

Very resistant

acle	mancono
calantas	merbau
liusin	molave
malabayabas	narra

Resistant

agaru	*Diospyros* spp. heartwood
agoho	mengkulang
aranga	*Palaquium* spp.
binggas	

Moderately resistant

amugis	kaki
apitong	mangachapuy
banuyo	paldao
calamansanay	tindalo
Diospyros spp. (sapwood)	yacal

TERMITE RESISTANCE *(continued)*

Very susceptible

alder	katsura
almaciga	larch
ash	malagai
batete	maple
beech	palosapis
birch	pine, benguet
cherry	pine, red
chestnut, horse	spruce
fir	sugi
hemlock	willow

AMENABILITY OF HEARTWOOD TO PRESERVATIVE TREATMENT

Extremely resistant

agoho	liusin
Albizia spp.	malabayabas
amugis	malagai
aranga	mancono
Diospysos spp.	merbau
Hopea spp.	molave
kaki	*Palaquium* spp.
guijo	

Resistant

agaru	larch
almaciga	lauan
banuyo	narra
batete	oak
baticulin	paldao
fir	spruce
hemlock	tindalo
katsura	

Moderately resistant

ailanthus	calantas
ash	keyaki
binggas	lumbayao
calamansanay	

Permeable

alder	maple
beech	pine, red
birch	willow
chestnut, horse	

AMENABILITY OF HEARTWOOD TO PRESERVATIVE TREATMENT

The above classification refers to the ease with which a timber absorbs preservatives under both open-tank (non-pressure) and pressure treatments. Sapwood, although nearly always perishable, is usually much more permeable than heartwood, accordingly, the above classification refers to the relative resistance of heartwood to penetration.

Extremely resistant
Timbers that absorb only a small amount of preservative even under long pressure treatments. They cannot be penetrated to an appreciable depth laterally, and only to a very small extent longitudinally.

Resistant
Timbers difficult to impregnate under pressure and require a long period of treatment. It is often difficult to penetrate them laterally more than about 3mm to 6mm.
Incising is often used to obtain better treatment.

Moderately resistant
Timbers that are fairly easy to treat, and it is usually possible to obtain a lateral penetration of the order of 6mm to 18mm in about 2-3 hours under pressure, or a penetration of a large proportion of the vessels.

Permeable
Timbers that can be penetrated completely under pressure without difficulty, and can usually be heavily impregnated by the open-tank process.

2
EUROPE

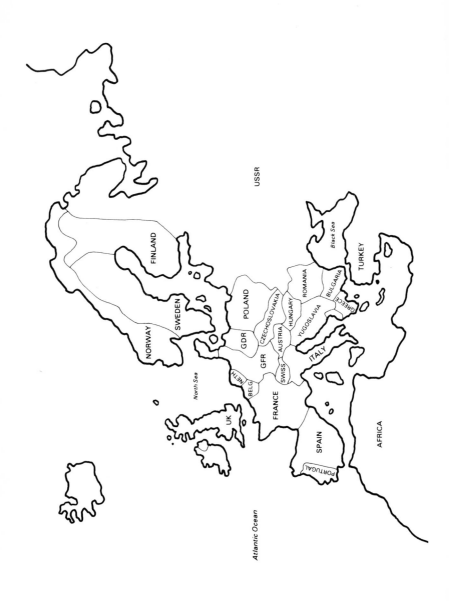

USSR

FINLAND

SWEDEN

NORWAY

POLAND

GDR

CZECHOSLOVAKIA

GFR

AUSTRIA

HUNGARY

ROMANIA

YUGOSLAVIA

BULGARIA

GREECE

TURKEY

Black Sea

SWISS

NETH

BELG

FRANCE

ITALY

North Sea

UK

SPAIN

PORTUGAL

AFRICA

Atlantic Ocean

INTRODUCTION

The geographical scope of this chapter is concerned with Europe bounded to the north by the Arctic Ocean, to the west by the Atlantic Ocean, and then extending southwards and eastwards to include the northern tip of North Africa, Turkey, and into the Soviet Union of Russia.

Europe is almost the smallest of the six continents, about the same size as Canada and slightly larger than Australia. An outstanding characteristic of the European forests is the presence of the same genera of trees as found in North America, although consisting partly of different species and partly of species introduced from there.

In approximate terms the forests of Europe are about 74 per cent coniferous, 24 per cent temperate hardwoods, and about 2 per cent mixed forests. The original forest cover of Europe has been severely depleted as the result of long utilization and the necessity of clearing the land for agriculture and other purposes, particularly in the British Isles, France, Spain, Italy and Greece. Sweden and Finland still have about half of their original forests available, and together with Soviet Russia are the most heavily forested regions in Europe.

Natural plant growth

From north to south of the continent the natural growth occurs in belts merging each into the next. Along the Arctic shore the tundra has stunted willows and a few annual plants; to the south lies the forest, at first coniferous, then deciduous; farther south the trees give way to the steppe or natural grassland; in the extreme south there is little grass, only evergreen shrubs, cypresses, and chestnut trees.

The vegetation zones are best marked in the east; in the west, Germany and the British Isles for example have had much of their natural forest cover removed by man, and reafforestation in these and other parts of western Europe is aimed at establishing forest reserves of relatively quick-maturing species such as conifers, rather than the re-establishment of deciduous forests which for centuries dominated much of the land in these areas. The deciduous species are not being ignored, however, but western Europe generally, and the British Isles particularly, have for centuries relied upon the importation of exotic hard-woods to satisfy the demands of industry to a great extent. At the present time Britain produces only about 8 per cent of her total timber requirements, and it is therefore logical for her to plant fast-maturing conifers partially to satisfy home demands and so reduce the cost of importing softwoods from elsewhere in Europe, and also to help to pay for costly hardwoods from the rest of the world.

Climate
The climate of Europe has a distinct effect not only on the growth-rate of trees indigenous to the area, but also, and perhaps more importantly, on the type of growth, and therefore the quality, of tree species introduced from overseas. Climate also has a bearing on the formation of ice in rivers and ports, which in winter slows down, or stops altogether, the movement of timber from one part of Europe to another.

Owing to its peninsular character, the climate of Europe is modified by oceanic conditions which affect it on the west. The prevalent surface air currents are the west winds which regularly carry moisture far into Europe. The prevalent surface oceanic movements are the drifts of wind-driven warm water, which prevent the coasts of west Europe south of the North Cape from becoming ice-bound in winter. In relation to its latitude, winter conditions on the west are abnormal. In January, the temperatures of Scotland are $20°C$ above the average for the latitude, so that Cape Wrath, with an average temperature of $5°C$ lies in a latitude where the average temperature is $- 15°C$.

Only in the extreme east of Europe on the Kirghiz steppe is the January temperature colder than the normal for the latitude. From Brittany through Szczecin on the river Oder to Leningrad the coastal strip is $6°C$ above the normal. The boundary line $0°C$, which limits the area frost bound in winter, starts at the North Cape in Norway, goes south to Hamburg and the Alps, and crosses the Balkans and the Crimea to Baku on the Caspian Sea. East and north of this line the winter frosts last from one to seven months, the period length-ening towards the north-east of Europe.

In summer, temperatures are normal for the latitudes, the Arctic circle has a temperature of $10°C$, latitude $55°N$ averages $21°C$, while the coast lands of the Mediterranean have three hot months when the temperature exceeds $21°C$.

Rainfall

Rainfall exceeds 1500mm annually on the highest areas and on parts of the west coast. The Pyrenees, Alps, Balkans and Caucasus include districts where the rain exceeds 1000mm, but most of Europe has an annual precipitation of between 500 and 1000mm. Spain, and east and north Russia receive less than 500mm, while in the Mediterranean areas most rain falls during the cool season, the summers being hot and dry. On the Atlantic coast rains are usually heaviest during late autumn, but in the east most rain falls during hot weather.

The climatic conditions accordingly influence tree growth since they can provide a long growing season in some parts of the continent and a short one in others, a factor reflected in the mild character of Kara Sea redwood occasioned by the long, cold, Siberian winters, and the coarser character of the same species grown under the influence of the Atlantic air streams.

Europe is an exporting area within itself, little lumber being shipped outside the continent, but the movement of timber from some parts of Europe, especially of softwoods, is controlled during the winter months by the quantity of ice built up in rivers and ports and its possible clearance by ice-breaking vessels, the date by which first open water (FOW) is declared, usually in late spring, deciding the period in which other parts of Europe can receive their timber from these areas.

Local preferences exist on the part of European timber users for species drawn from particular areas, but this is only valid if the preference is justified by results. A softwood species, slowly-grown because severe frosts have shortened the growing season, may not have such good strength properties as the same species grown in a warmer part of the continent, because here the growth can produce a higher proportion of dense, strong, late-wood. Conversely, a slowly-grown, ring-porous hardwood like oak and ash will be more coarse in texture by virtue of the closely-spaced rings of thin-walled early-wood pores. A medium growth-rate for both softwoods and hardwoods is generally the best for all-round use.

PART I   HARDWOODS

ALDER

Alnus glutinosa Gaertn.   Family : Betulaceae

Other names
common alder, black alder (UK) ; aune (France) ; els (Netherlands) ; erle (Germany).

Distribution
Alder occurs in Europe from Scandinavia and north Russia southwards. It is common throughout the British Isles and is found in north Africa and western Asia.

The tree
A small to medium-size tree, attaining a height usually between 15m and 27m and a diameter of 0.3m to 1.2m. It enjoys damp situations along streams, and reaches its best development when growing in moist loam upon which rain has washed down layers of humus from woods at higher elevations.

The timber
There is no distinction by colour between sapwood and heartwood, the wood being a dull, light reddish-brown colour, without lustre, soft, and light in weight, about 530 kg/m³ when dried.

Drying
The timber dries fairly rapidly with little degrade.

Strength
It has no reputation for strength, being comparable to poplar in general strength properties, although a little harder and rather more resistant in shear.

Durability
Perishable.

Working qualities
Easy to work and finish provided tools are kept sharpened.

It takes glue, stains and polish, and nails and screws satisfactorily, and is a fairly good turnery wood.

Uses
Plywood, broom and brush backs, hat blocks, rollers for textiles, toys, wooden clogs and soles, and since it is reputed to be very durable when totally submerged, it has been used for sluice gates and similar work.

Grey alder, *Alnus incana* Moench, occurs naturally in northern Europe and western Siberia, and has been planted in small amounts in the UK. Although distinguishable from the common alder in the tree, there is said to be no essential difference in the timber of either species.

ASH, EUROPEAN

Fraxinus excelsior L.   Family : Oleaceae

Other names
English, French, Polish, Slavonian etc ash, according to origin.

Distribution
Europe including the British Isles, north Africa and western Asia, growing best on loamy soils where both the soil and the atmosphere is moist and cool.

The tree
A tall, graceful tree, reaching a height of 30m to 42m on good sites, with a clear bole averaging 9m in length, and occasionally more. The diameter varies from 0.5m to 1.5m.

The timber
There is usually no distinction in colour between sapwood and heartwood, freshly cut wood being whitish to pale brown with a pink cast, turning to a slightly brownish-white after drying. In some logs, an irregular dark brown or black heartwood is found, but this is not necessarily a defect, as the timber is normally quite sound. Logs containing dark heart streaks are often enhanced in value because of the decorative nature of the wood which is known as olive ash.

European ash is typically straight grained, and this, combined with its toughness and flexibility, makes it one of the world's most valuable timbers for such uses as sports goods and striking tool handles. It is rather coarse textured, and varies somewhat in weight according to the growth conditions, from 528 kg/m³ to 816 kg/m³ when dried, but averaging 710 kg/m³.

Drying
Dries at a fairly rapid rate without excessive surface checking and splitting, but under the influence of severe temperatures, there is a tendency to distort and for end splitting to occur. Distorted stock responds well to reconditioning kiln treatment.

Strength
Similar to oak in general strength properties, but tougher and more resistant to splitting.

Durability
Perishable.

Working qualities
Although tough, ash works and machines quite well, and finishes to a reasonably smooth finish. It can be glued, stained, and polished.

Uses
One of the best bending woods, ash is used extensively in furniture and chair making. It is used for agricultural implements, vehicle bodies, wheelwright's work, plywood and decorative veneer, and for sports goods such as tennis racquets, hockey sticks, polo heads, and gymnasium equipment, and for tool and axe handles. The demand for so-called sports ash generally exceeds supply from a given area, and accordingly, it is not unusual for a relatively wide search to be made in order to locate suitable parcels.

BEECH, EUROPEAN

Fagus sylvatica L.   Family : Fagaceae

Other names
English, Danish, French, Slavonian etc beech, according to origin.

Distribution
Europe, especially central Europe and Britain.

The tree
Beech has been called the mother of the forest, since without it in mixed broad-leaved forests, other hardwood timber trees would have greater difficulties for survival. The rain drip from beech destroys many soil-exhausting weeds, its shade prevents over-evaporation of moisture from the soil, and its heavy crop of leaves provides humus to the soil.

In close forest, it can reach a height of 45m with a clear bole of 15m but on average this is usually about 9m with a diameter averaging 1.2m occasionally more.

The timber
Normally, there is no clear distinction by colour between sapwood and heartwood, the wood being very pale brown when freshly cut, turning reddish-brown on exposure, and deep reddish-brown under the influence of steaming treatment commonly applied in parts of the Continent before shipment.

Some logs show an irregular, dark reddish-coloured kern or heart, caused it is believed, by the effect of severe frosts, and occurring more frequently in Continental beech. The wood is typically straight grained, with a fine, even texture, but varying in density and hardness according to the locality of growth. Thus beech from central Europe, notably that from Yugoslavia (Slavonian), and that from Romania is milder and lighter in weight, about 672 kg/m^3, than beech from Britain, Denmark and northern Europe, which weighs about 720 kg/m^3 when dried.

Drying
Although it dries fairly rapidly and fairly well, beech is moderately refractory, tending to warp, twist, check and split, and shrink considerably. It therefore requires care both in air drying and kiln drying.

Strength
Green beech has general strength properties roughly equal to those of oak, but after drying, most values increase, and beech is stronger than oak in bending strength, stiffness and shear

by some 20 per cent, and considerably stronger in resistance to impact loads.

Durability
Perishable.

Working qualities
Beech varies somewhat in its ease of working and machining according to growth characteristics and dried condition. Thus, fairly tough material, or badly dried stock may tend to bind on the saw, or burn when cross-cut, or, if distorted due to drying, provide difficulties in planing. On the whole, however, it works fairly readily, and is capable of a good smooth surface. Beech turns well, takes glue readily, and takes stains and polish satisfactorily. It produces excellent veneer.

Uses
The uses for beech are innumerable, from furniture, both solid and laminated from veneer, to domestic woodware, shoe heels, toys, bobbins, tool handles, interior joinery, interior construction, and plywood, flooring, turnery.

The various types of beech tree used throughout Europe, mainly for decorative purposes are considered to be sports from the purple variety, which in turn was a natural sport from the common beech discovered in a German wood more than a hundred years ago. A sport is a tree that deviates strikingly from the type of its species, thus

F. sylvatica L. var. *cuprea* Loud. produces copper beech

F. sylvatica L. var. *heterophylla* Loud. produces fern-leaved beech

F. sylvatica L. var. *pendula* Loud. produces weeping beech

F. sylvatica L. var. *purpurea* Ait. produces purple beech

F. sylvatica L. var. *purpurea pendula* Rehd. produces weeping purple beech.

Fagus orientalis Lipsky is a separate species found in Asia Minor, the timber of which is known as Turkish beech, and which is similar in appearance and properties to those of common beech.

90

BIRCH, EUROPEAN

Betula spp.   Family: Betulaceae

Other names
English, Finnish, Swedish etc birch, according to origin, silver birch, white birch.

Distribution
Birch is found throughout Europe, including the British Isles. It penetrates farther north than any other broad-leaved tree, being found in Lapland, and it will grow where it is subject to great heat just as well as it will endure extreme cold.
It extends from Scandinavia and northern Europe down to central Spain, and throughout the British Isles.

The tree
Two forms are recognised, *Betula pendula* (silver or white birch), and *B. pubescens* (common birch). Silver birch is the form with rough bark at its base, the branches drooping, twigs warty, leaves short-pointed and smooth, as distinct from common birch with its smooth, often reddish bark at the base, branches closer and more horizontal, and twigs and leaves softly hairy.
   Both species may be little more than shrubs, particularly in very cold areas, or they may branch just above the ground, but in general, they produce a good clean bole, some 9m in length, especially in Finland and Sweden, with a diameter of 0.5m to 0.9m.
The trees reach a height of 18m or 20m sometimes more; in their first ten years of life they grow at a rapid rate of some 0.5m annually, putting on little girth during this period, and reaching maturity in fifty years.

The timber
There is no distinct heartwood, the wood being whitish to pale brown, without conspicuous features, fairly straight grained, fine-textured, and weighing about 670 kg/m^3 when dried.
Despite the normally featureless appearance of birch, changes in appearance occasionally take place due to beetle attack. An insect known as *Agromyzia carbonaria* is usually responsible, its larvae burrowing in the cambium of the tree create what are

91

known as pith flecks, pith-like cells which cause dark markings in the wood, and localized grain disturbances. Logs that have been severely attacked, when rotary peeled, can produce highly decorative veneer known as masur birch, the irregular dark markings appearing to stand out in relief against the silky white background.
Flame birch and curly birch veneer is likewise created by grain deviations.

Drying
Birch air dries. and kiln dries fairly quickly without undue difficulty beyond a tendency to warp. It should be dried quickly after conversion in order to avoid fungal discolouration, or decay.

Strength
The dried timber is similar to oak in most strength properties, and superior to that timber in compression along the grain, stiffness and toughness.

Durability
Perishable.

Working qualities
Works fairly easily but is inclined to be woolly. It can be planed and moulded to a good clean surface, and can be glued, stained and polished satisfactorily, and is a good turnery wood.

Uses
Plywood and blockboard, furniture, bobbins, dowels, fittings, turnery, veneer, and in twig form for brooms and pea sticks, and in pole form for posts after preservative treatment under pressure.

BOXWOOD, EUROPEAN

Buxus sempervirens L.   Family : Buxaceae

Other names
Abassian, Iranian, Turkish etc boxwood, according to origin.

Distribution
Southern Europe including the British Isles, Asia Minor, and western Asia. In England there are only a few places where the box is apparently indigenous, Surrey (Box Hill), Kent, Gloucester and Buckinghamshire.

The tree
A small tree on favourable sites, on others little more than a shrub. Reaching a height of 6m to 9m at best, with a diameter of 100mm to 200mm but rarely exceeding 150mm in Britain. Imported boxwood billets are generally about 1m in length.

The timber
A compact light yellow coloured wood, with a fine, even texture. The grain varies from fairly straight to irregular, and the wood weighs about 930 kg/m^3 when dried.

Drying
Difficult to dry, drying very slowly with a pronounced tendency to develop surface checks. It is liable to severe end-splitting if dried in the round, and end coatings should be applied or the billets should be converted to half-rounds, or to smaller dimensions which should then be carefully and slowly dried under covered storage conditions.

Strength
A heavy, hard timber, comparable to oak in most strength categories, but some 50 per cent stronger in compression along the grain.

Durability
Probably durable.

Working qualities
Rather hard to work, and requires sharp cutting edges in order to avoid burning. A cutting angle of 20° is preferable in planing because of the tendency for irregular grain to tear. It is an excellent turnery wood, and it can be stained and polished.

Uses
Rollers and shuttles, tool handles, mallet heads, rulers, pulley blocks, chess-men, fancy turnery.

CHERRY, EUROPEAN

Prunus avium L.   Family : Rosaceae

Other names
gean, wild cherry (UK) ; cerisier (France) ; kirsche (Germany) ;
kers (Netherlands).

Distribution
Europe including the British Isles. It occurs from Scandinavia
and south-west Russia southwards, and is found in western
Asia and the mountains of North Africa.

The tree
Cherry reaches a height of 18m to 24m and a diameter of about
0.75m. It has short, stout branches that take an upward direction.

The timber
The heartwood is pale pinkish-brown fairly well defined from
the lighter coloured sapwood. The wood has a fairly fine, even
texture, and a generally straight grain. It weighs about 630
kg/m^3 when dried.

Drying
Dries fairly well, with a tendency to warp.

Strength
A tough timber, its strength properties are similar to those of oak.

Durability
Moderately durable.

Working qualities
Works well, but this is dependent on the type of grain present ;
cross grained material tends to tear, and a cutting angle of 20°
is needed, but straight grained material finishes well. It is a
good turnery wood, and takes stain and an excellent polish.

Uses
With exposure and polishing, the wood assumes a beautiful red,
mahogany colour, and is suitable for cabinet-making and fur-

niture. It has been used for plywood in parts of Europe, and also for decorative veneer. If more attention was paid to its cultivation and grading, this timber would attract more users; at present, supplies are small, or are not continuous.

CHESTNUT, HORSE

Aesculus hippocastanum L.   Family: Hippocastanaceae

Distribution
This species is a native of the mountain regions of Greece, Bulgaria, Iran, and northern India, and· was introduced into Britain late in the sixteenth century. It should not be confused with the sweet chestnut, *Castanea sativa*, which it neither resembles, nor is related to. In the British Isles it is not met with in woodlands, yet it is constantly seen in parks and open spaces, and quite often, horse chestnut lumber is seen on the home grown market. Despite the sometimes unfavourable reports that have been published about this wood, it is nevertheless a valuable species not always appreciated and for this reason is included in this publication.

The tree
The stout, cylindrical bole is short, but its erect trunk reaches a height of 24m to 30m, the diameter of the bole being 1.5m or more. There appears a tendency for horse chestnut trees grown in Britain to develop spiral grain, but whether this is associated with the short bole having to support the usually enormous crown in open aspects subjected to prevailing winds is a matter for conjecture. It may be hereditary to the species, but this is not the case with other species of the genus, nor with the *Sapindales* group as a whole.

The timber
The wood is white to pale yellowish-brown, the rather rapid growth producing a soft, relatively light timber weighing about 510 kg/m^3 when dried. The grain may be straight, but is more commonly spiral and the wood has a fine, close, even texture caused by the fine rays and minute pores, and often shows a subdued mottle on longitudinal surfaces caused by the storied rays.

Drying
Because of the relatively isolated planting of horse chestnut in Britain, felling often takes place at varying times of year, and this has a bearing on the resulting colour of the wood. Trees felled early in winter have wood of extreme whiteness, but if felled later in the year, the wood assumes a yellowish-brown cast. The wood dries rapidly and well, but with a tendency to distort and for the ends to split. To retain the whiteness of the wood it should be treated in the same way as for sycamore, which is another member of the *Sapindales*, and that is to promptly stack the timber after conversion by end-racking, or by placing in stick and allowing plenty of ventilation between the boards. Kiln drying should be carried out at low temperatures.

Durability
Perishable.

Working qualities
A soft, easily worked timber which tends to tear in sawing and planing unless cutting edges are kept sharpened. It is a good carving wood, and can be converted to veneer. Although fairly absorbent, it takes stain well and can be finished to a high polish.

Uses
Its uses are dependent upon the dried quality of the wood, but it is suitable for cabinet-making, furniture, carving, brush-backs, turnery, and for fruit storage trays and racks, the porous nature of the wood, absorbing moisture from the fruit, which together with its non-tainting qualities, contributes to the preservation of the fruit.

CHESTNUT, SWEET

Castanea sativa Mill.   Family: Fagaceae

Other names
Spanish chestnut, European chestnut.

Distribution
The tree occurs from south-west Europe, including Britain, northwards to France, south-west Germany and Austria, in North Africa and Asia Minor.

96

The tree
In favourable situations sweet chestnut attains a height of 30m or more and a maximum diameter of 1.8m with a straight, unbranched bole of about 6m, but in less favourable conditions, the undivided bole is little more than 3m long after which it divides off into several huge limbs so that the general character of the tree is altered.

The timber
The sapwood is narrow, and distinct from the heartwood which is yellowish-brown in colour, closely resembling oak in appearance but lacking the silver-grain figure characteristic of that timber, resulting from the finer rays. The grain may be straight, but is more commonly spiral, particularly in wood from old trees, while logs are liable to cup and ring-shake. It weighs about 560 kg/m³ when dried. On account of its somewhat acidic character chestnut tends to accelerate the corrosion of metals, particularly when moist. It also contains tannin, as a result of which blue-black discolourations are prone to appear on the wood when it comes into contact with iron or iron compounds.

Drying
The timber is rather difficult to dry, retaining its moisture in patches, and tending to collapse and honeycomb; this form of defect does not respond well to reconditioning treatments.

Strength
Although resembling oak in appearance, chestnut is less hard and tough, and some 20 per cent inferior in all its strength properties to that timber.

Durability
Durable.

Working qualities
Easy to work and finishes excellently. Takes nails, glue, stains and polish well.

Uses
Furniture, coffin boards, turnery, sometimes as a substitute for oak. Chestnut poles are used for cleft fencing and hop poles.

ELM

Ulmus spp.   Family: Ulmaceae

Various species of the genus *Ulmus* occur in Europe, western Asia, North America and Japan. The following are those whose timber is found in Europe.

Ulmus procera Salisb. produces the English elm found mainly in England and Wales.
Ulmus hollandica Mill. var *hollandica* Rehd. produces Dutch elm found throughout the British Isles, and introduced from the Netherlands.
U. laevis Pall. produces European white elm found from Central Europe to western Asia.
U. carpinifolia Gleditsch. (*U. nitens* Moench *U. foliacea* Gilib.) produces smooth-leaved elm found in Europe including Britain.
U. stricta Lindl. produces the Cornish elm found not only in the west of England but also in Brittany.
U. glabra Huds. produces the wych elm of northern Europe including Britain.
English and Dutch elm are similar in their general characteristics. The trees grow to a height of 36m to 45m and a diameter as great as 2.5m but since large-diameter trees are frequently unsound in the centre, a diameter of 1m or slightly more is better commercially.

The timber
The heartwood is a dull brown colour, clearly defined when green from the lighter-coloured sapwood. The irregular growth rings together with the cross-grained character of the wood gives it an attractive appearance, but the large early-wood pores produce a rather coarse texture. The timber of these species when grown on the Continent is generally of more even and uniform growth with straighter grain. English elm weighs about 560 kg/m^3 and Dutch elm about 580 kg/m^3 when dried.

Drying
Although releasing its moisture fairly rapidly, there is a very marked tendency for the wood to distort, and there is some liability for collapse to occur in thick sizes. Care is therefore

needed ; sticks should be properly aligned, and tops of piles weighted down.

Strength
Both English and Dutch elm have similar strength properties, and in general are some 30 per cent below the strength of oak, although Dutch elm is appreciably tougher than English elm, and it is also a much better wood for bending.

Durability
Non-durable.

Working qualities
Elm is basically a fairly difficult timber to work, tending to pick up during planing and moulding, and to bind on the saw. Its working properties are however governed to an extent by the care with which it was dried, distorted wood being wasteful in planing and moulding. Dutch elm is not quite as refractory, but both species can be finished to a clean surface with care. The wood can be glued satisfactorily, and can be stained, polished or waxed. It takes nails without splitting, and can produce a good decorative veneer.

Uses
The attractive grain in elm renders it ideal for furniture, turnery and woodware such as salad bowls. It is used for chair seats, bent-wood backs, coffins and for domestic flooring. It is a good timber for use in boats for transoms and rudders, hatch covers, bottom planks etc, and is used in dock and harbour work for fenders, rubbers, keel-blocks, capping, wedges and for construction.

Wych elm
The wych elm attains a height of 30m to 38m and on favourable sites produces a bole of about 12m in length and a diameter up to 1.5m.

The timber
The heartwood is light brown in colour, often with a green tinge, or green streaks, and is clearly defined from the lighter coloured sapwood. The grain is usually straighter than in the

English and Dutch elms, and is considered not quite as coarse in texture. It weighs about 690 kg/m³ when dried.

Drying
Dries fairly rapidly and fairly well with less tendency to distortion and splitting than common elm. It still requires care in sticking and drying methods however.

Strength
Wych elm is similar to oak in most strength properties, and almost equal to ash in toughness. It is not such a good steam-bending timber as Dutch elm.

Durability
Non-durable.

Working qualities
Easier to work than both English and Dutch elm; there is less tendency to bind on the saw because of the straighter grain, and since distortion is relatively low, planing and moulding is more easily carried out. It can be worked to a good finish and it can be glued, stained and polished satisfactorily, while it takes nails without splitting.

Uses
While its uses are similar as those of English or Dutch elm, it is in greater demand for boat-building because of its straight grain and milder characteristics, for planking, keels, and deadwood.

The burrs that occasionally form on the boles of elm trees may produce highly decorative veneer, but even when carefully selected, the resultant veneer needs to be used carefully since if the finished article is used in situations where atmospheric conditions are subject to wide changes, as for example in ocean going ships, which might meet extremes of atmosphere in a single voyage, then panels and doors faced with elm burr could develop cracks and blisters due to the refractory nature of the wood.

HOLLY, EUROPEAN

Ilex aquifolium L.   Family: Aquifoliaceae

Distribution
The tree occurs in Europe from Norway, Denmark and north-west Germany southwards, and is found throughout the British Isles except in north-east Scotland. It is found in the Mediterranean region and in western Asia.

The tree
In the British Isles, the holly has been neglected for many years and is now mainly a tree of the hedgerows, under which conditions it grows to a height of about 10m with a bole of perhaps 3m and a diameter of 0.5m. Its maximum height is 24m and the diameter of the bole about 1m which it usually attains under Continental conditions.

The timber
There is no distinct heartwood, the wood being white with a green or grey cast. It has a fine, even texture, but the grain tends to be irregular. Hard and heavy, the wood weighs agout 800 kg/m³ when dried.

Drying
Fairly difficult to dry; there is a tendency for the timber to distort, and for end splitting to occur if dried in the round. The best results are obtained by converting to the smallest sizes permissible and drying these slowly with the top of the pile weighted down.

Durability
Perishable.

Working qualities
Fairly hard to saw, and because of the usually irregular grain, difficult to obtain a good smooth finish unless cutting edges are kept sharpened, and cutting angles reduced to 15° or 20°. It gives excellent results with stain and polish, can be glued satisfactorily and is a good turnery timber.

Uses
As a substitute for boxwood and, when dyed, as a substitute for ebony. It is used for turnery, fancy articles and inlay, engraving blocks and sliced into decorative veneer.

HORNBEAM, EUROPEAN

Carpinus betulus L.   Family : Betulaceae

Other names
charme (France) ; haagbeuk (Netherlands) ; hainbuche (Germany).

Distribution
Hornbeam occurs in Europe from Sweden southwards, in Asia Minor and in Iran. In the British Isles it occurs mainly south of a line drawn roughly from Worcester to Norfolk ie the south-east and midland counties. Elsewhere in Britain it appears to have been introduced, but in the British Isles generally, hornbeam is of irregular occurrence in woodlands and hedgerows. France is the main European area for commercially grown hornbeam.

The tree
The tree grows to a height of 15m to 24m and a diameter of 1m or slightly more. The bole is seldom clear for more than half the height, and the trunk is often fluted, but a characteristic of hornbeam is that the trunk is generally elliptical rather than circular.

The timber
The wood is dull white in colour with no clear distinction between sapwood and heartwood. The wood is often marked with greyish streaks, and the broad rays produce a fleck figure on radial surfaces. It has a fine, even texture, but the grain is commonly irregular. The wood weighs about 770 kg/m^3 when dried.

Drying
Hornbeam is said to dry well with little degrade.

Strength
A strong, tough timber, similar to ash in toughness, but in general strength properties superior to oak, being some 20 to 30 per cent higher than that timber in bending strength, stiffness, hardness, and shear strength, and much higher in resistance to splitting.

Durability
Perishable.

Working qualities
Green hornbeam converts fairly easily, but when dried, its toughness makes it fairly difficult to work, but it can be finished very smoothly, and it takes stains and polish very well. It can be glued satisfactorily, is very suitable for steam bending, and it turns well.

Uses
Piano actions, cogs, turnery, millwright's work, billiard cues, pulleys, dead-eyes, mallets, wooden pegs, violin bridges, brush-backs and for flooring, since it wears comparatively smoothly being suitable for light industrial use, as a substitute for maple.

LIME, EUROPEAN

Tilia spp. principally *T. vulgaris* Hay.   Family: Tiliaceae

Other names
linden (Germany).

Distribution
Several species and their variants of the genus *Tilia* occur throughout Europe, including the British Isles, where the tree may be found not only in pure stands as in Scotland, but also in mixed woodlands and as ornamental trees.
T. platyphyllos Scop. produces the large-leaved lime
T. cordata Mill. produces the small-leaved lime
T. vulgaris Hay. produces the common lime, generally considered to be a hybrid between the two preceding species, and the one commonly planted.
T. euchlora Koch. produces the large-leaved lime of the Caucasus. The basswood of North America is produced by *T. americana* Vent.

The tree
The average height of the tree is 30m but in some areas may reach 40m and a diameter of 1.2m. Under favourable conditions the bole is clear for about 15m.

The timber
There is no distinction by colour between sapwood and heartwood, the wood being pale yellowish-white when freshly cut, turning to pale brown when dried It is a soft, compact wood, with a fine, uniform texture, and a straight grain. It weighs about 560 kg/m³ when dried.

Drying
Dries fairly rapidly, and reasonably well with a slight tendency to distort.

Strength
Limited tests have indicated the general strength properties of lime to be similar to those of oak, but the principal uses for the wood are based more on its ability to resist splitting, together with its softness, rather than on general strength.

Durability
Perishable.

Working qualities
Works readily and easily, but is inclined to be woolly, and requires thin-edged, sharp tools in order to effect a smooth finish. It takes nails, stain and polish very satisfactorily, turns well, and carves extremely well.

Uses
In the past the most important use was for carving, the wood having the desirable property of resisting splitting no matter in which direction the wood is cut. It was a favourite timber for cutting-boards for leather work since it did not tend to draw or bias the knife away from the desired direction, nor did it dull the knife edge too rapidly. Although still used for these purposes, its present employment is for broom handles, bee-hive frames, hat blocks, sounding boards and keys for pianos, harps, turnery, bungs for oil casks, toys, artificial limbs, and wooden clogs and soles.

MAPLE, EUROPEAN

Acer spp.   Family : Aceraceae

The maples constitute a genus of over a hundred species spread over Europe, Asia, North Africa and North America, and include a number of important timber producing trees. The recommended standard name for all species is maple, with a qualifying name, except for *Acer pseudoplatanus* L.; sycamore.

Field maple, *Acer campestre* L. is found in Europe, including England and Wales, from southern Sweden to northern Greece and extending into Russia and Asia Minor. The timber has similar properties to sycamore, but while on good sites it forms a small tree 6m to 12m high, it is often little more than a bush.

Norway maple, *Acer platanoides* L. is also known as Bosnian maple or European maple. It occurs on the Continent from Scandinavia southwards into Asia Minor and the Caucasus, and is found throughout Great Britain where it was introduced from the Continent in 1683. On good sites it grows to a height of 21m to 27m with a diameter of 0.6m but it is often smaller, reaching a height of about 9m. The properties of the timber are very similar to those of sycamore, but it is not so hard, due probably to its very rapid early growth. It is used for turnery, brush backs, and domestic woodware.

When dried, the wood of field maple weighs about 690 kg/m^3, and that of Norway maple 660 kg/m^3, both being a little heavier than sycamore at 630 kg/m^3.

OAK

Quercus spp.   Family: Fagaceae

The genus *Quercus* with more than two hundred separate species produces the true oaks. Most of these are found in the northern hemisphere where, in temperate regions they may form pure stands, or may be dominant species in mixed woodlands, while in warmer countries they tend to occupy the mountain areas.

Most of the true oaks are trees but some are shrubs, the trees, on the basis of wood structure, falling into three groups, the red oaks, the white oaks, and the evergreen oaks or live oaks; the red and white oaks are deciduous.

Descriptions of the species that occur within the geographical scope of this publication are as follows.

European oak

Quercus petraea Liebl. (*Q. sessiliflora* Salisb.) and *Q. robur* L. (*Q. pedunculata* Ehrh.) known also as English, French, Polish, Slavonian, etc oak, according to origin.

Distribution

Q. petraea produces the sessile or durmast oak, while the pedunculate oak is produced by *Q. robur*; both species occur throughout Europe including the British Isles, and extend into Asia Minor and North Africa.

The tree

Both species reach a height of 18m to 30m or a little more depending upon growth conditions which also affect the length of the bole. When drawn up in forests at the expense of their branches, this may be 15m or so in length, but in open situations, the tree branches much lower down. Diameters are about 1.2m to 2m.

The timber

There is no essential difference in the appearance of the wood of either species. The sapwood is 25mm to 50mm wide and lighter in colour than the heartwood which is yellowish-brown. Quarter-sawn surfaces show a distinct silver-grain figure due to the broad rays. The annual rings are clearly marked by alternating zones of early-wood consisting of large pores, and dense late-wood. Conditions of growth accordingly govern the character of the wood to a great extent; for example, in slowly grown wood the proportion of dense late-wood is reduced in each annual growth-ring, thus tending to make the wood soft and light in weight.

The growth conditions in the various countries which export oak, vary considerably. Baltic countries, including northern Poland, produce oak which is generally hard and tough, but further south in Poland the growth conditions become more favourable to the production of milder, more uniformly-grown oak, the rich black soil of south-east Poland producing the famous Volhynian oak, the character of this type of wood changing but little in countries in Central Europe such as Czechoslovakia and Hungary, but being generally a little milder in character in Yugoslavia, from whence Slavonian oak is shipped.

The weight of oak varies according to type; that from the Baltic area, western Europe, and Great Britain being about 720 kg/m^3 and that from Central Europe about 672 kg/m^3 on average after drying.

So-called brown oak is the result of fungus attack in the growing tree. The fungus, *Fistulina hepatica*, causes the wood first to assume a yellow colour, then a richer brown or reddish-brown. A yellow-coloured streak sometimes appearing in oak is the result of another fungus, *Polyporous dryadeus*, but since very few tree diseases persist after the tree is felled, dried timber is no different from normal coloured wood, indeed, brown oak is often preferred for its decorative appeal.

Drying
Oak dries very slowly with a marked tendency to split and check, particularly in the early stages of drying, and there is considerable risk of honeycombing if the drying is forced, especially in thick sizes. End and top protection must be provided to freshly sawn stock exposed to sun and drying winds, and sticker thickness should be reduced to about 12mm for stock piled in the open air during early spring and onwards until winter.

Strength
Both the sessile and pedunculate oaks have well known and high strength properties, and those hybrid oaks developed from both types and common throughout Europe, are similar in their strength properties.

Durability
Durable.

Working qualities
The working and machining properties of oak vary with the mild to tough material which either machines easily or with moderate difficulty. These basic properties are concerned with growth conditions, but they may be exaggerated by indifferent drying methods which allow plain-sawn boards to cup, or severe case-hardening to develop, causing excessive wastage in planing and moulding, cupped stock in resawing, and a greater degree of blunting of cutting edges. These must be kept sharpened, particularly where cross grain is present, and especially in planing highly-figured quarter-sawn surfaces where there may be a liability for the grain to tear out at the juncture of the wide ray-figure thus producing a shelly appearance. In general, oak finishes well from the planer or moulding

machine although in some cases a reduction of cutting angle to 20° is preferable.

The wood can be stained, polished, waxed, and glued satisfactorily, takes nails and screws well, except near edges, when the wood should be pre-bored, and takes liming and fuming treatments well.

Uses

The sessile and pedunculate oaks fall within the white oak group, and since their structure greatly resists the passage of liquids, due mainly to the preponderance of tyloses in the pores, the wood is in demand for the manufacture of staves for tight cooperage. Oak is also a primary timber for furniture, either in the solid or veneer form, but preferences exist among users, the milder Slavonian oak, Volhynian oak, or Spessart oak from Germany, often being preferred for furniture and cabinet-making, to the harder and tougher English oak, which is often considered more suitable for constructional purposes.

Preference, in this context, means to choose, and is not an inference of superiority. English oak, when well-grown and well-graded is the finest of timbers. There is none better for boat-building for such purposes as keels, sterns, stems, knee-beams, ribs, gunwales, stringers and rudders, for docks, harbours and sea defence work, for railway waggon construction, ladder rungs, posts and rails, sills, and for all purposes of exposure and in contact with the ground. Oak generally is also used for high-class joinery, coffins, ecclesiastical work such as pews, rood screens, pulpits and for flooring. Brown oak is valued for panelling and joinery.

The character of oak is somewhat acidic and accordingly tends to accelerate the corrosion of metals, not only those that may be in contact with the wood, but due to the volatile nature of the acids they can evaporate rapidly and so extend their effect to adjacent metals not in direct contact with the wood, especially in enclosed spaces, where lead in particular may suffer severe deterioration.

Iron or iron compounds in contact with wet oak interact with the tannins in the wood thus causing unsightly blue-black staining. Because of the corrosive and staining characteristics of oak, metals should be protected by suitable coatings, or should be non-ferrous. Pure aluminium will usually stand up to the corrosive effect of moist oak better than will lead.

Holm oak
Quercus ilex L. is the evergreen oak of the Mediterranean area, but has been planted in the British Isles as an ornamental tree.

The tree
A medium-sized tree, reaching 15m to 18m in height, with a short bole, and a diameter of 1.8m.

The timber
The timber is entirely different from that of the deciduous oaks, the heartwood is slightly darker than that of European oak, being a warm brown colour and, since the rays are much broader, there is a distinctive ray-figure on all surfaces. It lacks the ring-porous structure so characteristic of the deciduous oaks, the growth-ring pattern being indistinct on longitudinal surfaces. It is a hard, compact, close-textured wood, weighing 800 kg/m^3 to 960 kg/m^3 when dried.

Drying
Requires care, particularly in the early stages of drying, being prone to surface checking and end splitting. It dries very slowly.

Working qualities
Its hardness makes it more difficult to work and machine than European oak but it is capable of a good finish, and stains and polishes well requiring less filling than the deciduous oaks.

Uses
Joinery and carpentry.

Turkey oak
Quercus cerris L. is native to southern Europe and south-west Asia, and has been introduced in various parts of the British Isles.

The tree
The Turkey oak is a tall tree with thick, greyish bark, attaining a height of 36m or more, and a diameter of 1.8m or more. It is of straighter growth and more pyramidal in form than the sessile and pedunculate oaks.

The timber
The sapwood is generally wide, often 150mm or more, and the heartwood is fairly dark brown in colour. The broad rays produce the typical silver-grain figure on quarter-sawn surfaces, but the growth is generally rapid, resulting in widely spaced annual rings with a rather loose zone of open early-wood pores and a dense, broad zone of late-wood, rendering the wood rather heavy, weighing from 800 kg/m^3 to 880 kg/m^3 when dried.

Drying
Dries very slowly, with a distinct tendency to check and distort.

Strength
It is reputed to be inferior to European oak in all strength properties.

Durability
Moderately durable.

Working qualities
Moderately easy to work, finishing well in most operations. It can be stained and polished, but tends to split on nailing.

Uses
Its bad drying reputation restricts its use as does its lack of durability. It is suitable mainly for rough work, but the permeability of the wide sapwood offers perhaps a wider scope for preservative treatment.

Cork oak
Quercus suber L. is an evergreen oak of southern Europe and North Africa. Although not a timber producing tree, its bark has a high commercial value and for that reason is included in this publication.

Distribution
The cork oak is found from the Atlantic to Asia Minor, and is especially abundant in Portugal, Spain, Algeria, Tunisia, southern France, Morocco and Corsica.

The tree

The tree thrives best on rocky siliceous soil on the lower slopes of mountains. It grows to a height of 6m to 18m and a diameter of 1.2m with a short trunk and densely spreading crown.

General characteristics

Cork consists of the outer bark of the tree. It is removed by making vertical and horizontal incisions and then prising off large pieces of bark. This can be done without injury to the tree provided the inner bark and cambium is not damaged. Bark is renewed, fresh layers being formed each year. Stripping is usually carried out in mid-summer, and cork is first removed when the tree is about 20 years old, this is of little value, being very coarse, and subsequent strippings, carried out at nine-year intervals, progressively improve in quality up to the third year, thereafter the quality is standard. The trees, which live for 100 to 500 years, yield from 18 kilos to 220 kilos per tree per year, the best grade of cork consists of 25mm layers obtained from young, vigorous trees.

After stripping, the pieces of cork are dried for several days, after which they are boiled in copper vats. This removes the sap and tannic acid, increases the volume and elasticity, and straightens and flattens the pieces. It also loosens the outer layer, which is scraped off by hand. The rough edges are trimmed, and the cork sorted and baled. Cork possesses many properties valuable in industry. Despite its bulk it is very light and exceedingly buoyant, owing to being composed entirely of dead, watertight cells. It is durable, a low conductor of heat, is resistant to the passage of liquids and moisture, absorbs sound and vibration, has certain frictional properties, and is readily compressed, but will recover most of its original volume after compression is released.

Persian oak

Quercus castaneaefolia C. A. Mey., or chestnut-leaved oak, is a deciduous species native to Asia Minor and the Caucasus. It is similar in appearance to North American red oak, but unlike the general run of red oaks, Persian oak contains a fairly high proportion of tyloses, making it relatively impermeable to liquids and accordingly suitable for staves for tight cooperage.

PEAR

Pyrus communis L.   Family: Rosaceae

Distribution
Found in Europe and western Asia growing singly or in small groups on dry plains.

The tree
A relatively small tree, usually 9m or 12m high, but occasionally reaching 18m with a diameter of about 0.5m. This is the wild pear, with harsh fruit unfit for eating.

The timber
A fine, even-textured wood, pinkish-brown in colour, weighing about 720 kg/m^3. It dries slowly and tends to warp, but with care can be a useful timber which finishes smoothly. A cutting angle of 20° is recommended for planing. The wood turns excellently, and is used for fancy goods, umbrella handles, set squares, T-squares, brush-backs, wooden bowls.

PLANE, EUROPEAN

Platanus hybrida Mill.   Family: Platanaceae
syn *P. acerifolia* Willd.

Other names
London plane, French, English plane, according to origin, lacewood (quarter-sawn wood only), platane (France, Germany).

Distribution
The London plane is believed to be of hybrid origin and to have first appeared about 1670 in Oxford. It is found in parks and squares in streets and cities, but is not known anywhere in the wild state. The oriental plane, *P. orientalis* L. occurs in south-east Europe and west Asia.

The tree
The plane grows to a height of 30m with a clear bole of some 9m and a diameter of 1m.

The timber
The timber resembles beech in colour, the heartwood being light reddish-brown, usually clearly defined from the lighter-coloured sapwood. The rays however, are broader and more numerous than those of beech, and produce on quarter-sawn surfaces, an attractive fleck figure, the reddish-brown rays contrasting with the lighter-coloured background, thus giving rise to the term lacewood. The wood is straight grained, with a fine to medium texture, and weighs about 640 kg/m^3 when dried.

Occasional logs appear much lighter in colour, a pinkish-brown, with a fairly small, and irregular, darker-coloured core.

Drying
Dries fairly rapidly and well, but with a tendency to distort.

Strength
Although some 30 per cent less stiff, plane has similar strength properties to European oak.

Durability
Perishable.

Working qualities
Works fairly readily with both hand and machine tools. It is capable of a good smooth finish, but sharp cutters are required in planing and moulding in order to avoid chipping out in the vicinity of the rays on quarter-sawn stock. The wood stains, polishes and glues reasonably well.

Uses
Fancy and decorative work, interiors to cabinets, inlay and decorative veneer.

POPLAR

Populus spp.   Family : Salicaceae

A number of poplars are found growing in the British Isles and Europe. Six main types are found in the UK, the grey poplar, the black poplar, and the aspen are usually regarded as indigenous species, while the white poplar, Lombardy poplar, and the hybrid black Italian poplar have been introduced. The botanical classification is as follows,

Populus canescens Sm. produces the grey poplar,

P. nigra L. produces the black poplar, or European black poplar,

P. tremula L. produces European aspen, or English, Finnish, Swedish aspen, according to origin,

P. alba L. produces the white poplar, or abele,

P. italica produces the Lombardy poplar, an ornamental tree whose timber is of little value,

P. canadensis Moench. var. *serotina* Rehd. produces black Italian poplar,

P. robusta Schneid. produces black poplar, or robusta.

The tree
With the exception of the white poplar and aspen, the trees reach a height of 30m ; the two former species seldom exceeding 18m. The diameter of all types is around 1m.

The timber
Poplar timber can be grouped with willow, lime and horse chestnut, since they are all soft, fine-textured woods, generally without lustre and without any very characteristic colour. Poplar wood is whitish or greyish in colour generally, but may be light brown, with no clear distinction between sapwood and heartwood. It is usually straight grained, without odour, uniform in appearance, rather woolly to the touch, and light in weight, the various species weighing about 450 kg/m^3 when dried, although the grey poplar is usually a little heavier at 480 kg/m^3.

Commercially, the general quality of poplar reaching the market varies considerably according to the area of production, and the degree by which the many species and their hybrid forms are mixed. Well-grown aspen is usually of particularly good quality, especially from northern Europe, but the wood of the white and grey poplars is generally of relatively low quality, with a very wide, whitish sapwood and a reddish-brown heartwood. Much of the poplar from France and Belgium is generally composed of timber of the black poplar group.

Drying
Dries rapidly and fairly well, with a tendency to retain local pockets of moisture, and for knots to split.

Strength
For their weight, poplar timbers are relatively strong and tough, and in the dried state, and depending on type, are only about 15 to 30 per cent inferior to European oak in all strength properties except hardness and shear, where they are about 50 per cent inferior.

Durability
Perishable.

Working qualities
Black Italian poplar is reputed to have the best working properties, and white and grey poplars the worst, tending to bind on the saw, and to produce a woolly surface. All types, with the exception of aspen, are slightly tough in working, aspen comparing more closely to lime in this respect. A good finish is obtainable with all species however, if thin, sharp-edged tools are employed. They can be glued satisfactorily, and take paint, polish and varnish quite well, but while they can be stained the wood accepts the stain with patchy results.

Uses
Its toughness and non-splintering, woolly nature makes poplar ideally suited to employment for the bottoms of lorries, railway waggons and carts subjected to rough usage. It produces good, constructional veneer for plywood, chip-baskets, and splints for matches. It is used in furniture for framing and drawers, for interior joinery, beer-cask hives, toys, industrial and domestic flooring, boxes and crates, and as an alternative to alder for hat blocks.

ROBINIA

Robinia pseudoacacia **L.**   **Family : Leguminosae**

Other names
false acacia (UK) ; black locust (USA).

Distribution
A native of North America, the tree has been introduced into Europe, Asia, North Africa and New Zealand. Although it had been planted in Britain as an ornamental tree during the seventeenth century, it was encouraged as a plantation tree in about 1820 by William Cobbett, but its timber is of limited use.

The tree
On good sites, mainly in Europe, the tree reaches its maximum height of about 24m but in the UK it is usually much shorter. The bole is short, due to the tree's inclination to fork close to the ground. The trunk is often twisted and usually fluted, and the diameter is about 1m.

The timber
The sapwood is narrow, about 12mm wide, and clearly defined from the heartwood, which is greenish when freshly cut, turning to a golden-brown colour after drying. The texture is rather coarse, due to the contrast between the porous early-wood, and the dense late-wood. The grain is usually straight, and depending on growth rate, the wood varies in weight from about 545 kg/m^3 to 860 kg/m^3 averaging about 740 kg/m^3 when dried.

Drying
The timber dries slowly with a tendency to warp badly.

Strength
Comparable to oak in general strength properties, and similar to ash in toughness.

Durability
Durable.

Working qualities
Fairly difficult to work and machine, due to the contrast between the softish early-wood bands and hard, horny late-wood. It can be glued satisfactorily, and takes stains and polish quite well, but is difficult to nail.

Uses
The tree is liable to wind-break, and old trees are often rotten at

the heart. In France and the Balkan countries, where the wood is used extensively, young trees of rapid growth are generally preferred. The wood is used for wheels for wine carts, barrows, waggon bottoms, posts and gates and planking in boats.

SYCAMORE

Acer pseudoplatanus L.   Family : Aceraceae

Other names
sycamore plane, great maple.

Distribution
Sycamore is native to central Europe and western Asia. It appears to have been introduced into Britain from the Continent in the fifteenth century.

The tree
Sycamore grows to a height of 30m or more and a diameter of 1.5m. It is tolerant of widely differing soil and exposure conditions, standing up well to the fumes of industrial areas and the salt-laden gales of coastal regions.

The timber
There is no difference by colour between sapwood and heartwood, the wood being white, or yellowish-white when freshly cut, with a natural lustre especially noticeable on quarter-sawn surfaces. It is generally straight grained but may be curly or wavy grained, and the texture is fine. The average weight is 630 kg/m³ when dried.

Drying
It air dries well, but is inclined to stain, and rapid surface drying is necessary to prevent this. The use of thick stickers helps, but kiln drying at low temperatures is probably the best treatment. Rapid air drying preserves the white appearance of the wood, sometimes achieved by end-racking the boards, while slow drying gives the wood a light-brown colour, referred to as weathered sycamore, but the aim must always be the avoidance of stick marks which penetrate well into the wood, and this can only be successful if the surfaces are dried rapidly.

Strength
Sycamore has high strength properties similar to those of oak.

Durability
Perishable.

Working qualities
Fairly easy to work and machine, and capable of a fine, smooth finish when straight grained; material with curly or wavy grain picks up in planing and moulding and a reduction of the cutting angle to 15° is needed in order to obtain a good finish. It turns excellently, can be glued, stained and polished.

Uses
Turnery, bobbins, textile rollers, brush handles, furniture, flooring and for decorative veneer. Harewood is sycamore that has been artificially dyed grey, and at one time was much in demand for panelling.

WALNUT, EUROPEAN

Juglans regia L.   Family: Juglandaceae

Other names
English, French, Italian, Turkish, Black Sea, Circassian, Persian etc walnut, according to origin.

Distribution
Walnut is a native of the Himalayas, Iran, Lebanon, Asia Minor, and extends into Greece. It was introduced into Britain about the middle of the fifteenth century. Commercial supplies of walnut are produced mainly in France, Turkey, Italy and Yugoslavia.

The tree
It attains a height of 24m to 30m and a diameter of about 1m or a little more, with a rugged bole rarely exceeding 6m in length.

The timber
Walnut timber varies very considerably in colour; the sapwood is a pale straw colour, clearly defined from the heartwood which is greyish or greyish-brown, but infiltrations of colouring matter

produce a darker-coloured streaky figure to the wood, sometimes irregularly distributed throughout the heartwood, at other times being concentrated in a relatively small core of inner heartwood. The darker streaks are usually of a smokey-brown or reddish-brown colour, the decorative appeal often being accentuated by natural wavy grain.

Local growth characteristics tend to vary the appearance of wood coming from certain areas, thus Italian walnut tends to show darker, and more elaborate markings than in walnut from France and Turkey, which are basically paler and greyer in colour, and in turn, paler than English walnut. Burrs, crotches and stumps provide valuable material for highly decorative veneer, and a good walnut tree should always be grubbed out and never sawn down above soil level, stumps often producing beautifully mottled wood.

The texture of walnut is rather coarse, the grain usually wavy, and the wood weighs about 670 kg/m^3 when dried.

While it is not possible to apply hard and fast rules to the type of walnut produced in a given country, the following is a rough guide to the overall characteristics.

French walnut; probably the largest class used. Usually rather lighter and more grey in colour than English.

Italian walnut; considered more valuable than French, being generally well figured and of a good colour. The best qualities used to come from Ancona, and the terms Italian and Ancona are now often used to denote any well-figured, dark and streaky walnut.

English walnut; lies between French and Italian in decorative appeal, but is often superior to both. Heavy cutting in the past has greatly reduced the availability.

Circassian walnut; represents the better-quality timber from the Caucasus; considerable amounts used to be exported, but little has been seen on the UK market in recent years.

Spanish walnut; the timber resembles French walnut, but is generally smaller, and of poorer quality.

Drying
Dries well, but slowly. There is a tendency for honeycomb checks to develop in thick material if the drying is forced.

Strength
A fairly hard to tough wood with a relatively high resistance to splitting.

Durability
Moderately durable.

Working qualities
Works easily and well with both hand and machine tools. It is suitable for hand carving and for turnery, finishing cleanly from the tool. It can be glued satisfactorily, and takes an excellent polish.

Uses
Furniture, decorative veneer, bank fittings, rifle stocks, fancy goods and turnery.

WILLOW

Salix spp.   Family : Salicaceae

Other names
saule (France) ; wilg (Netherlands) ; Weide (Germany), but see below specific common names.

Distribution
Europe, including the British Isles, western Asia and North Africa. The following are the main species found in these areas.

Salix alba L. produces the white willow or common willow (UK), found in the British Isles, and in Europe, Asia, and North Africa.
Salix fragilis L. produces the crack willow, found in the British Isles, Europe and north Asia.
Salix alba L. cultivar *calva* G. Mayer produces the cricket bat willow or close-bark willow (UK) found in the British Isles, Europe, Asia and North Africa.
Many species of the genus *Salix* are either pollarded, or are cut down low and induced to send out long slender shoots known as osiers, used for basket and wicker-work, but only two species are botanically recognised as osiers, *Salix purpurea* L. the purple

osier, and *S. viminalis* L. the common osier, the former being found in Europe, including Britain, and in central Asia, the latter being common to Europe and Britain, and Asia generally.

The tree
Willows will generally reach a height of 21m to 27m and a diameter of about 1m. When allowed to grow naturally they will branch at about 4m to 8m from the ground, but they are frequently pollarded at about 2.5m high or grown as coppice. Willows grown for cricket bats are felled at about 0.5m diameter, and are grown along the banks of streams in wet soil; in fact all willows are fond of moist, acid soils.

The timber
The sapwood is white and the heartwood pinkish in colour, and very similar to poplar in appearance. The sapwood varies in width according to species and growth conditions, and growth is generally rapid, the growth-rings appearing on longitudinal surfaces as faint zones caused by parenchyma marking each season's growth.
The wood is typically straight grained with a fine, even texture, and is comparatively light in weight, about 450 kg/m³ for the white and crack willow, with cricket bat willow varying from 340 kg/m³ to 420 kg/m³.

Drying
Willow dries fairly rapidly but often retains pockets of moisture. Degrade is minimal.

Strength
Although light in weight and soft, willow is a tough timber, being only about 15 per cent inferior to ash in this respect. In general strength properties it resembles poplar, but is some 20 per cent harder on side grain, 20 per cent more resistant to tangential splitting, and less stiff.

Durability
Perishable.

Working qualities
Willow of all species works easily with both hand and machine tools, although there is a tendency for woolliness, and sharp

tools are required in order to obtain the best results. Crack willow tends to split badly during conversion, a characteristic not necessarily associated with the common name; crack willow is so-called because its shoots, which grow obliquely and frequently cross each other, readily break off if struck at the base; hence the description, and the botanical name, *fragilis*. Willows can be glued satisfactory, and give good results with the usual finishing treatments.

Uses
The best butts of cricket-bat willow are used for cleft cricket bat blades, the remainder of the bole, or unsuitable boles, and other species, being used for artificial limbs, toys, sieve-frames, flower trugs, fruit baskets, bottoms for carts and barrows, boxes and crates.

PART II   SOFTWOODS

CEDAR

Cedrus spp.   Family: Pinaceae

Other names
Atlas cedar, Atlantic cedar, deodar, cedar of Lebanon. These are the true cedars, and they should not be confused with those timbers, both softwoods and hardwoods, often called cedar because their timber and fragrance recalls that of the true cedars.

Distribution
Cedrus atlantica Manetti produces Atlantic or Atlas cedar, a native of Algeria and Morocco.
Cedrus libani Loud. syn. *C. libanotica* Loud. produces cedar of Lebanon, a native of the Middle East.
Cedrus deodara Loud. produces deodar, an important timber tree of northern India.
All three species have been introduced into Britain where they are commonly planted for ornamental purposes.

The tree
Atlantic and Lebanon cedars grow to a height of 36m or rather more and a diameter of 1.5m. When grown on lawns and in

parks, it has a low, rounded, or flattened top, the great spreading branches having grown more rapidly than the trunk; thus the bole seldom has great length, the branches being thrown out 2m to 3m from the ground, and the trunk immediately being divided into several stems. In their natural habitat, the boles are usually cleaner and free from branches to a greater height.

The deodar cedar has a more pyramidal outline, and is a much larger tree reaching some 60m in height and a diameter of 2m in its native habitat. In the UK it rarely exceeds 21m in height, and its branches are usually thrown out quite near to the ground.

The timber

The timber of the true cedars is similar in colour for all species; the heartwood is light brown, usually distinct from the narrow, lighter-coloured sapwood. The wood has a pungent cedar odour, and growth rings clearly marked by the contrast between early-wood and dense late-wood zones. It is rather resinous, and the texture of the wood is medium fine, while the grain is generally straight, although straight grain is more usually found in deodar. The Atlantic and Lebanon cedars grown under parkland conditions are fairly knotty with consequent grain disturbances.

A characteristic of the true cedars is a tendency to produce bark pockets in the wood. The average weight of all these species is about 580 kg/m^3 when dried.

Drying

Dries easily, but with a tendency to warp.

Strength

No data are available for Atlantic and Lebanon cedar, but they are soft, brittle woods, presumably with low strength. Deodar is similar to European redwood in bending strength and stiffness, but it lacks shock resistance and toughness.

Durability

Durable.

Working qualities

Easy to work, with little effect on the cutting edges of tools. A good finish can be obtained, although knots and bark pockets are sometimes troublesome. The timbers take paints and varnish well, and have good nailing properties.

Uses
Joinery, construction, bridges, garden furniture, gates, fences, doors, furniture, railway sleepers, according to quality of the timber.

'DOUGLAS FIR'

Pseudotsuga menziesii (Mirb) Franco
syn *P. taxifolia* Brit. *P. douglasii* Carr.

Distribution
Although a native of North America, the tree has been extensively planted in Europe and the UK.

The tree
A large tree attaining a height of 45m to 60m and a diameter of 1m to 2m, occasionally much taller and larger.

The timber
The heartwood is light reddish-brown in colour, usually quite distinct from the lighter-coloured sapwood. The abrupt change and contrast in colour between early-wood and late-wood bands, produce a prominent growth ring figure which is a feature of plain-sawn surfaces and of rotary-cut veneer. The wood from trees grown in the UK appears to have rather less resin than the North American wood, and to some extent is of more rapid growth. The average weight of dried timber from either source is about 530 kg/m^3.

Drying
Imported 'Douglas fir' is not a difficult timber to dry on arrival in this country or in Europe, because the moisture content has already been reduced prior to shipment with some selecting out of degraded boards. Drying degrade is generally confined to surface checking, splitting and loosening of knots, and splitting in the vicinity of knots. Accordingly, stock from trees grown in the UK and in Europe when dried from the green state, needs care, particularly because of the generally higher preponderence of knots which are hard, often loose, and which encourage more wavy grain than in imported stock.

Strength

Grade for grade, there is approximately the same strength properties in European or home-grown 'Douglas fir' and that imported from the mountain areas of North America. Compared with European redwood, it is some 60 per cent stiffer, 40 per cent harder and more resistant to suddenly applied loads, and 30 per cent stronger in bending and in compression along the grain.

Durability

Moderately durable.

Working qualities

'Douglas fir' grown in Europe and the UK on the whole is rather more difficult to work and machine than imported material due to the greater incidence of hard knots which can be troublesome especially when loosened, while fast grown stock can cause problems in sawing, drilling, morticing, and planing, due to tearing and splintering of the relatively soft early-wood. A characteristic feature of 'Douglas fir' is the abrupt transition between the early-wood and the dense late-wood, which appears to lift, and stand proud of the wood surface. Strictly speaking, it is the early-wood that becomes compressed, thus creating this effect, and in planing and moulding, dull cutters will cause this compression. A similar effect can also be created when finishing treatments are applied; in this case the greater absorbency of the early-wood can cause this to sink slightly and be held by the finishing media. Care must therefore be taken in finishing, but good results can be obtained. It can be glued satisfactorily, and although tending to split, can be nailed and screwed.

Uses

Heavy construction, piling, house building, vats and tanks, laminated members, roof trusses, interior and exterior joinery, edge-grain flooring.

The above uses are applicable to imported stock in the sense that long experience has proved their suitability. Home grown or European stock is just as suitable by selection; in some cases of an introduced timber species, the material may not be considered quite as good as its imported counterpart, but 'Douglas fir' is a tree that is tolerant of extreme variations in climatic

125

conditions, and in its natural habitat will endure both the long, severe winters of North America, and the almost perpetual sunshine of the Mexican Cordilleras, producing excellent timber in either case. The tree has a pyramidal outline, with the lowest branches bending to the ground under open conditions and which would obviously tend to encourage knotty timber, but under controlled forestry conditions this should not eventually apply, bearing in mind that the full life of a 'Douglas fir' is many centuries, something like 700 years in fact, and the timber so far on the European market is relatively young, and fairly fast grown and often knotty.

LARCH, EUROPEAN

Larix decidua Mill. syn. *L. europaea* DC.   Family: Pinaceae

Distribution
The natural habitat of larch is the mountainous areas ascending to great elevations, generally from the Bavarian to Swiss Alps, through western Poland and the Moravian Heights to the Carpathians. It has also been extensively planted elsewhere in Europe including the UK where it was introduced early in the seventeenth century.

The tree
Larch attains a height of 30m to 45m and a diameter of 1m or slightly more, and in favourable situations with a long, clean, cylindrical bole for two-thirds of its length. Essentially a natural tree of the mountains, it requires long, really cold winters for its best development; it is deciduous, and appears to depend upon a long winter rest for the ripening of its wood. In the UK the winters are either short or mild, and neither provide ideal growth conditions. For this reason, English larch is generally inferior to that grown naturally in the mountains.

The timber
The heartwood is pale reddish-brown to brick-red in colour, sharply defined from the narrow, lighter-coloured sapwood. It is a very resinous wood, with clearly marked annual rings, a straight grain, and a fine, uniform texture. It is rather heavy, weighing 590 kg/m³ when dried.

Drying
Dries fairly rapidly with an inclination to distort and for knots to split and loosen.

Strength
A hard tough timber, it is about 50 per cent harder than Scots pine and slightly stronger in bending and toughness; in other strength categories it is about the same as for Scots pine.

Durability
Moderately durable.

Working qualities
Saws, machines and finishes fairly well, but loosened knots may be troublesome. The wood takes the usual finishing media quite well, but it tends to split in nailing.

Uses
Pit props, posts, transmission poles, piles, boat planking, and other uses where durability and strength are prime requirements.

LARCH, JAPANESE

Larix kaempferi (Lamb) Carr   Family: Pinaceae
syn. *L. leptolepis* (Sieb & Zucc) Endl.

Distribution
This tree occurs naturally in Japan, but has been extensively planted in Europe and the UK.

The tree
A smaller tree than European larch, attaining a height of 18m to 30m and a diameter of 0.6m or slightly more, while the bole is usually not as straight as that of European larch.

The timber
The colour of the wood closely resembles that of European larch, being reddish-brown with clearly marked annual rings. Under European growth conditions the growth is often fairly rapid, resulting in a generally lighter weight than that of European larch and averaging 560 kg/m^3 when dried.

Drying
Dries fairly rapidly but with a tendency to warp, split and check.

Strength
Similar to European larch, but about 30 per cent softer, and 20 per cent less stiff.

Durability
Moderately durable.

Working qualities
Generally milder than European larch, with a tendency for the soft, early-wood zones to crumble and tear during sawing and planing. Cutting edges must be kept sharpened, when a clean finish can be obtained. The wood can be stained, varnished and painted, but care is needed in nailing to avoid splitting.

Uses
General construction, mine timber, bridge construction, sleepers, poles, and when suitable, for boat-building.

Note; *Larix eurolepis* Henry produces Dunkeld larch, a natural hybrid between *L. decidua* and *L. leptolepis*. When young, it grows at a much more rapid rate than European larch. Its timber weighs 480 kg/m³ when dried, and is usually employed for general construction and posts.

LAWSON'S CYPRESS

Chamaecyparis lawsoniana Parl.   Family: Cupressaceae
syn *Cupressus lawsoniana* Murray

Other names
Port Orford cedar (USA).

Distribution
Lawson's cypress is native to the USA but has been introduced into Britain mainly as an ornamental tree, but to a minor extent also in plantations. It produces a valuable wood under North American conditions, and since it is perfectly hardy with good freedom of growth, it may, in time become regarded in the UK as a timber producer also.

General characteristics
There is little difference by colour between sapwood and heartwood, the wood being pale pinkish-brown, to all intents and purposes non-resinous, but occasionally exuding a slight orange-coloured resin. The wood possesses a characteristic spicy odour, has a fine, even texture, and weighs 500 kg/m³ when dried. Depending on site conditions, growth is usually rather more rapid than that of imported material which encourages the grain to tear during planing and moulding. The wood takes stains, paints and polish satisfactorily, and nails and screws well.

Uses
The wood is durable, and in America it is used for boat building, oars, paddles, cabinet-work and in organ-building.

AUSTRIAN PINE

Pinus nigra Arnold var. *nigra*   Family: Pinaceae
syn *P. laricio* Poir. var *austriaca* Loud.

Distribution
The natural habitat of Austrian pine extends from Austria, to Hungary and Yugoslavia, but it has been planted elsewhere in Europe and in the UK, but in this latter case, mainly as a shelter tree.

The tree
A smaller tree than the associated Corsican pine, it reaches a height of 23m to 30m and a diameter of 1m or slightly more. *Pinus nigra* and its varieties will thrive in pure sand, and furthermore, when exposed to strong winds develops a dense branch system which affords a good wind break, hence its use in the UK in seaside areas and elsewhere for shelter purposes.

The timber
The sapwood is wide and lighter in colour than the heartwood which is reddish-brown and resinous. The timber grown in Yugoslavia is denser and more resinous than that grown in the UK and has been exported under the misleading name of Bosnian pitch pine.

It is a coarse textured wood, generally knotty and of relatively low quality. That grown in Europe is generally heavy, weighing about 800 kg/m³ when dried, while that grown in the UK is much lighter, about 510 kg/m³.

Uses
Owing to its generally low grade, its main uses are for rough carpentry, shuttering and crates.

CORSICAN PINE

Pinus nigra Arnold subsp. *laricio* (Poir.)   Family: Pinaceae
Maire syn *P. nigra* Arnold var. *calabrica* Schneid

Distribution
Corsican pine is widely distributed throughout the Mediterranean area, occurring in Spain, Italy, Greece, and extending into southern Russia. Pure forests are found in Corsica and Sicily. It was introduced into the UK in 1759 in the belief that it was a maritime form of Scots pine. It grows vigorously on the poorest of soils, and with Austrian pine furnishes a good example of fixing sand dunes and providing shelter.

The tree
It attains a height of 45m and a diameter of 1m or more.

The timber
The heartwood is light yellowish-brown clearly demarcated from the yellowish-white sapwood. It is similar in appearance to Scots pine, but the sapwood is wider, much wider in material grown in the UK while the texture is fairly coarse. The wood weighs 510 kg/m³ when dried, and often contains a greater number of large knots than Scots pine.

Drying
Dries very rapidly and well, with little degrade except slight checking around knots and some splitting of these. The wide sapwood is liable to fungal staining unless dried quickly after conversion.

Strength
Similar to Scots pine.

Durability
Non-durable.

Working qualities
Works and machines well, but cutting edges must be kept sharpened. Takes the usual finishing treatments quite well, and nails satisfactorily.

Uses
Used for the same purposes as Scots pine, but owing to the wide permeable sapwood, Corsican pine will take a deeper penetration of preservatives for uses where treatment is essential. Selected material from trees grown in Europe is suitable for high-class joinery.

LODGEPOLE PINE

Pinus contorta Dougl.   Family: Pinaceae

Other names
contorta pine

Distribution
A natural tree of the North American flora, it has also been introduced to the UK and other parts of Europe.

The tree
A slender tree, 15m to 30m high with a diameter of up to 0.6m.

The timber
The wood is pale brown with little distinction between sapwood and heartwood. A characteristic of the wood is its small, tight knots, which because of the small size of the tree generally reduces the yield of high-grade timber, and causes the dimpled appearance of the tangential surface. It has a fine, fairly even texture, and a straight grain. The wood is soft, and weighs about 470 kg/m^3 when dried.

Drying
Dries easily and uniformly without serious splitting and checking. Resin exudation is said to be fairly general in home grown material.

Strength
Similar to Scots pine in all strength categories.

Durability
Non-durable.

Working qualities
Works and machines easily although the resin content may in some cases be troublesome. A good finish is obtainable, and the wood takes paints and varnish fairly well. It has good nailing properties.

Uses
Suitable for boxes and crates, mining timbers, light and medium construction, fencing, sleepers and transmission poles and for paper pulp.

MARITIME PINE

Pinus pinaster Ait.   Family : Pinaceae

Distribution
Generally confined to the coastal regions in the Mediterranean area, in Greece, and along the Atlantic coasts of France and Portugal, and has been planted to a small extent on sandy coastal areas in the UK.

The tree
This tree attains a height of 36m and a diameter of 1m.

The timber
Similar to Scots pine in appearance, but more resinous, coarser-textured, with a greater preponderance of knots, and a wider sapwood. It is an important source of resin extraction in parts of Europe, and since tapping encourages the formation of resin within the tree, this results in variations in the weight of the wood; consequently the weight can vary from 510 kg/m^3 to about 730 kg/m^3 in the dried state.

Strength
Similar to those of Scots pine.

Durability
Moderately durable.

Working qualities
Generally works readily with both hand and machine tools with variable dulling effect on cutting edges depending on the resin content. A clean finish is obtainable provided cutting edges are kept sharpened.

Uses
Packing cases, sleepers, pit-props, and for building construction in France and Portugal.

SCOTS PINE

Pinus sylvestris L.   Family : Pinaceae

Other names
European ‘redwood ; Baltic, Finnish, Swedish, Archangel, Siberian, Russian, Polish redwood ; red deal, yellow deal ; red pine (Scotland).

Distribution
Widely distributed in Europe and northern Asia. It is found in the mountains of Spain and in the UK, especially in Scotland, at its westerly limits, in the north-west of Norway in a northerly direction, spreading east through northern Europe into Asia, and reaching the Verkhoyansk Range, while its extreme southerly point is in Spain, in the Sierra Nevada in Andalusia. It is found in the Maritime Alps in France, and in the eastern Pyrenees, and in the Caucasus and Transylvanian Alps. It is the only true pine indigenous to the British Isles, being native to Scotland and just over the border ; elsewhere in the UK the forests are generally the result of planting.

The tree
The tree is generally 30m high with a diameter of about 1m but larger trees may be found on favourable sites.

The timber
The sapwood is creamy-white to yellow in colour, narrow, especially in northern environments, becoming wider in the

southern areas, and the heartwood is pale yellowish-brown to reddish-brown, resinous, and usually distinct from the sapwood. The growth rings are clearly marked by the denser late-wood. The quality of the timber is affected by the conditions of growth, climate, soil, elevation, etc, more than most timbers because of its wide and varying distribution, and these factors affect the texture, density, size and number of knots. The weight of dried timber is about 510 kg/m³.

Drying
The timber dries rapidly, and without undue degrade, but owing to its tendency to develop sap stain, it should either be anti-stain dipped, cr dried quickly after conversion.

Strength
For its weight, the timber is strong, and moderately hard, although that grown in the UK is some 20 per cent harder on side grain than that grown elsewhere, and is also rather tougher. In other respects however, there is practically no difference in comparable grades.

Durability
Non-durable.

Working qualities
In general, the timber works easily and well with both hand and machine tools, but ease of working and quality of finish is dependent upon the size, and number of knots, and degree of resin present. The wood is capable of a smooth, clean finish, and can be glued, stained, varnished and painted satisfactorily, and takes nails and screws well.

Uses
Constructional work, joinery, furniture, telegraph poles, piles, pit-props, turnery, sleepers, vehicle bodies, plywood, carcassing, housebuilding.
It is customary to refer to timber imported into the UK as red-wood, as for example, European, Finnish or Swedish redwood, and to call the timber Scots pine when grown in the UK. The end uses depend very much upon rate of growth, and number and size of knots permitted within the grading rules operated by a given country or area.

SIBERIAN YELLOW PINE

Pinus sibirica Du Tour   Family : Pinaceae
syn *P. cembra* L. var. *sibirica* Loud.
P. koraiensis Sieb. and Zucc.

Other names
Siberian, Korean, Manchurian pine.

Distribution
Siberia and Manchuria.

General characteristics
This is a soft pine, similar in some respects to the yellow pine of eastern North America, *Pinus strobus* L .and of the same weight, about 420 kg/m^3 when dried. It is a soft, yellowish-brown wood, usually with a little resin, although thin dark lines can be observed on longitudinal surfaces due to resin canals. It is straight grained, with a fine, even texture.
It is not a large tree, and although capable of producing some very fine timber, this is confined to relatively narrow widths and much of the timber is rather knotty.
Good quality timber was seen on the European market some forty years ago in sizes up to about 75mm x 200mm but little has been forthcoming in recent years.
Its softness and low density renders it ideal for carving, pattern making, and panelling when selected with a suitable complement of decorative knots.

SILVER FIR

Abies alba Mill syn. *A. pectinata* DC.   Family : Pinaceae

Other names
whitewood (in part) see *Picea abies*

Distribution
Its natural habitat is in the mountain regions of Central and Southern Europe. It occurs in northern Spain, Corsica, and in the Balkans across Bulgaria to the Black Sea. In the east, it is found from Poznan in Poland, and south through Warsaw to the Carparthians. The tree was introduced into England in 1603.

The tree
It grows to a height of about 37m with a diameter of about 1m but under favourable conditions it is often a larger tree. In open conditions of growth, it retains its lower branches for 40 or 50 years, but after that age they begin to fall off.

The timber
The timber closely resembles that of Norway spruce (*Picea abies*) but is slightly less lustrous. It is almost white in colour, with a yellowish-brown cast and faintly marked annual rings. The grain is straight, and the texture fine. The wood weighs 480 kg/m^3 when dried.

Drying
Dries rapidly and well, with little tendency to warp. There is a distinct tendency for knots to loosen and split.

Strength
Its general strength is similar to that of Norway spruce, but it is harder on side grain.

Durability
Non-durable.

Working qualities
The wood works and finishes in similar manner to that of Norway spruce.

Uses
Used for the same purposes as Norway spruce. It is usual practice for silver fir to be included in shipments of spruce from central and southern Europe.

Other firs introduced into the UK include the following,

Abies grandis Lindl. produces grand fir, a native of British Columbia and western USA. Also known as lowland fir, white fir and western balsam fir.
The tree grows to a height of 30m to 37m with a diameter of about 0.75m and with a long, straight, clean bole.
The wood is similar to European spruce in appearance, but is less lustrous and rather coarser in texture. Straight-grained and non-resinous, it weighs about 450 kg/m^3 when dried.

Non-durable, easy to work and finish, it is used for carpentry, crates and boxes, slack cooperage, light construction and for pulp.

Abies procera Rehder. syn. *A. nobilis* Lindl. produces noble fir, native to western USA. Under favourable growth conditions this is a large conifer, often reaching 60m or more in height and a diameter of 2m or slightly more.

Firs, spruces and hemlocks, are all associated botanically and where fir occurs with spruce in their natural habitat, the two are often mixed for commercial purposes, and the same applies where fir occurs with hemlock. Noble fir is not unlike western hemlock in appearance, being pale buff-coloured, but a little lighter in weight, and coarser in texture. It weighs about 420 kg/m^3 when dried, is non-durable. It is used for interior joinery and trim, and for packing cases. Selected logs are used for plywood manufacture.

SITKA SPRUCE

Picea sitchensis Carr.   Family: Pinaceae

Other names
silver spruce.

Distribution
The natural distribution of Sitka spruce is Canada and the USA, but the tree has been extensively planted in the UK particularly in Wales.

The tree
The tree does not attain the same size in the UK as it does in its natural habitat, being smaller, and reaching a height of 33m and a diameter of 0.75m or slightly more.

The timber
The sapwood is pale pink in colour, merging gradually to the light, pinkish-brown heartwood. It is non-resinous, without odour and therefore non-tainting, is soft and light in weight, and generally of fast growth under UK conditions. The grain varies from straight to spiral, and the texture is coarse; the

wood weighs about 400 kg/m³ when dried (imported Sitka spruce weighs 450 kg/m³).

Drying
The timber dries rapidly, but is liable to twist and cup, and thick material varies considerably in its ability to give up its moisture. There is also a tendency for collapse to occur.

Strength
Although light in weight, its strength properties are relatively high, being similar to those of Scots pine when selected.

Durability
Non-durable.

Working qualities
Works easily, but the soft, broad bands of early-wood tend to crumble and tear in sawing and planing, and knots can be troublesome. It is difficult to obtain a really good finish. The wood can be nailed satisfactorily.

Uses
Carpentry and construction, but since the strength properties vary considerably according to the growth conditions, selective grading is necessary in order to obtain timber suitable for say joists and rafters. Lower grade material is used for packing cases and boxes.

SPRUCE, NORWAY

Picea abies Karst. syn *P. excelsa* Link.   Family : Pinaceae

Other names
European whitewood (in part) see *Abies alba* ; European spruce ; Baltic, Finnish, Swedish, Russian, Yugoslavian whitewood ; the common names, white deal and white fir (UK), and white pine (Scotland) are confusing and should be discontinued.

Distribution
Widely distributed throughout Europe with the exception of Denmark and the Netherlands. Although classed as an intro-

duced species to the UK there is ample evidence that the spruce was native when the upper beds of the Tertiary formations were laid down. There is no true record of its modern introduction, but it is known to be prior to 1548.

The tree
Its average height is 36m with a diameter of 0.75m or more, but its best development is in the Carpathian mountains where it reaches 60m in height and up to 1.8m in diameter.

The timber
There is no difference by colour between sapwood and heart-wood, the colour varying from almost white to pale yellowish-brown. The growth rings as seen on plain-sawn surfaces are less prominent than those of Scots pine (European redwood), and the wood is more lustrous. It has a straight grain and a rather fine texture. The weight of the wood is generally about 470 kg/m^3 when dried, but is usually a little lower than this for timber grown in the UK and in parts of south-east Europe, due to the faster growth resulting from the relatively lower elevations and climatic conditions of these areas.

Drying
Dries rapidly and well, but with a tendency for knots to split and loosen.

Strength
Norway spruce in general is similar to Scots pine in all strength categories. That grown in the UK is rather weaker when green, but after drying there is little difference between the two types.

Durability
Non-durable.

Working qualities
The timber works easily both by hand or machine tools, and is capable of a smooth, clean finish. It takes stain, paint, varnish and glue satisfactorily, and nails and screws well.

Uses
Joinery and interior construction, boxes, packing cases, veneer for plywood, flooring and carcassing.

The uses for this timber are wide, ranging from thinnings sold as Christmas trees, to poles used for masts, scaffold poles, pit-props, ladder stringers, and flag poles, to the high-class material used for piano sound boards and the bellies of violins. The so-called Romanian pine, used for violin manufacture is spruce which grows in what is probably the best conditions high in the Carpathians; it is the growth conditions that govern the overall quality, and which is reflected in preferences for timber from northern areas rather than southern areas of the same country. This is not necessarily valid, since not only altitude, but growth density of the forest stand has a distinct effect on the quality of the wood; quality grade variations can occur at both high and low elevations.

THUYA

Tetraclinis articulata Mast.   Family : Cupressaceae

Distribution
Morocco, Algeria and Malta.

General characteristics
Although botanically related to the cypresses and to the genus *Thuja*, these should not be confused with commercial thuya, which is mainly met with in the form of burrs. The colour of the wood is brownish-red with a yellowish tinge, the burr wood being marked with very small twisted curls and knots similar to bird's eye maple, except in colour, and more varied in effect. It is a relatively soft wood, fairly easily worked, and has a sweet, aromatic odour.

The burrs are used in veneer form for small items of furniture and fancy boxes and the solid wood is also used locally for constructional purposes under the name of alerce or alcerce, but again, alerce should not be confused with the Chilean timber of that name, produced by *Fitzroya cupressoides*.

WELLINGTONIA

Sequoiadendron giganteum (Lindl.)   Family : Taxodiaceae
Buch. syn *Sequoia gigantea* (Lindl.) Decne.,
S. wellingtonia Seem.

The wellingtonia is a native of California, and along with its botanically associated *Sequoia sempervirens*, or Californian redwood, has been extensively planted in the UK mainly as ornamental trees, and occasionally in clumps.

General characteristics
Wellingtonia grown in the British Isles has a very wide sapwood, and a heartwood varying from pale yellow in colour to warm red. It is soft, spongy, and rather brittle timber, very light in weight, about 340 kg/m³ when dry. Because of its comparative rareness and rather poor quality timber, it is of no real economic value, but occasional trees do come on the market, and are used for unexacting work such as fencing, and for stuff-over furniture in interior parts where strength is not a requirement, but lightness helps reduce the over-all weight.

The wood of *Sequoia sempervirens* grown in the UK is similarly much lighter in weight than that grown in America, and of faster growth.

'WESTERN RED CEDAR'

Thuja plicata D. Don   Family: Cupressaceae

Distribution
Although indigenous to North America, 'western red cedar' grows well in the UK and has been planted to a limited extent.

The tree
On favourable sites it reaches a height of 45m to 75m and a diameter of 0.9m to 2.5m.

The timber
The sapwood is narrow, whitish in colour, distinct from the heartwood, which varies when freshly cut from dark brown to salmon-pink, assuming a fairly uniform reddish-brown colour after drying, and turning a grey colour after prolonged exposure to weather. The wood has a prominent growth-ring figure, is non-resinous, and coarse textured, and weighs about 390 kg/m³ when dried. The timber from home grown trees generally contains numerous small knots as opposed to the more or less knot-free imported timber, but since the species has not been

established in the UK long enough to produce really large trees, it is probable that in time the proportion of high-class wood will increase considerably.

Drying
Home grown material is rather difficult to dry; thin sizes dry quite well, without much degrade, but there is a distinct tendency for collapse to develop in thick stock, the wood retaining its moisture at the centre for a relatively long time. Drying must therefore be carried out slowly and progressively.

Strength
A soft, lightweight, rather brittle timber, with correspondingly low strength properties.

Durability
Durable.

Working qualities
A fairly easy timber to work and machine, although knots may be troublesome and the soft, early-wood bands generally tend to tear in planing and moulding. It takes stain and paint readily and screws and nails reasonably well.

Uses
According to quality, it is suitable for exterior cladding, greenhouses, sheds, bee-hives, shingles, light construction. The wood is acidic and tends to corrode ferrous metals in contact with it; protective coatings should therefore be applied to metal fittings and fixings eg hot-dipped galvanized, or they should be non-ferrous, eg copper.

YEW

Taxus baccata L.   Family: Taxaceae

Other names
common yew, European yew.

Distribution
Yew has a very wide distribution in Europe, North Africa, Asia

Minor, the Himalayas and Burma. It extends in Europe from Scandinavia to the Mediterranean, and from the Atlantic to the western provinces of Russia, and is found in Algeria and northern Iran.

The tree
Although a large tree it is by no means tall, growing to a height of 12m to 15m but with a short bole which is never cylindrical because of its characteristic form of growth. The tree is continually pushing out new shoots from the lower part of the bole ; these grow upwards and coalesce with the old wood, thus producing a fluted appearance to the bole, or as a series of fused stems.

The timber
The sapwood is very narrow and white in colour, sharply demarcated from the heartwood which varies in colour from orange-brown to dark purplish-brown, the lighter-coloured wood often containing darker streaks. Although the natural growth tendency is to produce narrow growth rings, which account for the hard, compact, and elastic nature of yew wood, the irregular growth pattern results in widely varying ring widths, even in the same ring, and this, combined with the narrow zone widths of dense late-wood, often produces a valuable decorative appearance in the wood. It is a hard, relatively heavy softwood, weighing about 670 kg/m^3 when dried.

Drying
The timber dries fairly rapidly and well, with little degrade, but care is needed initially to avoid shakes developing. Where these occur in air drying, they usually tend to extend in further drying.

Strength
A tough, resilient wood, equal to oak in hardness and in compressive strength along the grain, but rather inferior to oak in resistance to splitting.

Durability
Durable.

Working qualities
A moderately difficult to difficult timber to work and machine,

depending greatly on the type of grain present; when this is straight, the wood can be machined and finished to a good surface, but irregular and cross-grain can tear out in planing and moulding, and a reduced cutting angle is recommended, generally to about 15°. The wood is inclined to be oily, which sometimes interferes with good gluing, and care is therefore needed. It takes stains satisfactorily, and a high polish. It is a good turnery wood.

Uses
Decorative work restricted only in scope by the size of available timber. Chairs, doors, tables, veneer, sometimes from burrs that occasionally form. It is also used for posts because of its durability.

USE GUIDE FOR EUROPEAN TIMBERS

AGRICULTURAL IMPLEMENTS

ash   hornbeam
elm   oak

BOAT AND SHIP CONSTRUCTION

Decking
                    'Douglas fir' (selected, edge-grain)
                    larch
                    Scots pine (European redwood)
Framing
                    oak
Keels and stems
                    elm
                    oak
Masts and spars
                    'Douglas fir' (selected)
                    Sitka spruce (selected)
Oars and paddles
                    Lawson's cypress
                    Sitka spruce (selected)
Planking
                    'Douglas fir' (selected)
                    elm
                    larch (European)
                    larch (Japanese when selected)
                    robinia
                    Scots pine (European redwood)
Tillers, boat-hooks, cleats, etc.
                    ash

COOPERAGE

oak, European and Persian   fir, grand (slack cooperage)

BOXES AND CRATES

chestnut, horse
'Douglas fir'
fir, grand
fir, noble
fir, silver
lime
pine, Austrian
pine, lodgepole

pine, maritime
pine, Scots (E. redwood)
poplar
spruce, Norway
  (E. whitewood)
spruce, Sitka
willow

CONSTRUCTION

Heavy
beech
Douglas fir
elm
larch
oak
Light
beech
birch
cedar
'cedar, western red'
chestnut, sweet
cypress, Lawson's

fir, grand
fir, noble
fir, silver
pine, lodgepole
pine, maritime
pine, Scots (European
  redwood)
pine, Siberian yellow
plane
poplar
spruce, Norway (European
  whitewood)
spruce, Sitka (selected)

DOORS

oak
pine, Corsican (selected)
pine, Scots (European
  redwood)

pine, Siberian yellow
walnut

FANCY GOODS

boxwood
cherry
holly (natural or dyed)
pear

plane
thuya
walnut
yew

FLOORING

beech
birch
elm
fir, silver
hornbeam
oak
pine, Corsican

pine, Scots (European
  redwood)
poplar
spruce, Norway (European
  whitewood)
sycamore

FURNITURE AND CABINET MAKING

ash
beech
birch
cedar (garden furniture)
cherry
chestnut, sweet
elm
oak

pine, Scots (European
  redwood)
plane
poplar
sycamore
walnut
yew

JOINERY

High-class

beech
birch
chestnut, sweet
elm
maple
oak

pine, Corsican (selected)
pine, Scots (European
  redwood)
pine, Siberian yellow
sycamore

Utility

beech
birch
cedar
'cedar, western red'
chestnut, horse
cypress, Lawson's
'Douglas fir'
fir, silver
larch

lime
pine, Corsican
pine, Scots (European
  redwood)
pine, Siberian yellow
poplar
spruce, Norway (European
  whitewood)
spruce, Sitka

MARINE PILING AND CONSTRUCTION

Under water

(a) Teredo infested waters

beech (pressure treated with preservative)
'Douglas fir (pressure treated with preservative)'

(b) Non-Teredo waters, in addition to above,

pine, Corsican (pressure treated with preservative)
larch
oak (preferably desapped)
pine, Scots (pressure treated with preservative)

Above water

(a) docks, wharves, bridges, etc

cedar	oak
'Douglas fir'	pine, Corsican (preservative treated)
elm	pine, Scots (preservative treated)
larch	

(b) decking

'Douglas fir' (selected, edge-grain)
oak

MUSICAL INSTRUMENTS

cypress, Lawson's	spruce, Norway (selected)
hornbeam	

PATTERN MAKING

pine, Siberian yellow (selected)

SPORTS GOODS

ash	walnut
hornbeam	willow

148

TURNERY

alder
ash
beech
birch
boxwood
chestnut, horse
chestnut, sweet
cherry
elm
holly

hornbeam
lime
maple
oak
pear
pine, Scots (European
 redwood)
sycamore
walnut
yew

VEHICLE BODIES

ash
hornbeam
pine, Scots (European
 redwood)

poplar
robinia

VENEER AND PLYWOOD

Corestock
alder
ash
beech

birch
poplar

Decorative
ash
birch (masur, flame, curly,
 etc.)
cherry
elm
holly
maple

oak
plane
sycamore
walnut
thuya burr
yew

Utility (plywood, chip baskets, small laminated items, etc)
alder
ash
beech
birch
cherry

fir, noble
fir, silver
pine, Scots
spruce, Norway

AMENABILITY OF HEARTWOOD TO PRESERVATIVE TREATMENT

Extremely resistant

chestnut, sweet
oak

robinia

Resistant

cedar
'cedar, western red'
'Douglas fir'
elm, wych
fir, grand
fir, noble
larch, European and Japanese
pine, Austrian
pine, lodgepole

pine, maritime
poplar, black and grey
spruce, Norway (European whitewood)
spruce, Sitka
walnut
willow
yew

Moderately resistant

ash
elm, English and Dutch
fir, silver
Lawson's cypress

pine, Corsican
pine, Scots (European redwood)
pine, Siberian yellow

Permeable

alder
beech
birch
hornbeam
lime

poplar, black Italian (permeable sapwood comprises most of the log)
sycamore

The above classification refers to the ease with which a timber absorbs preservatives under both open-tank (non-pressure) and pressure treatments. Sapwood, although nearly always perishable, is usually much more permeable than heartwood, accordingly, the above classification refers to the relative resistance of heartwood to penetration.

Extremely resistant

Timbers that absorb only a small amount of preservative even under long pressure treatments. They cannot be penetrated to an appreciable depth laterally, and only to a very small extent longitudinally.

Resistant
Timbers difficult to impregnate under pressure and require a long period of treatment. It is often difficult to penetrate them laterally more than about 3mm to 6mm.
Incising is often used to obtain better treatment.

Moderately resistant
Timbers that are fairly easy to treat, and it is usually possible to obtain a lateral penetration of the order of 6mm to 18mm in about 2-3 hours under pressure, or a penetration of a large proportion of the vessels.

Permeable
Timbers that can be penetrated completely under pressure without difficulty, and can usually be heavily impregnated by the open-tank process.

3
NORTH AMERICA

INTRODUCTION

The geographical scope of this chapter is concerned with North America, ie Canada and the United States, bounded to the north by the Bering Sea, Beaufort Sea and Baffin Bay, to the south by the Gulfs of Mexico and California, and extending west to east from the Pacific to the Atlantic.

Climate and forests

The climates vary in different regions, owing to the size of the continent; the northern regions are in a zone where winters are long and severe, while its southern extremities lie near the tropics, but for the most part the climate is temperate, though the summers are hotter and the winters colder than in western Europe. The prevailing winds of the north-west are from the Pacific Ocean; they give the west coast a mild and fairly uniform climate. Rainfall is abundant on this and most other coasts; inland it is mostly in smaller quantity; over the barren lands very little falls at any time of year.

In Florida and Texas there are regions where tropical vegetation flourishes; in California and the states along the Gulf of Mexico and the Atlantic, as far as Virginia, sub-tropical plants are found. The trees and shrubs are immensely varied, many native species are largely unknown in Europe, but many European species have been introduced. In the mountain areas the forests are magnificent, while on the prairies there are not many trees except willows and cotton-wood growing by the streams.

The forest areas of North America are now less than half of what they were at the time of the first English settlements 300 years ago, but they occur in at least five fairly well-defined areas, a rough assessment of timber types being as follows; Canada, Alaska and Newfoundland are predominatly coniferous, with about 90 per cent softwoods and 10 per cent temperate hardwoods, while the USA has about 70 per cent conifers and 30 per cent temperate hardwoods.

The five principal forest areas can be summarized as follows :-

1 From Newfoundland to the lower Hudson Bay, and sweeping north-west to Alaska south of the treeless arctic tundra, are found spruce, balsam fir and larch, with some paper birch, aspen and poplar. In the east, from Nova Scotia to northern New England and

Minnesota, and southwards along the summits of the Appalachian Mountains, a transitional region exists between conifers and hardwoods with both types intermingled. The principal trees of this area include white pine, red spruce, white cedar, beech, sugar maple, eastern hemlock, yellow birch, and locally red pine and jack pine.

2   A deciduous tree area occurs from Ontario and southern Quebec, extending into much of the central and eastern parts of the USA, and attaining its best development in the lower Ohio valley and on the slopes of the southern Appalachians. The most important species are oak, hickory, chestnut, black walnut, basswood, ash and elm, while towards the northern limits of the area beech and maple become prominent.

3   To the south-east along the Atlantic coastal plain and extending from Virginia to the Gulf states and into Texas, there occurs pitch pine on the uplands, while on lower ground are found red gum, tupelo, live oak and magnolia; southern white cedar and cypress occur in the swamps.

4   The Rocky Mountain forests extend from northern British Columbia southward across the USA to Mexico, the tree species varying considerably according to altitude and latitude, but principal among these are Douglas fir, white fir, western larch, Engelmann spruce, lodgepole pine, alpine fir, western hemlock, western red cedar and white pine.

5   The Pacific Coast regions of North America incorporate a number of distinct forest areas. From Alaska south to Washington the coastal forest strip is dominated by Sitka spruce. In southern British Columbia, around Puget Sound, eastern Oregon and Washington, and as far east as the summits of the Cascades, there is situated one of the finest coniferous forests extant, which for many years has been the centre of the North American softwood lumber industry. The density of the stands and the large sizes of the trees in these areas have largely been due to the mildness of the winters, owing to the nearness of the ocean and the very high precipitation. Douglas fir and associated western hemlock and red cedar are dominant species, together with Sitka spruce and several firs. South of Washington, from Oregon to San Francisco, the forests along the Coastal Range were for centuries dominated by redwoods (Sequoia sempervirens), but the area has been exploited for many years and much of the cleared land has been given over to agriculture, although a few red-

wood reserves have been retained.

East of the Cascade Range the forests tend to merge with those of the Rocky Mountains, and here are found pines, larch, Douglas fir, alpine fir and Engelmann spruce. This forest also extends southward along the Sierra Nevadas in California. The Big Trees (Sequoia gigantea) are found locally along the lower slopes of the Sierras, and at higher elevations are found sugar pine, incense cedar, Douglas fir, and red and white fir.

These five areas describe in broad outline the forest trend of North America; to a degree many areas within the forests so described have either been severely exploited, or have been cleared to satisfy increases in population, to cater for economic industrial activity and for agriculture, and to some extent formerly lacked adequate protection, particularly from fire.

While the annual growth and removal of softwood types throughout North America would appear compatible with economic timber harvesting, at least for the next few decades, the position regarding hardwoods is rather different; the trends in inventory, growth, and removal indicate that the gradual growth in forest management programmes such as planting and timber stand improvement in recent decades has provided a vastly improved hardwood situation. For example, the saw-timber inventory in the USA for 1968 was 5 per cent above that for 1963, and 14 per cent higher than in 1953. In 1967 the net annual growth of growing hardwood trees was some 67 per cent higher than removals, while saw-timber size trees increased in net annual growth, some 31 per cent above removals.

The net annual growing stock growth in northern USA in 1967 was 2.3 times the amount removed, while the largest surplus was in the Middle Atlantic area where growth was more than three times that of removals.

Although these figures indicate that hardwood production, at least in the USA, should be improving rapidly, they conceal some problems. Much of the increased growth is on less desirable species such as upland oak, beech, cottonwood and soft maple, while preferred species like black walnut and yellow birch dropped by 11 per cent and 17 per cent respectively, and select white and red oak increased only by 6 per cent, and hard maple by 10 per cent.

157

Furthermore, much hardwood saw-timber volumes are dispersed over wide areas, and in many cases exist as single trees or scattered groups of trees mixed with softwood types, and are not economically harvestable.

It would seem that over the next decade much of the projected increased demand for hardwoods in North America could be met from domestic forest resources, provided there is a greater intensification of improved utlization of less preferred species, but beyond the next few years there is likely to be·a progressive narrowing of the margin between demand and supply, accentuated by a further loss of forest land due to expansion of cities and clearing for highway construction, thus placing a greater emphasis on the increased importation of tropical hardwoods.

Another factor limiting expansion of North American domestic hardwood production has been the development of corporations with international market structures which apparently find economic advantage in controlling some overseas hardwood processing capacity.

This leads to the conclusion that North America, like western Europe and Japan, has pressed the domestic forests for hardwood supplies to a stage where additional expansion to meet the needs of increased demand for preferred species, particularly in large sizes of quality timber, is likely to be limited in the foreseeable future.

It is obvious that if the world's hardwood resources are to be suitably exploited in the fullest manner, a flow of information between producers and sellers on the one hand, and buyers and consumers on the other, must be maintained, not only on those timbers well-known to the trade, but also on the lesser-known species.

It is the aim of this book and its companion volume to assist this flow of information by presenting in convenient form the most important aspects of the commercial timbers of the world, both broad-leaved and coniferous, in order that their accepted roles are sustained or, what is more important, that new ones are acquired.

This present chapter deals only with the North American timbers of temperate origin, but as demands for tropical timbers increase, a fuller appraisal of American and Canadian industrial timber needs can be made by reference to other chapters.

PART I HARDWOODS

ALDER, RED

Alnus rubra Bong.   Family : Betulaceae

Other names
western alder, Oregon alder.

Distribution
Found in the Pacific coastal district of British Columbia, and in Oregon and Washington west of the Cascade Range.

The tree
A fairly small tree, 9m to 15m high with a diameter of 0.3m.

General characteristics
The wood is pale yellow to reddish-brown in colour with a fairly straight grain, and uniform texture. It is of medium hardness and weight, about 529 kg/m³ when dried, and often shows a pleasing subdued figure. It dries easily and well, is a soft, weak wood, which works well but with a tendency for the grain to pick up in planing. It has good nailing properties, takes stain, paint and polish satisfactorily, and can be glued.

Uses
Typical uses for red alder include turnery, furniture, corestock, wooden ware and plywood. Current interest in North America is for the use of the wood in decorative veneer form for plywood panelling, where natural defects such as knots, burl clusters and minor stain emphasise the growing trend to modern – contemporary styles.

ASH, AMERICAN

The natural order *Oleaceae* includes a number of species of the genus *Fraxinus* or ash, whose timber is characterised by good strength, elasticity, toughness, stiffness and hardness, allied to relatively light weight. The following are the principal species found in North America.

BLACK ASH

Fraxinus nigra Marsh.

Other names
brown ash.

Distribution
An eastern species; it occurs mainly from the Gulf of the St Lawrence to Manitoba.

General characteristics
A slender, medium sized tree reaching a height of 18m to 21m growing in swamps and by rivers, its timber is greyish-brown to brown in colour, darker than that of white ash, (*F. americana*), and inferior to that timber in general strength properties, and lighter in weight, about 560 kg/m^3 when dried. A certain amount of this species is used for interior trim and fittings. It takes a good finish.

GREEN ASH

Fraxinus pennsylvanica Marsh.

Other names
red ash.

Distribution
Found in fairly limited quantities from south-eastern Quebec throughout southern Ontario to eastern Saskatchewan, and also in the southern states of America to the Mississippi River.

General characteristics
A small tree, some 12m to 15m in height, producing timber similar to American white ash in appearance, but inferior to that timber in hardness, strength and toughness. It weighs about the same as white ash, about 670 kg/m^3 when dried, and is used for similar purposes as white ash, except for striking tool handles.

WHITE ASH

Fraxinus americana L.

Other names
Canadian ash (UK).

Distribution
Occurs in Canada from Nova Scotia to south-western Ontario, and in America from New England, the Middle Atlantic and Central States.

General characteristics
The tree reaches a height of 15m to 18m or a little more, and a diameter of about 0.75m. The sapwood is almost white in colour, and the heartwood varies from light brown to reddish-brown, rather similar to European ash, but a little lighter in weight, about 670 kg/m³ when dried.

Uses
The three species given are the principal ones making up commercial American ash, but there are several minor species which provide ash timber. Because of the differences in density, rate of growth, and general strength properties, the various species are usually segregated into tough and soft grades, the former being suitable for work which demands toughness and elasticity, while the latter type, with its milder nature is more suitable for interior joinery, cabinets and furniture.
The tough grades are used for skis, striking tool handles, boat frames, vehicle bodies, church pews and shop fitting.

BASSWOOD

Tilia americana L. syn. *T. glabra*   Family: Tiliaceae

Other names
American lime.

Distribution
In Canada it is found from the Atlantic coast westward to southern Manitoba, and extending southwards into the eastern deciduous forests of the USA.

The tree
Although sometimes reaching a height of 30m with a diameter of 1.2m it is more usually about 18m to 21m tall and about 0.75m in diameter.

The timber
The wood is light-coloured, varying from creamy-white to pale brown, with a straight grain and fine, even texture, due to the uniform growth and lack of contrast between early-wood and late-wood zones. It is soft, light in weight, about 416 kg/m^3 when dried, and is weak and lacks toughness.

Drying
Dries without undue checking and distortion.

Strength
Similar in most strength categories to poplar, but a little more resistant to shock loads.

Durability
Non-durable.

Working qualities
Works extremely easily, and finishes smoothly. It takes nails and screws well, glues satisfactorily, and can be stained and polished without difficulty.

Uses
Constructional veneer, plywood, carving, louvres, drawing boards, pattern making, piano keys, turnery, barrel heads, bee-hives, food containers, match splints and wood wool.

BEECH, AMERICAN

Fagus grandifolia Ehrh.   Family : Fagaceae

Distribution
It occurs in Canada from Nova Scotia to the north shore of Georgian Bay, and is found in the USA in northern New England and in the eastern deciduous forest.

The tree
Sometimes attaining a height of 24m it is more commonly 12m to 15m tall, with a diameter of 0.5m.

The timber
There is generally little distinction by colour between sapwood and heartwood, the sapwood being light brown and the heartwood, reddish-brown, similar to European beech, but of coarser quality. It is also a little heavier, weighing about 740 kg/m^3 when dried.

Drying
Dries fairly rapidly and fairly well, but with a tendency to warp, surface check and end split.

Strength
A hard, heavy and strong timber, with general strength properties similar to those of European beech.

Durability
Perishable.

Working qualities
Works fairly readily, but there is a tendency for the wood to bind on the saw, and to burn in cross-cutting and drilling. It can be worked to a good finish however, and it turns well. It has good nailing qualities, and can be stained, polished and glued satisfactorily.

Uses
Flooring, furniture, cooperage, woodware, joinery, handles and turnery, brushes, vehicle parts and for wood distillation.

BIRCH

The Betulaceae family contains nine or more species of the genus *Betula* found in North America, but only two or three are considered commercially important. The timber is diffuse porous, and is hard, heavy, strong and tough. The following are the principal species producing North American birch.

PAPER BIRCH

Betula papyrifera Marsh.

Other names
American birch (in part) (UK) ; white birch (Canada).

Distribution
It has a very wide range from the Yukon to Hudson Bay and Newfoundland, spreading to the eastern parts of the USA.

The tree
Although the tree may reach a height of 21m with a diameter of 0.5m it is more commonly 15m to 18m tall with a diameter of 0.3m usually with a clear cylindrical bole.

The timber
The wood is creamy-white in colour, with a fine, uniform texture, weighing about 640 kg/m³ when dried.

Drying
Dries rather slowly, but quite well and with little degrade.

Strength
A medium-hard timber with general strength properties some 10 to 20 per cent inferior to those of yellow birch.

Durability
Non-durable.

Working qualities
Works reasonably well with all hand and machine tools, with only moderate dulling of cutting edges. Curly-grained material is liable to pick up, but a good finish can be obtained with care. The wood glues satisfactorily.

Uses
The best butts are used for plywood, otherwise the timber is used for spools, bobbins, dowels, woodware, hoops and crates. Western paper birch, *B. papyrifera* Marsh var. *occidentalis* Sarg. occurs in western Canada and the USA and is similar in appearance, properties and uses to paper birch, although it is a little lighter in weight, about 610 kg/m³ when dried.

YELLOW BIRCH

Betula alleghaniensis Britt. syn
B. lutea Michx. (principally) and *B. lenta* L.

Other names
hard birch, betula wood (Canada); Canadian yellow birch, Quebec birch, American birch (in part) (UK).
Note: North American specifications sometimes refer to selected, and unselected; these refer to colour and not to grade, and means the timber has or has not been selected for uniformity of colour. Thus sapwood may be called white birch (and is sometimes confused with *B. papyrifera*), and the heartwood, red birch.

Distribution
It is found from the Maritime Provinces of Canada westward to the east side of Lake Superior, and from the west end of this lake to the Lake of the Woods, extending southwards over the border into USA reaching Long Island, northern Delaware and Tennessee.

The tree
It is the largest of the North American birches, reaching a height of 30m and a diameter of 1m on favourable sites, but more often it is from 18m to 24m tall with a diameter of 0.75m having a clear bole with moderate taper.

The timber
The sapwood is light yellow in colour and the heartwood a distinct reddish-brown, with the growth-rings marked with a narrow line of darker colour. There is a wide range of colour differences in unselected parcels, but yellow birch is one of the few woods which when finished with a medium or dark-coloured stain will not show a marked difference between sapwood and heartwood, hence there is a saving in cost in using unselected stock as opposed to selected white or red birch.
The wood is straight-grained, and the texture is fine, and even. The weight is about 710 kg/m³ when dried.

Drying
Dries slowly, but with little degrade.

Strength
Yellow birch is a stronger and harder wood than European birch, being about 60 per cent harder when dry, and about 15 per cent stronger in compression along the grain and stiffer in bending. It equals European ash in toughness and in resistance to shock loads.

Durability
Perishable.

Working qualities
Works fairly easily with only a moderate dulling effect on cutting edges, and finishes smoothly and without difficulty if the stock is straight-grained and clear. Curly-grained material, and disturbed grain in the vicinity of knots is liable to tear and pick up during planing and moulding, and a cutting angle of 15° or less is needed. The wood turns well, and with care glues satisfactorily. It takes stains and polish extremely well, and on account of the light tone of birch wood, it is well adapted to delicate colour stains. It is unexcelled as a base for white enamel, because its uniform, dense surface, free from large groups of pores, guarantees a permanent smooth surface.

Uses
Furniture, flooring, high-class joinery, turnery, bobbins, shuttles, spools, cooperage, high-grade plywood.

CHERRY, AMERICAN

Prunus serotina Ehrh.   Family: Rosaceae

Other names
black cherry, cabinet cherry (USA).

Distribution
Occurs in the deciduous forest areas from Ontario to Florida and from the Dakotas to Texas, but only in small quantities or as scattered trees.

The tree
A medium-sized tree, 18m to 21m tall, with a diameter of 0.5m.

The timber
The timber is hard, with a fine, straight, close grain, the heart-wood varying in colour from reddish-brown to rich red, the narrow sapwood being pinkish. Fine, narrow, brown-coloured pith flecks, and small gum pockets are a common feature of the wood, which weighs about 580 kg/m³ when dried.
It is moderately durable, works fairly easily, turns well, and takes an excellent polish.

Uses
Because of its beautiful grain and colour it is favoured for furniture and cabinet-making, but it is also used for pattern-making, tobacco pipes, musical instruments, interiors for boats and high-class joinery.

CHESTNUT, AMERICAN

Castanea dentata Borkh.   Family : Fagaceae

Distribution
At the beginning of this century, American chestnut was an important timber tree in North America, particularly in southern New England, and much lumber was exported to Europe for use as a substitute for oak, and in a wormy grade for solid veneer cores, the worm holes affording a particularly good key to the animal glues then in use. Unfortunately, at some time prior to 1904, a bark-inhabiting fungus had inadvertently been imported into America from Asia, and this caused a devastating chestnut blight which caused a ring-girdling effect in the trees, progressively killing off many natural stands. Tests at Madison while establishing that timber from infected trees was not reduced in strength, failed to evolve an effective means of controlling the blight, which persisted for many years. Some trees showed varying degrees of resistance to the infection, but wholesale felling took place, with replanting of other species of forest trees in the cleared areas. Present day supplies of chestnut are limited ,and appear to be confined to a small area of southern Ontario, and in the USA to the southern Appalachians.

The tree
The tree may reach a height of 30m but more commonly it is 21m to 24m tall with a diameter of about 0.5m.

The timber
The sapwood is narrow, and lighter in colour than the heartwood which is pale brown, usually characterized by wide growth-rings which give the wood a pronounced figure. It resembles oak in general appearance but lacks the broad rays which produce the silver-grain in oak. It is lighter in weight than European sweet chestnut, weighing about 480 kg/m^3 when dried.
It has moderate strength, is durable, works readily and finishes excellently.

Uses
Furniture, office desks and equipment, coffins, tanks, posts and sleepers. It is rich in tannin, and is liable to cause staining when wet wood is in contact with unprotected ferreous metals.

DOGWOOD

Cornus florida L.   Family : Cornaceae

Other names
cornel (USA).

Distribution
Eastern USA.

The tree
A small tree producing a merchantable bole 1.2m to 2.4m in length and 150mm or a little more in diameter.

The timber
Only the sapwood is used, and this is pinkish to pale pinkish-brown in colour; the heartwood is a small, dark brown core. The wood is hard and heavy, with a fine, lustrous, close grain, which is usually straight. The wood weighs about 830 kg/m^3 when dried.

Drying
Dries very slowly without a marked tendency to warp and split.

Uses
The wood is rather hard to work, but it turns well and finishes smoothly. It is used primarily for shuttles for cotton mills, as it is very resistant to wear. Other uses include mauls, wedges, bobbins, golf-club heads, engraver's blocks and cogs.

ELM, AMERICAN

The Ulmaceae family is represented in North America by five species of the genus *Ulmus* or elm, but only three of these are commercially important. These are described below.

Ulmus americana L. produces **white elm**, otherwise known as water elm, swamp elm and American elm. It occurs in all provinces of eastern Canada and as far west as Saskatchewan, and in the eastern and central parts of the USA. It is a large tree, which under favourable conditions reaches a height of 37m and a diameter of 2m, but more generally it is 15m to 27m in height, with a diameter of 0.5m or a little more. The timber weighs about 580 kg/m³ when dried.

Ulmus fulva Michx. produces **slippery elm**, otherwise known as soft elm, red elm, and slippery-barked elm. It has a rather restricted distribution in North America, and is found mostly in the St Lawrence River valley. It is a smaller tree than white elm, reaching a height of 15m to 18m and a diameter of about 0.3m to 0.5m. It is a little heavier than white elm.

Ulmus thomasii Sarg. syn *Ulmus racemosa* Thomas. produces **rock elm**, otherwise known as cork elm, hickory elm and cork-bark elm. This tree grows to a height of 15m to 18m and a diameter of 0.5m. It is found in the southern parts of the provinces of Quebec and Ontario, and extends into the USA.

General characteristics
White elm and slippery elm are similar in appearance and properties, and in the North American trade are marketed together. The heartwood is pale reddish-brown in colour, and the sapwood is paler. The wood is strong and tough, and has

good bending properties. The grain is usually straight, but occasionally is interlocked, and the texture is coarse, and inclined to be woolly. The timber is said to dry well, with medium shrinkage, and its strength generally is superior to that of European common elm, being some 50 per cent stiffer and harder, 30 per cent stronger in compression parallel to the grain, and more than twice as resistant to shock loads.

It works fairly easily, finishes well if sharp cutting edges are employed, and takes stains and polish satisfactorily, nails and screws well, and is said to glue well.

Uses

A non-durable type, white elm along with slippery elm is used for purposes where good strength, toughness and bending properties are essential, eg staves and hoops for slack cooperage, coffins, church pews, furniture, agricultural implements, cheese boxes, crates and in boat building. It is a favoured timber for fenders and rubbing strips in dock and harbour construction.

Rock elm differs considerably in appearance from white and slippery elm. There is no sharp distinction between sapwood and heartwood, the wood being light brown in colour, the grain is straight, the texture is finer, and it is appreciably heavier, averaging about 705 kg/m^3 when dried, but varying from 640 to 800 kg/m^3.

The appearance of the early-wood vessels on end grain also is different; white elm and rock elm may have only a single row of vessels in the pore ring. In the former species, these vessels are easily visible to the unaided eye, and further, contain few tyloses, whereas the vessels in rock elm are much smaller, usually requiring the use of a hand lens in order to distinguish them clearly, and containing abundant tyloses, hence the higher density, finer texture, and straighter grain of rock elm.

The timber is said to tend to check and twist during drying and therefore to require care. It is also a rather difficult timber to work by hand, and moderately difficult to machine, there being a tendency for cutting edges to dull rather quickly, and for the wood to burn during drilling, cross-cutting and mortising. A good finish can be obtained with care, and the wood can be stained, polished, nailed and screwed satisfactorily.

Uses

A non-durable wood, it is used in boat and ship building for keels, gunwales, bilge stringers, in dock and harbour work for fenders and rubbing strips, agricultural implements, chair rockers, gymnasium equipment, vehicle bodies for bent work, ladder rungs and for sleigh runners. The outstanding features of rock elm are its toughness and resistance to shock loads.

GUM, RED, AMERICAN

Liquidambar styraciflua L.   Family : Hamamelidaceae

Other names

sweet gum, bilsted (USA) ; red gum (heartwood) sap gum (sapwood), (USA) ; the UK names of hazel pine (sapwood) and satin walnut (heartwood) are confusing and should be discontinued.

Distribution

The tree ranges from New England to Mexico and Central America, but reaches its best development in the south-eastern States. It is a source of storax or styrax, a pathological balsam product formed in the bark by wound stimulation.

General characteristics

The sapwood is creamy white and the heartwood varies from pinkish-brown to deep reddish-brown. The texture is fine and uniform, and the grain is generally irregular ; the wood, which has a satiny lustre, weighs about 560 kg/m^3 when dried. Some trees produce an attractive mottle figure. The timber dries readily, but with a distinct tendency to warp and twist, and unless carefully dried to a suitable moisture content, is highly susceptible to in situ atmospheric changes, the wood tending to shrink, swell and split. Quarter-sawn stock is less liable to distortion in service.

Uses

The timber has a wide range of uses, either as red (sweet) gum, or in sapwood form (sap gum). These range from furniture and panelling, to doors, interior trim, plywood, boxes and crates.

HACKBERRY

Celtis occidentalis L.   Family: Ulmaceae

Distribution
Eastern USA.

General characteristics
Hackberry is botanically associated with the elms of North America, and is often marketed with white and slippery elm, although the colour of hackberry, which is greyish or yellowish-grey, with little difference in colour between sapwood and heartwood, distinguishes it from the elms, with their brownish heartwood, clearly defined from the lighter coloured sapwood. The anatomical features of both hackberry and elm are similar, each having a conspicuous early-wood pore-ring one, or more vessel wide, with the late-wood vessels in undulating tangential lines. Hackberry has an irregular grain, occasionally straight, a fairly fine and uniform texture, is tough, strong and moderately hard, and weighs about 640 kg/m³ when dried.

Uses
It is a non-durable wood, used for furniture, cooperage, vehicle bodies, woodware; generally for the same purposes as elm.

HICKORY

The Juglandaceae produces various tree species well known for their timber and in most cases also for the valuable nuts they produce. Among these are walnut, pecan and hickory. Originally, hickory and pecan were classified under the genus *Hicoria*, but they have now been reclassified as *Carya* spp. The following are the important species of this genera found in North America; walnut, *Juglans* spp. will be found elsewhere in this publication.

Hickory is produced by,
Carya glabra Sweet. also known as pignut hickory.
C. tomentosa Nutt. also known as mockernut hickory.
C. laciniosa Loud. also known as shellbark hickory.
C. ovata K. Koch. also known as shagbark hickory.

172

Pecan is produced by,
Carya illinoensis K. Koch. also known as sweet pecan and pecan hickory.
C. aquatica Nutt. also known as bitter pecan and water hickory.

All are sold as hickory and used for the same purposes, but the true hickories are a little superior in strength. Both types are often separated into white hickory (sapwood) and red hickory (heartwood), but this is a distinction by colour, and not by strength, since this is more dependent on density and rate of growth.

Distribution
The four true hickories are found from Ontario to Minnesota, Florida and Mexico, mainly in the eastern deciduous forests. The pecans are native to south-eastern USA and Mexico, and are now extensively cultivated in the southern States, particularly in Texas and Oklahoma, principally for the nuts they produce.

The tree
The trees vary according to species, from 18m to 30m or a little more in height, with diameters ranging from 0.5m to 1.0m.

The timber
All the species are similar in appearance; the sapwood is white, and usually wide, and is generally preferred, while the heart-wood is brown or reddish-brown in colour. The grain is straight, and only occasionally wavy or irregular, and the texture is coarse, not unlike ash in general appearance. The true hickories weigh about 830 kg/m^3 and pecan weighs about 750 kg/m^3 when dried.

Although for practical purposes it is usually unnecessary to distinguish between the various species, except where high strength is required, when high density and a growth rate of less than 20 rings to 25mm is usually preferred, it is possible to separate true hickory from pecan by observing the position of the narrow bands of parenchyma in the early-wood as seen on clean cut end-grain. These bands appear like ladder rungs between the rays; in the true hickories the first band appears beyond the first row of early-wood pores, while in pecan it occurs between these large pores.

173

Drying
All types dry fairly rapidly without much tendency to warp and twist, but shrinkage is said to be high.

Strength
Compared with ash, hickory is much tougher, stronger in bending, stiffer, and more resistant to shock loads, and although pecan is slightly inferior, both types exceed in importance all other North American woods, where a combination of such properties is required.

Durability
Non-durable.

Working qualities
Rather variable in working properties, the general run of hickory working with moderate ease, but the fast-grown wood, mostly preferred because of its higher density and strength, is relatively hard, and combined with its natural toughness tends to make it rather difficult to work. There is a tendency for the grain to tear in planing, and a reduction of cutting angle to about 20° is often necessary to overcome this. Cutting edges are inclined to dull fairly quickly, but the wood can be finished to a smooth surface, and can be glued satisfactorily.

Uses
Striking tool handles, rims, spokes and felloes for wheels, chairs, ladder rungs, sports goods, turnery, shafts for golf clubs, shunting poles, vehicle bodies. It has excellent steam bending properties.

HOP HORNBEAM, AMERICAN

Ostrya virginiana K. Koch   Family: Betulaceae

Other names
ironwood (Canada and USA); this name is confusing and should be discontinued; by comparison with other woods of this name, the timber of *Ostrya* does not merit the description.

Distribution
Canada and eastern USA.

General characteristics
This is a minor species, of limited availability, but locally important as a hard, tough and strong timber, associated in use with the hickories.

The tree grows to a height of 18m with a diameter of 0.5m. The wood varies from white to light brown in colour, is usually cross-grained, and is heavy and hard, weighing about 800 kg/m^3 when dried. It is difficult to work, and is used locally for tool handles, vehicle parts, agricultural implements, levers and fence posts.

MAGNOLIA

Magnolia spp. principally   Family : Magnoliaceae
M. grandiflora L. and *M. virginiana* L.

Other names
cucumber (USA).

Distribution
The Atlantic coastal plain forests extend from Virginia to Texas and contain conifers at the higher elevations, while on lower ground magnolia occurs along with red gum and tupelo.

The tree
The tree varies in size according to species but on average it is about 18m high with a diameter of 0.5m or more.

General characteristics
The sapwood is creamy white and the heartwood is light straw-coloured, with a greenish or sometimes purplish tinge, often with dark, almost purple streaks caused by mineral deposits, and fine, light-coloured lines of terminal parenchyma. The grain is straight, the texture fine and uniform, and the wood has a satiny lustre. It is similar in appearance to American whitewood (*Liriodendron*). and not unlike tupelo (*Nyssa*) and red gum (*Liquidambar*), especially in anatomical characteristics. Magnolia weighs about 560 kg/m^3 when dried.

It works easily and well, can be nailed, screwed, glued, stained and polished excellently.

Uses

It has a small movement in changing atmospheres and accordingly is used for louvres, interior joinery, doors, boxes, woodwool and for panelling, especially when streaked with variegated mineral stain.

MAPLE

The Aceraceae family includes some ten species of the genus *Acer* found in North America, but of these, only about five species are important sources of maple timber; these are given below.

Acer saccharum Marsh. produces rock maple, hard maple or sugar maple.

A. nigrum Michx f. produces black maple, rock or hard maple.

A. saccharinum L. produces soft maple or silver maple.

A. rubrum L. produces soft maple or red maple.

A. macrophyllum Pursh. produces Pacific maple or Oregon maple.

Distribution

Found generally in Canada and eastern USA; Pacific maple being confined to the Pacific Coast of Canada and USA.

The tree

A. saccharum and *A. nigrum* grow to a height of 27m or more and a diameter of 0.5m to 0.75m.

A. saccharinum is of similar height but is often of slightly larger diameter, about 1.0m.

A. rubrum reaches a height of 15m to 23m and a diameter of 0.75m.

A. macrophyllum is a smaller tree, some 12m to 24m high, and a diameter of 0.5m.

The timber

Hard maple is strong, heavy, hard, straight-grained and fine textured. The heartwood is light reddish-brown with deeper-coloured late-wood bands. The sapwood is white in colour, and furnishes the white maple prized for certain uses. It differs mainly from the soft maples in its greater density and finer texture. The weight of dried timber is as follows; *A. saccharum* and *A. nigrum* (rock maple) 740 kg/m³; *A. rubrum* (soft maple) 630 kg/m³; *A. saccharinum* (soft maple) 550 kg/m³; *A. macrophyllum* (Pacific maple) 560 kg/m³.

Drying
All types dry without undue difficulty but rather slowly, particularly rock maple.

Strength
Compared with European beech, rock maple is about equal in bending strength and in compression along the grain, and some 15 to 20 per cent superior in hardness, resistance to shock loads and resistance to splitting. Soft maple is inferior to rock maple in all strength categories; it is 40 to 50 per cent softer, about the same amount less resistant to shock loading and in shear strength, 20 per cent less stiff, and 20 to 30 per cent weaker in bending and compression along the grain, and less resistant to splitting.

Durability
All types are non-durable.

Working qualities
Hard maple is rather difficult to work, the timber tending to cause saws to vibrate, and for cutters to ride on the wood during planing. A reduction of cutting angle to 20° assists the finishing operation particularly when curly grain is present. The timber can be stained, polished and glued satisfactorily, but it is hard to nail or screw, although these are held firmly.
Soft maple works and machines with less difficulty in all operations.

Uses
The uses for hard and soft maple are practically the same except for most exacting requirements of hardness and strength. Hard maple is generally preferred for flooring and for shoe lasts, but soft maple is also used. Typical uses for maple include flooring, furniture, piano actions, turnery, musical instruments, sports goods, butcher blocks, bowling alleys, dairy and laundry equipment ,panelling, veneer and plywood. Figured forms of maple include bird's eye, fiddle-back, blister and curly maple.
Note : a small proportion of *Acer negundo* L. is sometimes mixed

with shipments of soft maple. This timber, known as box elder, Manitoba maple or ash-leaved maple is rather inferior to the other maples, being lighter in colour, softer, and weak. It is used locally for boxes, drawer-bottoms and for rough construction.

OAK

The Fagaceae family includes some fifty species of the genus *Quercus*, producing the true oaks of North America, but many of these are so small in size, or are found in such limited quantities that they are of no commercial importance. Some twenty species are important, but since it is difficult to distinguish between the wood of the individual species, it is the practice to group them either as red or white oak. The following are the principal species comprising these groups.

Red oak group; timbers characterized by the small, late-wood pores larger and less numerous than in the white oaks. Large pores of the early-wood mostly open and free from tyloses.

Quercus rubra Du Roi. syn *Q. borealis* Michx f. produces northern red oak.
Q. falcata Michx f. var. *falcata* produces southern red oak or Spanish oak.
Q. falcata Michx f. var. *pagodaefolia* Ell. produces swamp red oak or cherrybark oak.
Q. shumardii Buckl. produces shumard red oak.

White oak group; timbers characterized by the small, late-wood pores fine and numerous, not easily distinguished without a hand lens. Large pores of the early-wood filled with tyloses in heartwood.
Quercus alba L. produces white oak.
Q. prinus L. syn. *Q. montana* Willd. produces chestnut oak.
Q. lyrata Walt. produces overcup oak.
Q. michauxii Nutt. produces swamp chestnut oak.

RED OAK

Distribution
Eastern Canada and USA. In Canada it is more abundant than white oak, and covers a wider range.

The tree
The trees vary according to species but average about 18m to 21m in height with a diameter of 1.0m.

The timber
The timber varies in colour from pink to pale reddish-brown, there is usually a reddish cast to the wood although sometimes it approaches white oak in colour. The large rays do not produce such an attractive figure as they do in white oak, and generally speaking, the wood is coarser in texture. The quality of red oak depends greatly on growth conditions, northern red oak, with its comparatively slow rate of growth, compares favourably with northern white oak, while red oak from the southern States is generally of faster growth, and consequently more coarse and open in texture. Red oak weighs about 790 kg/m^3 when dried.

Durability
Non-durable.

Uses
Less esteemed than white oak, it is too porous for tight coop-erage, and its lack of durability, and tendency to warp and check, limit its uses to some extent. It is used for flooring, furniture, interior joinery and veneer.

WHITE OAK

Distribution
From southern Quebec and Ontario to eastern Minnesota and Iowa, extending eastward to the Atlantic and southward through the lower western slopes of the Allegheny and Appalachian Mountains.

The tree
The white oaks vary in size and form according to species and soil conditions, some are unsuitable for timber production, but others vary in height from 15m to 30m, well-grown specimens having a clear cylindrical bole of up to 15m with a diameter of about 1.0m.

The timber

Although generally resembling European oak, American white oak is more variable in colour, ranging from pale yellow-brown to pale reddish-brown, often with a pinkish tint. The multi-seriate rays are generally higher than those of the red oaks producing a more prominent and attractive silver-grain figure on quarter-sawn surfaces. The grain is generally straight, and the texture varies from coarse to medium coarse. As with the red oaks, the quality depends greatly on the conditions of growth; slowly-grown northern white oak usually being lighter in weight and milder, than that from the southern states. The Appalachian Mountains used to provide beautiful mild white oak greatly esteemed for furniture and cabinet-making, but much of this forest area has been destroyed in recent years due to open-cast coal mining activities. Southern white oak is typically fast grown, and with its wide growth-rings is relatively coarse and more suited to constructional use. White oak weighs about 770 kg/m^3 when dried.

Drying

Like all the true oaks the timber dries slowly, with a tendency to split, check and honeycomb.

Strength

It compares fairly closely with European oak in general strength, but on the whole, its higher density provides rather higher strength.

Durability

Durable.

Working qualities

Variable in working properties according to rate of growth, slow-grown material being easier to work than fast-grown, but either type can be finished smoothly if care is taken. A reduction of cutting angle to 20° is often helpful in planing. The timber can be glued, stained and polished, and takes nails and screws well.

Uses

Heavy construction, flooring, furniture, pews and pulpits, doors, counters, boats, ladder rungs, agricultural implements, waggon bottoms, coffins, veneer and cooperage white oak barrels being the only satisfactory containers for beer, wine and alcoholic spirits.

Note: *Quercus virginiana* Mill. produces the live oak of the southern USA. This is quite a distinct, evergreen species, and has the hardest, strongest and toughest wood of all the American oaks. It is used in the construction of waggons, ships and farm implements, but is not in much demand owing to low availability.

PERSIMMON

Diospyros virginiana L.   Family: Ebenaceae

Distribution
Central and Southern USA.

General characteristics
Although persimmon belongs to the ebony family, the tree produces only a small, dark brown or black core, the commercial wood being the straw-coloured sapwood, although selected material containing dark heartwood streaks of yellow-brown, brown, and black, is occasionally used for small, decorative items. ·The wood is tough, hard, strong, elastic, resistant to wear and very heavy, weighing about 850 kg/m^3 when dried. It is used chiefly for textile shuttles, shoe lasts, golf-club heads, turnery, and other items demanding a close, compact wood with an ability to wear smooth.

PLANE, AMERICAN

Platanus occidentalis L.   Family: Platanaceae

Other names
sycamore, buttonwood (USA).

It should be noted the British standard name for species of *Platanus* is plane, whereas in the USA the timber of *Platanus occidentalis* is commonly called sycamore. The wood of plane does not resemble that of sycamore, nor is it botanically related, sycamore being classified as *Acer pseudoplatanus*, a member of the Aceraceae family.

Distribution
Eastern USA.

General characteristics
The wood is a uniform light reddish-brown in colour, resembling beech, but with more of a reddish cast. Plain-sawn surfaces are fairly plain in appearance, with little figure excepting for lighter-coloured narrow bands of parenchyma marking the season's growth. The large rays produce a figure on quarter-sawn surfaces, showing reddish-brown against the lighter background, and giving rise to the distinctive and highly decorative wood known as lacewood. The wood weighs about 560 kg/m³ when dried.
It dries easily, but with a tendency to warp and check, and therefore requires care. It works fairly easily, but the large ray flecks on quarter-sawn surfaces tend to flake out in planing unless sharp cutting edges are employed. The wood can be glued, stained and polished quite well.

Uses
Joinery, doors, panelling, butcher's blocks, brush-backs and veneer.

POPLAR

The Salicaceae family contains a number of species of the genus *Populus*, which produces commercial aspen, cottonwood and poplar. Since the English equivalent of *Populus* is poplar, and the timber of the various species is similar in appearance and properties, these are included here under the heading of poplar, with the exception of yellow poplar, *Liriodendron tulipifera*, which belongs to the Magnoliaceae family and is described elsewhere in this publication. The most important species of *Populus* found in North America are as follows,

Populus tremuloides Michx. produces **Canadian aspen**, otherwise known as aspen or quaking aspen. This occurs fairly widely from Newfoundland and Nova Scotia to Alaska, and from northern New England to Minnesota and southwards along the Appalachians. The tree is normally from 15m to 18m tall, with a diameter of about 0.3m. The weight of dried timber is about 450 kg/m³.

Populus trichocarpa Hook. produces **black cottonwood**, otherwise known as western balm or balsam cottonwood. This occurs in western Canada and western USA. It is a large tree, 24m to 37m in height, with a diameter of 1.0m to 1.5m. The weight of dried timber is about 400 kg/m³.

Populus deltoides Bartr. ex Marsh. produces **eastern cotton-wood**, which occurs in eastern Canada in limited quantities and in small areas from Quebec westward through southern Ontario, extending into the USA. This is one of the largest of the poplars, averaging 23m to 30m and a diameter from 0.6m to 1.2m. The weight of dried timber is about 430 kg/m³.

Populus balsamifera L. syn. *P. tacamahaca* Mill. produces **Canadian poplar**, otherwise known as tacamahac poplar, and balsam poplar in the USA and as balm poplar, and black poplar in Canada. This species occurs widely in Canada and the USA in approximately the same areas as aspen. It is generally larger than aspen, reaching 18m to 21m in height, and occasionally reaching 27m with a diameter of 0.6m or more. The weight of the dried timber is about 470 kg/m³.

Populus grandidentata Michx. also produces **Canadian poplar**, otherwise known as big-tooth aspen or aspen. This occurs in eastern Canada and eastern USA. The wood is a little lighter in weight than that of *P. balsamifera*, about 450 kg/m³ when dried.

The timber
All the above species are similar in appearance; the sapwood is creamy-white in colour; in some species, notably *P. trichocarpa*, rather wide, and the heartwood is greyish-white to light brown. The wood is free from appreciable odour and taste, is inclined to be woolly, but generally fine and even textured, with a straight grain.

Drying
The various species have an inherent tendency to warp and twist during drying, and accordingly require care.

Strength
The various timbers are tough, with good shock resistance, but in general strength properties they are similar to eastern Canadian spruce.

Durability
Non-durable.

Working qualities
The timber works easily, although there may be a tendency to bind on the saw. A smooth surface can be obtained, but there is a tendency for the fibres to tear in sawing, and sharp, thin-edged tools are needed to avoid woolly surfaces in planing. The wood can be nailed, screwed, glued, stained and finished with the usual treatments, satisfactorily.

Uses
The uses for all the species is wide, ranging from match splints, wood wool, boxes and crates, to brake blocks for iron wheels, bottoms for carts, lorries and waggons, interiors of furniture and interior fitments.

TUPELO

Nyssa spp.   Family : Nyssaceae

Other names
water tupelo or tupelo gum *Nyssa aquatica* L. and *N. ogeche* Bartr. black gum or black tupelo *N. sylvatica* Marsh.

Distribution
Nyssa sylvatica is found from Maine to Michigan and south to Florida and Texas, while *Nyssa aquatica* and *N. ogeche* are restricted to the swamps of the southern States.

The tree
The trees reach a height of 24m to 30m and a diameter of 1.0m.

The timber

The timber of these species is similar in character and appearance, the sapwood is wide, and of a greyish-white colour, and the heartwood is pale yellow to pale brown. The grain is generally interlocked or twisted, and the texture is fine; the wood weighs about 560 kg/m³ when dried. The timber is either marketed collectively, or may be separated into black gum, which is the harder material, with the softer wood being sold as tupelo.

Drying

Although the wood dries readily and without undue splitting, it is prone to warping, particularly the harder, tougher, black gum. Care is therefore required, and piles should be weighted down to reduce warping.

Uses

The timber is soft, light, tough, stiff and resistant to wear, and is used for flooring, wheel hubs, wooden ware, interior trim, bridge and pier decking and rough construction.

WALNUT, AMERICAN

Juglans nigra L.   Family : Juglandaceae

Other names

black walnut.

Distribution

Black walnut is widely distributed throughout North America, from south Ontario southward to Texas, and in the east, from Maine to Florida, but it is not plentiful, firstly because its growth is scattered, and secondly, because of the clearing of ground for cultivation and the demands for the timber have exhausted the supply in many areas.

The tree

Under favourable conditions, the tree attains a height of 30m and a diameter of 1.5m or more, the bole often being clear for 15m to 18m.

The timber
The sapwood is usually narrow, and pale brown in colour, the heartwood varying in colour from rich chocolate-brown to a purplish-black. The wood has a fine even texture and a rather coarse grain, and weighs about 660 kg/m³ when dried.

Drying
Dries rather slowly with a tendency to honeycombing.

Durability
Moderately durable.

Working qualities
The timber is moderately hard, tough, strong and is easily worked. It finishes well and takes an excellent polish.

Uses
Furniture, cabinets, gun stocks, musical instruments and decorative veneer.

Juglans cinerea L. produces butternut, sometimes called white walnut. This occurs throughout the hardwood region of Ontario to Georgian Bay, and from New Brunswick to Minnesota and south to Georgia and Arkansas. The tree is 12m to 15m in height, with a diameter of 0.3m to 0.75m. The heartwood is a medium to dark brown colour, but not as dark as that of black walnut which it resembles somewhat in general appearance and texture. It is a rather soft and light, weak timber, which takes stain well, and is sometimes used as a substitute for black walnut, but its main uses are for boxes and crates, interior trim for ships and boats and wooden ware.

WHITEWOOD, AMERICAN

Liriodendron tulipifera L.   Family : Magnoliaceae

Other names
yellow poplar, tulip poplar (USA) ; tulip tree (UK and USA) ; canary wood, canary whitewood (UK).

Note : The BSI standard name, whitewood should not be confused with the softwood of that name, nor should the

American trade name, poplar be confused with the true poplars, *Populus* spp. *Liriodendron* is associated botanically with *Magnolia* spp., both trees carrying tulip-like flowers.

Distribution
Eastern USA and Canada. Owing to the enormous demand for the timber in past years, supplies at the present time are limited.

The tree
A large tree attaining a height of 37m or more, and a diameter of 2m or more.

The timber
The sapwood is white, and in second-growth trees, very wide; the heartwood is variable in colour, ranging from olive green to yellow or brown, and may be streaked with steel-blue. The annual growth terminates in a white band of parenchyma, giving a subdued figure to longitudinal surfaces. The wood is straight-grained, fine-textured, fairly soft and light in weight, about 510 kg/m^3 when dried.

Drying
Dries easily and well, with little degrade.

Strength
Similar to idigbo (*Terminalia ivorensis*) in general strength properties.

Durability
Non-durable.

Working qualities
Easy to work, and finishes to a fine, smooth surface. Takes nails without tending to split, glues well, can be stained, polished or painted, and holds hard enamel finishes excellently.

Uses
Joinery, including doors, interior trim, light construction, boats, toys and plywood.

MINOR SPECIES

Malus spp. (Rosaceae) ; **apple wood**, usually obtained from old orchards, is strong, hard and compact, with a uniform close grain, light reddish-brown in colour, weighing about 720 kg/m^3 when dried.

Uses
tool handles, tobacco pipes, rulers, turnery, mallet heads.

Aesculus octandra Marsh. syn. *A. flava* Ait. (Hippocastanaceae) ; **buckeye** or sweet buckeye; similar to the European horse chestnut, but the buds are not resinous. A tree of the Middle West USA it furnishes a soft, light wood, yellowish-white in colour weighing about 520 kg/m^3 when dried.

Uses
boxes, wood wool, artificial limbs, furniture interiors.

Catalpa speciosa Ward. (Bignoniaceae) ; **catalpa** is a small tree, native to the lower Ohio valley, and planted extensively throughout the Middle West. The brown wood is cross-grained and durable, and is much used for fencing posts and rails.

Gymnocladus canadensis Lam. syn. *G. dioica* Koch. (Leguminosae) ; **Kentucky coffee tree**; a strong, durable wood used for furniture, sills, bridges, posts, ties and interior finish.

Ilex opaca Ait. (Aquifoliaceae) ; **American holly**; similar in appearance to European holly, it is a characteristic tree of the southern coastal states and the lower Mississippi and Ohio valleys. The tough, close-grained, whitish coloured wood is used for inlay, brushes, wooden ware, fancy articles, and is often stained to imitate ebony.

Maclura pomifera Schneid. (Moraceae) ; **osage orange**, a small tree, native to the Gulf States, but cultivated elsewhere. Its wood is a bright orange colour, darkening on exposure, hard and tough, weighing about 768 kg/m^3 when dried. Because of its durability it is used for wheel felloes, tree-nails, fence posts and wood ware.

Sassafras officinale Nees & Eberm. syn *S. variifolium* Kuntze. (Lauraceae) ; **sassafras**, is a small tree of the eastern USA producing fragrant, durable, and soft wood, used for furniture, fencing, boxes and cooperage.

Salix nigra Marsh. (Salicaceae) ; **black willow**, occurs in Canada and the USA reaching its best development on the flood plains in the Mississippi and Ohio valleys. This is the only one of the numerous North American willows which is of commercial importance. The wood is whitish in colour, typically straight-grained, with a fine even texture, soft, tough, fairly strong, and light in weight, about 430 kg/m^3 when dried.

Uses
boxes and crates, wood wool, water wheels and for charcoal. The young, long, pliable shoots are used for wicker baskets and furniture.

PART II SOFTWOODS

CEDAR

The Coniferae plant order includes the Pinaceae family among whose genera is found *Cedrus*, the various species of which produce the true cedars, eg Atlantic, Lebanon and deodar cedars, indigenous to North Africa, Asia Minor and the Himalayas. A further family is the Cupressaceae, comprising certain genera and species which possess a natural fragrance reminiscent of the true cedars, and whose timbers have been given the commercial name cedar, for example, *Thuja* (arbor vitae), *Chamaecyparis* (false cypress) and *Juniperus* (junipers). Since many of these are found in the Northern Hemisphere, the principal genera and species occurring in North America are dealt with individually under their commercial name of cedar in the notes that follow.

'INCENSE CEDAR'

Calocedrus decurrens (Torr) Florin syn.
Libocedrus decurrens Torr.

Other names
'Californian incense cedar' (USA).

189

Distribution
East of the Cascade Range at the higher altitudes, being most abundant on the Sierra Nevada of Central California.

The tree
A tall, straight tree, attaining a height of 24m to 30m, occasionally reaching 45m, with a irregularly lobed bole, and a diameter of about 1m but sometimes larger.

The timber
When freshly sawn the wood varies in colour from salmon-red to dark chocolate-brown, but tones down after drying to a fairly uniform light brown colour. Although the wood generally resembles western red cedar in character, its less prominent late-wood zones, lack of lustre, and lighter colour as opposed to the reddish-brown colour of western red cedar, serves to distinguish 'incense cedar' from the latter wood. A common characteristic of 'incense cedar' is its slight peppery odour, and a tendency to peckiness; small, decayed areas caused by heart rot in the tree, which sometimes cause severe loss in conversion. The wood weighs about 400 kg/m^3 when dried.

Drying
Dries readily, with little degrade in general, although there is a tendency for thick sizes to retain patches of moisture, and for honey-comb checking to develop if the drying is forced.

Strength
A soft, light, weak wood, with strength properties similar to those of 'western red cedar', but slightly heavier.

Durability
Very durable.

Working qualities
Works easily with little dulling effect on cutting edges. It is capable of a good, smooth finish, but cutters must be kept sharpened. It can be stained, takes a fair polish and paints well.

Uses
Building purposes, shingles, laths, posts, interior trim, pencils, piling and for the construction of flumes.

'PORT ORFORD CEDAR'

Chamaecyparis lawsoniana Parl. syn.
Cupressus lawsoniana Murray.

Other names
Lawson's cypress (UK).

Distribution
This tree is restricted generally to the coast of southern Oregon and California.

The tree
A large, tall tree, reaching a height of 60m and a diameter up to 3.5m above the large, swollen base.

The timber
The heartwood is pale pinkish-brown in colour, barely distinct from the lighter-coloured sapwood. It is the hardest of the so-called cedars, with a fine, even texture, is typically non-resinous, but possesses a high, spicy scent. It weighs about 500 kg/m³ when dried.

Drying
Dries well with little degrade.

Strength
A strong, stiff timber, with general strength properties similar to those of Douglas fir, although a little lighter in weight.

Durability
Durable.

Working qualities
Works easily with all hand and machine tools, and generally finishes cleanly. It takes nails and screws well, and can be stained, polished and painted.

Uses
'Port Orford cedar' is used for exterior cladding, boat and ship-building, canoe paddles, organ pipes, match splints, shingles, and because of its high fragrance, for chests and closet-

linings, but the scent is lost after a while, and is only restored when the wood is sawn or planed again. The timber is also used in rough construction products such as posts, poles and piling.

'SOUTHERN WHITE CEDAR'

Chamaecyparis thyoides B.S.P. syn.
Cupressus thyoides L.

Other names
'white cedar', 'Atlantic white cedar' (USA).

Distribution
Occurs with cypress in the swamps along the sandy Atlantic coastal plain from Virginia to Texas.

General characteristics
The wood is pinkish in colour, with a fine grain and texture, soft, weak and light in weight, weighing about 370 kg/m^3 when dried. The wood is more highly scented than 'northern white cedar *Thuja occidentalis*.

Uses
The timber is durable and is used for boat-building, shingles, posts, ties and to a minor extent for building and construction. In colonial days, it was used for timber frame houses, but was considered too light and weak to support the weight of second storeys.

'NORTHERN WHITE CEDAR'

Thuja occidentalis L.

Other names
'white cedar' (BSI standard name) ; eastern arbor vitae (USA) ; 'eastern white cedar' (Canada).

Distribution
A common tree of New England, the Lake States, and adjacent Canada, it occurs from Nova Scotia and northern New England to Minnesota, and southwards along the summits of the Appalachians.

The tree
A smaller tree than 'southern white cedar', it reaches a height of 15m to 18m and a diameter of about 0.75m.

General characteristics
The sapwood is narrow, and almost white in colour, and the heartwood is light or pale brown, with narrow, inconspicuous late-wood bands. The wood has a faint spicy odour, is light in weight, about 340 kg/m^3 when dried, has a fine texture, but is soft, brash, and weak. Although much less stiff than 'western red cedar', it is much tougher, and has a higher resistance to shock.

Uses
The timber is easily worked, and owing to its durability, is used for shingles, fence posts, poles, tanks and silos.

'VIRGINIAN PENCIL CEDAR'

Juniperus virginiana L. and
J. silicicola (Small) Bailey

Other names
'eastern red cedar' (USA).

Distribution
'Pencil cedar' has a wide distribution in North America. It is found in Canada in southern Ontario along the St. Lawrence and Ottawa rivers, and in the eastern USA from Maine to Georgia, spreading westerly to a line from North Dakota to eastern Texas, and reaching its best development in rich, damp soils throughout the southern part of its range, with its best growth being obtained in Tennessee.

The tree
The tree generally averages 12m to 15m in height, but may reach 30m and a diameter of 1m but more generally, diameters of about 0.5m are found. The tree tends to develop a buttress, more noticeable in old specimens.

The timber
The sapwood is narrow and creamy-white in colour, and the

heartwood is purplish or pinkish-red when freshly cut, assuming a uniform reddish-brown colour after drying, occasionally with lighter streaks. A thin dark line of late-wood marks the boundary of each growth ring, and the wood is typically cedar-scented. It is soft, with a fine even grain, and it can be whittled easily, constituting the standard wood for lead pencils. The dried timber weighs about 530 kg/m³.

Drying
The timber should be allowed to dry slowly in order to reduce its natural tendency to fine surface checking and end splitting.

Strength
Although of similar weight to Douglas fir, its general strength properties are only about half those applicable to that timber, but 'pencil cedar' is harder and more resistant to splitting.

Durability
Durable.

Working qualities
The timber works easily, but much depends upon the quality of the wood fed to the machines. Selected material for pencil slats works without difficulty, but much material is knotty, and in a sense it is one of the few timbers where this defect adds to its value for use as decorative panelling. This type of material contains disturbed grain in the vicinity of the frequent knots and this tends to tear during planing, so that care is needed to ensure cutting edges are kept sharpened in order to obtain a good finish. The wood can be stained and polished, but tends to split in nailing.

Uses
It is one of the best timbers for pencil making; the chips and shavings from this manufacture are recovered and used to distil an essential oil. The fragrant, aromatic wood is also used for cigar boxes, linen and blanket chests, ship-building, coffins, panels, veneer and interior trim.

'WESTERN RED CEDAR'

Thuja plicata D.Don.

Other names
giant arbor vitae (USA) ; 'red cedar' (Canada).

Distribution
A tree of the northern Rocky Mountains and Pacific North-west; its full range extends from Alaska southwards to California, and eastwards along many of the interior ranges of British Columbia, northern Washington, Idaho and Montana, to the western slope of the continental divide.

The tree
The largest of the so-called cedars, it grows to a height of 45m to 75m with a diameter of 1m to 2.5m.

The timber
The sapwood is narrow and white in colour, and the heartwood is reddish-brown. When freshly felled, the heartwood often displays a marked variation in colour; that from the centre of the log may be a dark chocolate-brown changing to salmon pink nearer the sapwood, or the wood may be variegated with alternate dark and light zones. After drying, the wood assumes a uniform reddish-brown tone, but after long exposure to weather the colour is lost, and the wood becomes silver-grey. This weathered appearance is sometimes purposely sought by architects, but a further peculiarity of the wood is its ability to take and hold stain of the finest tint without discolouration. The wood is non-resinous, straight-grained, somewhat coarse-textured and exhibits a fairly prominent growth-ring figure. It is soft, rather brittle, aromatic, especially when wet, and light in weight, about 390 kg/m^3 when dried.

Drying
Thin sizes dry readily with little degrade, but the timber generally tends to hold its moisture at the centre, and care is needed with thick stock to avoid internal honey-combing and collapse. The timber holds its position well after drying, with practically no tendency to warp and check, while movement due to shrinking and swelling in changing atmospheres is small.

Strength
Its light weight and soft timber contributes to low strength properties and compared with European redwood (*Pinus sylvestris*) it is some 20 to 30 per cent inferior in bending strength, and about 15 per cent less stiff. It is also much less resistant to splitting and indentation on side grain than redwood.

Durability
Durable.

Working qualities
The timber works easily with both hand and machine tools, but its relatively brittle nature, which can cause splintering during some operations, and its soft character, which can lead to chip-bruising, usually means that care is needed in order to obtain the best results during mortising, planing and moulding. A good finish can be obtained, but cutters must be kept sharpened.

Uses
Shingles, exterior cladding, weather boarding, greenhouses, bee-hives, interior trim, poles, posts and fences.
Owing to its acidic properties, the timber tends to accelerate the corrosion of metals, and to cause unsightly black staining, ie when wet wood is in contact with unprotected ferreous metal, the wood becomes stained, and the metal begins to corrode. Suitable precautions should be taken—either to use metals which are relatively resistant to corrosion, for example, brass, or in extreme exposure conditions, pure aluminium—or by means of protective coatings such as hot dip galvanized, but these must be adequate, since cuts and scratches which penetrate the protective coating, caused during the application of metal fixtures and fittings, will impair the efficiency of the coating.

'YELLOW CEDAR'

Chamaecyparis nootkatensis Spach. syn
Cupressus nootkatensis Lamb.

Other names
'Alaska yellow cedar', nootka false cypress (USA); 'Pacific

coast yellow cedar' (Canadian standard name), yellow cypress (Canada).

Distribution
A typical Pacific coast species, it ranges from Alaska to Oregon.

The tree
A medium-size tree, reaching a height of 24m and a diameter of 0.75m with a sharply tapering bole.

The timber
A pale yellow-coloured wood, with a fine, even texture. Unlike the related 'Port Orford cedar', it lacks the persistent fragrant scent when dry, but green timber is said to have a strong odour reminiscent of rotten potatoes.' Yellow cedar' weighs about 500 kg/m^3 when dried.

Drying
Dries without undue difficulty, but there is a tendency for surface checking to occur in thick stock with some end splitting if the drying is forced.

Strength
A light, stiff, hard timber, with strength properties in most categories equal to, and in some cases a little superior to, those of European redwood (*Pinus sylvestris*), but rather less resistant to splitting.

Durability
Durable.

Working qualities
Works easily with all hand and machine tools, and finishes excellently. It can be glued, stained, polished and painted satisfactorily.

Uses
'Yellow cedar' has low movement values when used in fluctuating atmospheric conditions and is valued for high-class joinery, doors, window frames, boat-building, drawing boards, greenhouses, cabinet work, shingles, veneer for use in panelling, posts, poles and marine piling, Since it is resistant to acids and possesses other suitable properties, it is one of the best woods for battery separators.

197

'CYPRESS, SOUTHERN'

Taxodium distichum Rich.   Family: Taxodiaceae

Other names
'Louisiana cypress', 'bald cypress', 'swamp cypress'.

Distribution
This is a characteristic tree of the swamps along the Atlantic coast from Delaware to Texas, and in the lower Mississippi valley. It also occurs in Florida and the Gulf States.

The tree
The tree reaches a height of 24m to 32m and a diameter of 1.5m above the knees, which are conical outgrowths from the roots for the purposes of aeration. These are a conspicuous feature of swamp cypress, and unlike most conifers, it sheds its leaves.

The timber
The colour of the heartwood varies from pale yellowish-brown to dark reddish-brown, sometimes being quite a rich red, to almost black. The dark-coloured wood usually comes from the coastal swamps and is sometimes called 'black' or 'tidewater cypress', as distinct from the lighter-coloured timber growing further inland, often called 'yellow' or 'white cypress'. There is usually a marked contrast in colour between the early-wood and late-wood zones, which produces a rather pronounced figure on tangential surfaces. The wood when freshly cut has an unpleasant rancid smell, particularly the dark-coloured wood, while dried timber has a greasy feel and a somewhat grubby appearance. Dark-coloured resin is contained in rather frequent parenchyma cells as seen on end-grain surfaces, the resin being just discernible on longitudinal faces. The grain is typically straight, the texture rather coarse and the wood weighs about 510 kg/m^3 when dried.

Drying
The timber requires care in drying, and should be regarded as refractory, especially when drying thick sizes. There is a distinct tendency for the wood to split and for checks to occur if drying is hurried. Air drying prior to kiln drying is usually beneficial.

Strength
Although heavier than European redwood, it has similar strength properties.

Durability
Durable.

Working qualities
Works easily and generally finishes cleanly. The abrupt change from the relatively soft early-wood to the dense, hard, latewood must be considered in relation to planing and moulding, since they can cause grain raising problems when dull cutting edges are used. The timber can be glued satisfactorily, and takes nails and screws well. It can also be painted, but again, the growth-ring differences must be considered, and it may be necessary for several coats to be applied in order to obtain the best results.

Uses
'Southern cypress' is used for joinery and panelling, and because of its durability is a principal timber for mining and for poles and piling. It is also used for tight cooperage, and is a highly favoured wood for the construction of chemical vats and tanks. Other uses include, railway sleepers, general construction, boats, greenhouses, fencing and shingles.

'DOUGLAS FIR'

Pseudotsuga menziesii (Mirb) Franco. syn.
P. taxifolia Brit. syn. *P. douglasii* Carr.

Other names
'British Columbian pine', 'Columbian pine' (UK) 'Oregon pine' (USA).

Distribution
Particularly abundant in British Columbia, Washington, and Oregon, its range extends over a wide territory from the Rocky Mountains to southern Mexico.

The tree
Occasionally 'Douglas fir' reaches a height of over 90m and a diameter of 4.5m, but more commonly in good forest it is from 45m to 60m with a diameter of 1m to 2m. In such forests the bole is clear of branches for about two-thirds or more of its height. It has very little taper, and therefore produces a high percentage of sawn material clear of knots and other defects.

The timber
The sapwood is generally narrow, usually less than 50mm wide, and lighter in colour from the heartwood which varies from a decided yellow tinge to a reddish-brown colour. The timber from the coastal region is generally lighter in colour, and more uniform in texture than that grown in the mountainous areas. There is a pronounced difference in colour between early-wood and late-wood zones which gives the wood a very distinctive figure on plain-sawn surfaces and rotary-cut veneer. The average weight of dried timber is about 530 kg/m^3. Although there is sometimes a tendency for wavy or spiral grain to be present, the wood is generally straight-grained.

Drying
A relatively easy timber to dry, particularly in clear grades, little trouble occurring from checking, warping, and splitting. Lower grades require a little more care because of the tendency for knots to split and loosen, and in thick sizes for a small degree of fine surface checks to develop, but the drying of such timber is now fairly standard practice, and degrade is generally very small.

Strength
A very strong wood in relation to its weight, and by comparison with European redwood, is about 60 per cent stiffer, 30 per cent stronger in bending and in compression along the grain, and about 40 per cent harder and resistant to suddenly applied loads. The timber from the Pacific coastal districts is heavier, harder and generally stronger than that from the mountain areas. On the whole, the strength of 'Douglas fir' is comparable to commercial pitch pine.

Durability
Moderately durable.

Working qualities

Works readily and fairly easily, but with a slight dulling effect on cutting edges, which unless kept sharpened, tend to compress the softish early-wood zones which later expand and produce ridged surfaces. With care, a good finish is obtainable, and the wood can be nailed, screwed, glued, stained and polished satisfactorily. Resin canals tend to bleed with small pin-head exudations if the wood dries further in service. Care should be taken to ensure that timber intended for a varnished finish, especially for interior joinery, is kiln dried to a suitable moisture content.

Uses

Heavy construction, piling, masts and spars, dock and harbour work, barges, railway sleepers, slack and tight cooperage, joinery, transmission poles, flooring and flooring blocks (edge-grain), windows and doors, mine timbers, ship-building, vats and tanks in chemical plants, distilleries, and breweries, constructional purposes in houses, roof trusses, laminated arches, and for veneer and plywood.

FIR, TRUE

The Pinaceae family includes two genera whose species produce fir, ie *Pseudotsuga* and *Abies*, but distinctions are made in their botanical classification because of certain differences in the floral formula, which is a method of compressing information and is used by botanists to apply the laws of classification to trees. This takes into account differences in flower formation, and other aspects of tree growth. Thus, the various species of the genus *Abies*, collectively differ in their botanical aspects, including the appearance of the cones, which are held erect on the tree, from the single species of *Pseudotsuga*, whose flowers are different from *Abies*, and whose cones are pendant.

Accordingly, the various species of *Abies* are classified as true firs, while *Pseudotsuga menziesii* produces 'Douglas fir', the timber, and its properties and characteristics, being entirely different, in fact, Douglas fir (*Pseudotsuga*), is more closely related to hemlock (*Tsuga*), the formation of the flowers and pendant cones having closer similarity than the catkins and erect cones of the true firs.

The following notes apply to the principal species of true fir found in North America.

ALPINE FIR

Abies lasiocarpa Nutt.

Other names
mountain fir, western balsam fir, white fir, Rocky mountain fir.

Distribution
In Canada it occurs in British Columbia, Alberta, and the Yukon, associated with 'Douglas fir', Englemann spruce, and lodgepole pine. It also occurs in the USA along the Sierra Nevadas in California.

The tree
A relatively small tree, attaining a height of 18m to 21m and a diameter of 0.5m.

The timber
A whitish wood, resembling spruce in appearance, but coarser in texture, and lacking the lustre found in spruce. As with all the true firs, the early-wood is nearly white in colour, and the late-wood darker, sometimes light to dark brown, the growth rings showing rather inconspicuously on longitudinal surfaces. The late-wood bands are generally scanty, and the wood is therefore soft, and light in weight, being about 370 kg/m³ when dried.

Drying
Dries readily with little degrade.

Strength
A light-weight, soft, weak wood, with low strength properties.

Durability
Non-durable.

Working qualities
Works easily with all hand and machine tools, but due to the usually wide bands of soft early-wood, there is a definite tendency for these to tear in sawing, drilling and mortising operations, and to become compressed during planing, later lifting to give a ridged surface. A smooth finish depends upon cutting edges being kept sharpened. The wood takes nails well and can be stained and painted.

Uses
Boxes and crates, light construction and carpentry.

AMABILIS FIR

Abies amabilis Forbes.

Other names
Pacific silver fir, white fir (USA) amabilis fir (Canadian standard name).

Distribution
From Alaska down to British Columbia, generally on the western slope of the coast range, and on Vancouver Island, extending southwards to the northern part of California.

The tree
Grows to a height of 50m and a diameter of 1m but in the forest it is more commonly 24m to 30m tall with a diameter of 0.5m or a little more.

The timber
Similar to spruce in appearance, but rather darker in colour with fairly prominent brown late-wood bands. The wood weighs about 420 kg/m³ when dried.

Drying
Dries well, without excessive degrade.

Strength
The strength properties are similar to those of European silver fir, (*Abies alba*).

Durability
Non-durable.

Working qualities
Works readily, but sharp tools are needed in order to overcome the tendency for grain tearing. Takes nails well, and can be stained, polished, varnished and painted.

Uses
Pulp and paper, boxes and crates, general carpentry, house building, light construction. This timber is sometimes mixed in shipments of western hemlock as western balsam.

BALSAM FIR

Abies balsamea Mill.

Other names
balsam (USA).

Distribution
In Canada it is widely distributed from the Atlantic seaboard through the eastern provinces and the northern part of the Prairie Provinces to Great Slave Lake and northwards almost to Alaska. It extends southwards into the USA to Minnesota and into the northern part of New York State.

The tree
Balsam fir is not a large tree. It reaches a height of 15m to 21m with a diameter of about 0.5m.

The timber
The timber is very similar to spruce in colour and general appearance, but is coarser and less lustrous. There is practically no difference by colour between sapwood and heartwood, but the ends of logs usually show a wide sapwood band and a darker core, although this is not really noticeable once the log is converted. The wood is fairly light in weight, softer than spruce, and weighs about 400 kg/m^3 when dried.

Drying
Dries without excessive degrade.

Strength
Weaker in strength than Canadian spruce, and appreciably weaker in resistance to shear.

Durability
Non-durable.

Working qualities
As with the general run of the true firs, the timber works easily, but knots are liable to become loosened and become trouble-some during planing, and there is a distinct tendency for the grain to tear. A good finish is possible if cutting edges are kept sharpened. It nails well, and can be stained, polished, varnished and painted.

Uses
Carpentry, interior joinery, building, pulp, pit props. Since the tree grows in association with white, red, and black spruce, it is often mixed and sold as spruce lumber.

GRAND FIR

Abies grandis Lindl.

Other names
lowland fir, (Canada) ; white fir, western balsam fir (USA).

Distribution
In British Columbia it is found only in the southern coastal district and in limited quantities in the interior wet belt of the province, generally associated with 'Douglas fir', 'western red cedar', and western hemlock. In the USA it extends along the coastal belt into California and in the mountain area of Washington and Idaho to northern Montana.

The tree
Grows to a height of 30m to 37m and a diameter of 0.75m.

The timber
There is no distinct heartwood, the wood being almost white to light brown in colour, closely resembling spruce, but less lustrous, and generally more coarse in texture. The grain is

typically straight, the wood is non-resinous and non-tainting and weighs about 450 kg/m³ when dried.

Drying
Dries without undue difficulty.

Strength
The strength properties of grand fir are similar to those of silver fir (*Abies alba*) except in bending strength and resistance to splitting, where it is about 15 per cent weaker than silver fir. It is also some 25 per cent inferior in hardness and shear strength.

Durability
Non-durable.

Working qualities
The timber works easily and generally finishes cleanly, but sharp cutting edges are needed to avoid the tendency for the grain to tear. Because of the size of the trees, knots are less troublesome than in alpine, amabilis, and balsam firs. Grand fir can be stained, painted, polished and varnished, takes nails well and glues satisfactorily.

Uses
Crates and boxes, general carpentry, interior construction and pulp. The timber is sometimes mixed with western hemlock as western balsam.

NOBLE FIR

Abies procera Rehder. syn. *A. nobilis* Lindl.

Other names
None.

Distribution
Found in northern Washington and extending south into California. It is most abundant in the Cascade Mountains.

The tree
A large tree, attaining a height of 45m to 60m or more and a diameter of 2m.

The timber
Similar to western hemlock in appearance, but coarser-textured, and a little lighter in weight. The wood is buff-coloured with darker late-wood bands. It weighs about 420 kg/m^3 when dried.

Drying
Dries easily and with little degrade.

Strength
Similar to silver fir (*Abies alba*) in all strength categories.

Durability
Non-durable.

Working qualities
Works easily, and because of its generally straight grain and clearer timber (due to its large size), more easy and straight-forward to work than other true firs. It can be glued, nailed, stained and polished, or painted satisfactorily.

Uses
Interior joinery, boxes and packing cases, and plywood from selected logs.

HEMLOCK

Two species of the genus *Tsuga* as represented in the Pinaceae are recognised as timber trees in North America.

EASTERN HEMLOCK

Tsuga canadensis Carr.

Other names
white hemlock, 'hemlock spruce' (USA). The name 'hemlock spruce' is confusing and should be discontinued.

Distribution
Found from Nova Scotia westerly to Lake Superior, and extending from southern Quebec and Ontario to eastern Minnesota and south to Georgia and Alabama.

The tree
It reaches a height of 15m to 21m and a diameter of about 0.5m.

The timber
The wood is pale brown in colour with a reddish-brown tinge, the growth rings being prominent and reminiscent of 'Douglas fir'. It is inclined to be splintery and cross-grained, and is generally inferior to western hemlock. The texture is coarse, and the wood weighs about 470 kg/m³ when dried.

Drying
Rather difficult to dry as the timber warps and twists badly.

Strength
It is about 20 to 30 per cent inferior to western hemlock in all strength categories excepting shear where it is some 30 per cent more resistant.

Durability
Non-durable.

Working qualities
Works relatively easily with both hand and machine tools, but its cross-grained tendency and splintery nature makes machine operations less satisfactory than with western hemlock. Since the wood is more often used in a sawn state or a hit and miss finish off the planing machine, difficulty in obtaining a good finish is not usually important. Nailing properties are not so good as those of western hemlock.

Uses
Bridge planks, concrete forms, boxes and crates, structural timbers, rough carpentry and pulp.

WESTERN HEMLOCK

Tsuga heterophylla Sarge.

Other names
Pacific hemlock, British Columbia hemlock (USA).

Distribution
This species ranges from Alaska southward along the whole British Columbia coast, and is also found in the interior of British Columbia in certain areas of heavy rainfall. It extends into northern Washington, Idaho, and to the western slopes of the Cascades.

The tree
A much larger tree than eastern hemlock, it reaches a height of 60m and a diameter of 2m or more, with a straight bole that is often clear of branches for about three-quarters of its length.

The timber
Neither the tree nor the timber bears close similarity to eastern hemlock. The timber of western hemlock is pale brown in colour and somewhat lustrous, with a straight grain and fairly even texture, non-resinous and non-tainting when dried, it has a faint sour odour when freshly sawn. The darker-coloured late-wood bands have a reddish or purple cast and produce a well-marked growth-ring figure on plain-sawn surfaces, with an occasional short, purplish-coloured line here and there on the wood. The growth-rings are less prominent than those of 'Douglas fir'. The timber weighs about 500 kg/m^3 when dried.

Drying
The initially high moisture content of this species requires care in drying processes in order to avoid surface checking, and to ensure uniform drying throughout the thickness. Warping and twisting tendencies are usually low.

Strength
The timber is not as hard as 'Douglas fir,' but compared with that species, it is about 30 per cent less stiff and 50 per cent less tough, and in respect of general strength properties it is more closely comparable to European redwood (*Pinus sylvestris*).

Durability
Non-durable.

Working qualities
The timber works readily with all hand and machine tools with little dulling effect on cutting edges. A good finish is obtained in planing and moulding, but cutters must be kept sharpened. It can be glued, stained, painted and varnished, and takes a good polish. It can be screwed and nailed, but although it is less inclined to split in nailing than 'Douglas fir', it should be pre-bored if nailing takes place close to the ends of dry boards.

Uses
Western hemlock is one of the most valuable of North American timbers. It is used for general construction, joinery, including doors, interior finish, floors, fitments, suspended ceilings, and for broom handles, vehicle bodies, railway sleepers (treated), pulp and plywood. It can be obtained in large baulk or flitch sizes.

LARCH

The larches are deciduous trees of the Pinaceae family producing timbers characterized by their resinous wood with conspicuous late-wood darker and harder than the early-wood, with a more or less abrupt transition from one to the other. The following are the two most important North American species.

TAMARACK LARCH

Larix laricina K. Koch.

Other names
tamarack (Canada and USA) ; eastern larch (USA).

Distribution
The tree is found from Labrador and the Maritime Provinces to the Rocky Mountains and north to the mouth of the Mackenzie River. It extends south to West Virginia, and westwards through north Indiana and Illinois to the eastern foot-hills of the Rocky Mountains.

The tree
Tamarack attains a height of 18m to 21m and a diameter of about 0.5m with a straight and cylindrical bole with little taper.

The timber
The sapwood is narrow and yellowish in colour, and the heartwood is yellowish-brown to reddish-brown, rather coarse in texture, with fairly wide, but irregular growth-rings, characterized by alternate bands of softish early-wood and darker-coloured, hard late-wood. The wood is resinous and weighs about 580 kg/m³ when dried.

Drying
It is said to dry well with little degrade.

Strength
Softer, and a little lighter in weight than western larch, it is a relatively weak timber, and compared with European larch (*Larix decidua*) is some 20 per cent inferior in general strength properties.

Durability
Moderately durable.

Working qualities
Fairly easy to work and similar to European larch in this respect. It has a tendency to split in nailing, and is not always a good wood for painting, but this depends upon the amount of resin present.

Uses
One of the less important species of North America but valued for special purposes such as sleepers, tanks and silos, boxes and crates, posts and poles and planking.

WESTERN LARCH

Larix occidentalis Nutt.

Other names
western tamarack.

Distribution
In Canada western larch is confined to the south-eastern part

of British Columbia. It is seldom found in pure stands, but is usually mixed with 'Douglas fir', western hemlock and lodge-pole pine. It extends south into northern Oregon, and attains its largest size in northern Montana and northern Idaho.

The tree
A tree with a long, clean, cylindrical bole, reaching a height of 30m to 54m and a diameter of 1m or more.

The timber
The timber resembles 'Douglas fir' more closely than any other North American softwood. The sapwood is narrow, yellowish-brown in colour, and sharply defined from the deep reddish-brown heartwood. There is considerable contrast in colour between the early-wood and late-wood, which gives a pronounced figure when the timber is plain-sawn or rotary-cut. It weighs about 610 kg/m³ when dried.

Drying
Dries fairly well, but with some tendency to warp and surface check.

Strength
Similar to European larch in general strength properties, but some 20 to 30 per cent stronger in compression along the grain, and stiffer in bending.

Durability
Moderately durable

Working qualities
Works fairly readily with only a small blunting effect on cutting edges. It is similar to European larch in respect of knots, which are hard, and tend to fall out during machining and damage cutting edges. The wood can be glued satisfactorily, but it tends to split in nailing, and there is sometimes difficulty in staining or painting the more resinous material.

Uses
Heavy construction, sleepers, flooring, ceilings, tanks, posts, piling, interior and exterior finish and plywood.

PINE

The genus *Pinus* produces the true pines, the timber of the various species belonging either to the soft-pine or the hard-pine class. These classifications can be summarized as follows. Soft pines have inconspicuous late-wood, and have a straight-grained, soft wood that is comparatively free from resin and is easy to work and carve across the grain. Used for joinery, furniture, patterns, toys, packing cases and light construction. Hard pines have conspicuous late-wood which is darker in colour and harder than the early-wood, and have resinous, often hard, heavy, strong, and durable wood, more regularly used for buildings, bridges, ships and other types of heavy construction.

The following are the principal pines found in North America.

JACK PINE

Pinus banksiana Lamb.

Other names
princess pine (Canada).

Distribution
It occurs in the USA in Indiana and in parts of Michigan, but is more prevalent in Canada where it ranges from Nova Scotia to the Rocky Mountains and northern Alberta.

The tree
A medium-sized tree, it reaches a height of about 24m on good sites, but is more usually about 15m tall with a diameter of 0.3m.

The timber
A timber of the hard-pine class, with a sapwood yellowish in colour and about 38mm wide, and a heartwood varying in colour from pale brown to reddish-brown. It is not unlike European redwood (*P. sylvestris*) in appearance, but is more resinous, brittle, and coarser in texture, and is inclined to be knotty. The wood weighs about 500 kg/m^3 when dried.

Drying
Generally dries without difficulty, but material from trees grown

in open forest is inclined to warp owing to the higher incidence of knots and disturbed grain.

Strength
Similar to that of European redwood.

Durability
Non-durable.

Working qualities
Works reasonably well and a good finish can be obtained provided cutters are kept sharpened. As the tree is small, it produces little clear timber and accordingly, the generally knotty quality of the wood influences the quality of the finish. It can be screwed and nailed satisfactorily, and takes stains, polish and paint quite well, although the resinous nature of the wood may make this difficult at times.

Uses
General construction, railway sleepers and telephone poles (treated), silos, pit props, piling (treated) and for pulp.

LODGEPOLE PINE

Pinus contorta Dougl. var. *latifolia* S. Watson syn.
P. contorta Dougl. var. *murrayana* Engelm.

Other names
contorta pine (UK).

Distribution
Extends from the Yukon territory over most of British Columbia, and in Alberta on the eastern slope of the Rocky Mountains, and over the northern part of Alberta west of the Lesser Slave Lake. It also extends from the Rocky Mountains into Montana and Colorado.

The tree
In the eastern parts of its range, the tree is slender and reaches a height of 15m to 30m and a diameter of 0.5m, but on less favourable sites, mainly in western areas, the tree is much smaller.

The timber
A pale yellowish-coloured timber, soft, straight-grained, with a fine, fairly even texture, weighing about 470 kg/m³ when dried. Although on account of its size it does not produce much high-grade timber, it yields a good grade of wood with small, tight knots.

Drying
Dries rapidly and well, with only slight distortion.

Strength
Similar to European redwood.

Durability
Non-durable.

Working qualities
Works easily and finishes cleanly, but resin exudation may be troublesome. It has good nailing properties, can be glued and gives reasonable results with the usual finishing materials.

Uses
Railway sleepers, telephone poles and piling (treated), mining timbers, boxes and crates, light and medium construction.

PITCH PINE, AMERICAN

Pinus palustris Mill. and *P. elliottii* Engelm.

Other names
Gulf Coast pitch pine, long leaf pitch pine (UK); southern yellow pine, southern pine, long leaf yellow pine, longleaf (USA).
Note: the term southern yellow pine or southern pine covers the timber of several allied species of which the most important are *P. palustris* Mill. (long leaf pine), *P. elliottii* Engelm. (slash pine), *P. echinata* Mill. (short leaf pine), and *P. taeda* L. (loblolly pine). The term long leaf yellow pine or long leaf is now restricted to the heavier, stronger material of *P. palustris* and *P. elliottii* as defined in paragraph 7 of the Rules of the

Southern Pine Inspection Bureau, USA 1963 Edition. Material that does not come up to this specification (formerly classified as short leaf) is now classified as southern pine. Thus the trade name short leaf is now obsolete.

Distribution
P. palustris ranges from south-east Virginia to Florida and Texas occurring along the coasts of the Atlantic and Gulf of Mexico in a forest belt some 200 kilometres deep. *P. elliottii* occurs in the same area but is more restricted, ranging from South Carolina to Florida and along the Gulf to eastern Louisiana.

The tree
Both species attain a height of 30m and a diameter of 0.75m or slightly more.

The timber
The sapwood is narrow in the better grades, sometimes up to 50mm wide, lighter in colour than the heartwood which is yellowish-brown to reddish-brown. Both species are typical of the hard-pine class, being resinous, with the growth-rings usually well-marked by the contrast between the light-coloured early-wood, and the dense, darker-coloured late-wood, which produces a rather coarse texture in the wood, especially in fairly rapidly grown material with its wide growth-rings. The timbers weigh about 670 kg/m^3 on average when dried.
The lower density material of *P. palustris* and *P. elliottii* together with other species termed southern yellow pine, is lighter in weight, coarser in texture, inferior in strength, and usually has a wider sapwood, sometimes as wide as 150mm.

Drying
All these species dry well with little degrade.

Strength
The general strength properties of *P. palustris* and *P. elliottii* compare closely with those of 'Douglas fir'.

Durability
Moderately durable.

Working qualities

Works moderately easily, but the resin is often troublesome, tending to clog saw-teeth and cutters, and to adhere to machine tables. Saws with teeth of fairly long pitch reduce the effect of resin. A good finish is obtainable, and the wood can be glued satisfactorily, takes nails and screws well, and gives fair results with paint and other finishing treatments.

Uses

Heavy construction, exterior finish, flooring, ship-building for spars, masts, decking, dock work. The lower density grades are used for joinery, light construction, boxes and crates.

PONDEROSA PINE

Pinus ponderosa Laws.

Other names

Western yellow pine, Californian white pine (USA); British Columbia soft pine (Canada).

Distribution

In Canada, ponderosa pine is confined to the drier portions of the southern interior of British Columbia and to the lower altitudes of this district, sometimes in almost pure stands. In the USA it extends from Montana through western Nebraska and Texas into Mexico and westwards to the Pacific coast.

The tree

Generally attaining a height of 30m and a diameter of 0.75m although occasionally it is much larger and taller.

The timber

The wood varies considerably in colour; mature trees have a very thick, pale yellow sapwood, soft, non-resinous, uniform in texture, and similar to yellow pine (*P. strobus*). The heartwood is much darker, ranging from a deep yellow to a reddish-brown, and is considerably heavier than the sapwood. Resin ducts are fairly prominent on longitudinal heartwood surfaces, appearing as fine, dark brown lines. The average weight of the wood is about 480 kg/m³ when dried.

Drying
The wide sapwood is susceptible to fungal staining and care must be taken during air drying to ensure suitable piling. The timber dries rapidly and well, and since the sapwood is particularly valuable, anti-stain treatment is helpful.

Strength
Ponderosa pine grown in Canada has similar strength properties to those of European redwood (*P. sylvestris*) ,but that grown in the USA is a little lighter in weight and some 15 per cent inferior in average strength to the Canadian wood.

Durability
Non-durable.

Working qualities
The wood works easily and smoothly, and takes nails and screws well, glues satisfactorily and can be painted, although resin exudation may be troublesome. It is the most resinous of the Canadian commercial pines.

Uses
The sapwood is used for pattern-making, kitchen furniture, turnery, and doors, the wood resembling yellow pine (*P. strobus*) otherwise the timber is used for building, light and medium construction, window frames, interior trim, boxes and crates.

RED PINE, CANADIAN

Pinus resinosa Ait.

Other names
Norway pine (USA).

Distribution
In Canada it extends from Nova Scotia to Lake Winnipeg, and southwards over the border to Minnesota and Wisconsin, and eastwards to Massachusetts.

The tree
It reaches a height of 23m to 37m and a diameter of 0.5m to 0.75m.

The timber
The tree receives its name from the colour of its bark which is a distinctive reddish-brown, the timber resembling European redwood (*P. sylvestris*). The sapwood is wide, often 75mm, of a pale yellow colour, the heartwood being pale brown with a reddish tinge to reddish-yellow, with a straight grain and medium to fine texture. The wood is somewhat resinous, but not enough to spoil the wood surface. There is a good deal of contrast in colour between the early-wood and late-wood in the growth-rings, especially in the heartwood, producing a figure on longitudinal surfaces. The wood weighs about 450 kg/m^3 when dried.

Drying
Dries easily and uniformly, with little checking, twisting or cupping. Kiln-drying improves its finishing qualities by setting the resin.

Strength
Although softer than European redwood, its general strength properties are about equal to that species.

Durability
Non-durable.

Working qualities
Works easily with both hand and machine tools, and finishes smoothly. It can be stained, painted, varnished or polished, takes nails and screws satisfactorily and can be glued.

Uses
Its wide, permeable sapwood enables it to be readily treated with preservatives. It is used for constructional work, tanks and silos, windows and doors, general joinery, piles, posts and poles.

SUGAR PINE

Pinus lambertiana Dougl.

Other names
Californian sugar pine.

Distribution
Principally in Oregon and California, especially along the Sierra Nevadas.

The tree
Attains a height of 24m to 45m and a diameter of 1m or more.

The timber
A typical soft pine, the sapwood is white in colour, and the heartwood varies from pale straw colour to reddish-brown. The change from early-wood to late-wood is gradual, and the late-wood is usually neither very extensive nor very dense. The wood is light in weight, about 430 kg/m^3 when dried.

Drying
Dries easily and uniformly without undue degrade.

Strength
No information.

Durability
Non-durable.

Working qualities
The timber works very easily and has little dulling effect on cutting edges. It is capable of a good smooth finish, but because of its soft nature is inclined to crumble under dull cutting edges; these should be kept sharpened to obtain the best results. It can be glued, stained, polished and painted satisfactorily, and it holds screws and nails well.

Uses
Joinery, doors, window frames, light construction, interior trim, boxes.

WESTERN WHITE PINE

Pinus monticola Dougl. ex Lamb.

Other names
Idaho white pine.

Distribution
In Canada it is found mainly in southern British Columbia, but it also occurs in parts of the interior of British Columbia, and on Vancouver Island. Its range extends south into California, and east into Montana, and is most abundant in northern Idaho.

The tree
A tall tree with a clean bole almost without taper, it is usually from 23m to 37m high with a diameter of 1m but occasional specimens are much larger.

The timber
The sapwood is white in colour and up to 75mm wide, and the heartwood is a pale straw colour varying to shades of reddish-brown, with fine brown lines appearing on longitudinal surfaces due to resin ducts, similar to those in yellow pine (*Pinus strobus*). There is little contrast in colour between the early-wood and late-wood zones. The grain is straight, the texture even and uniform, and the wood weighs about 450 kg/m³ when dried. Although western white pine bears some similarity to yellow pine, and both timbers are used for similar purposes, western white pine is slightly the heavier wood, and has narrower growth-rings as a rule. It should be noted that yellow pine (*P. strobus*) is invariably called white pine both in the USA and Canada.

Drying
Dries easily and well, with little checking or warping, but with a slightly higher shrinkage value than yellow pine.

Strength
Since its uses are similar, its strength must be compared to that of yellow pine, and in this respect, white pine is some 30 per cent harder, 25 per cent stronger in compression along the grain, 15 per cent stronger in bending and 25 per cent more

resistant to shock loads; both species have about the same resistance to splitting.

Durability
Non-durable.

Working qualities
Very easy to work, and provided cutting edges are sharp, finishes excellently. Takes nails, screws, stains and paint well, and glues satisfactorily.

Uses
Western white pine is used for joinery such as doors and windows, interior trim, fitments, shelving, wooden-ware, light and medium construction, pattern-making, drawing-boards, cabinets, match splints, and in boat and ship-building. It is also used for plywood.

YELLOW PINE

Pinus strobus L.

Other names
white pine, eastern white pine (Canada and USA); northern pine, northern white pine (USA); Quebec yellow pine, Weymouth pine (UK).

Distribution
In Canada it is found in Newfoundland and in eastern Canada from the Maritime Provinces to eastern Manitoba, but the commercial forests lie mainly in the area of the St Lawrence River. It reaches its best development in the Ottawa Valley in Ontario and Quebec. In the USA it is found south of the Great Lakes and along the Appalachian Mountains down to northern Georgia.

The tree
Usually not more than 30m high and a diameter of 0.75m or a little more, but under favourable conditions can reach a height of 52m to 60m with a diameter of 1.5m.

The timber
The sapwood is almost white, and the heartwood varies from creamy-white to light straw-brown, or light reddish-brown. The wood is not particularly resinous, but resin ducts produce short, brown-coloured, thin lines on longitudinal surfaces. The grain is straight, and the texture is fine and even, planed surfaces have a satin-like appearance; the growth-rings are rather inconscpicuous. The wood weighs about 420 kg/m³ when dried.

Drying
It dries readily and well, but suitable precautions should be taken to avoid sap-stain.

Strength
A soft, weak timber, which compared to European redwood is 45 per cent softer, 25 per cent less resistant to shock loads, 30 per cent weaker in bending and in compression along the grain, and 20 per cent less resistant to splitting, and less stiff.

Durability
Non-durable.

Working qualities
Works very easily, but the soft nature of the timber encourages crumbling under dull cutting edges, which must therefore be kept sharpened in order to obtain the best results. It takes glue, stains, polish, varnish and paint well, and can be screwed or nailed.

Uses
An important characteristic of yellow pine is its low shrinkage, and in this respect it is superior to all other North American softwoods except the cedars. It is therefore particularly well-suited to pattern-making, drawing-boards, doors, and other forms of high-class work. It is also used for musical instruments, cabinets, ship and boat-building, shelving, light and medium construction, interior trim, wooden-ware, match splints and wood flour. It should be noted that second-growth timber is usually of coarser texture, and is prone to be knotty and cross-grained.

SEQUOIA

The Taxodiaceae family produces the genus *Sequoia*, with two well-known species indigenous to the USA. The best known is probably *Sequoia gigantea* Decne. the Big Tree of California, whose dimensions and age are equalled by no other living organism. Its wood is of little commercial value, and accordingly these giants of the forest have been spared destruction. Its only rival is *Sequoia sempervirens* Endl. the Californian redwood, or to give it its standard name, sequoia, a tree which has been extensively exploited in recent years, and only the efforts of conservationists have resulted in a few stands being set aside with a view to protection for all time. The following is a description of sequoia (*Sequoia sempervirens* Endl.).

Distribution
It is found in southern Oregon extending southwards near the coast to Monterey, California.

The tree
The tree is often heavily buttressed and reaches a height of 60m to 100mm and a diameter of 3m to 4.5m or more. A characteristic feature is the cinnamon-brown coloured bark which is often 300mm thick.

The timber
The sapwood is very narrow, almost white in colour, and the heartwood is a rich dull red or reddish-brown, with a growth-ring figure produced by the contrasting early-wood and late-wood zones. The wood somewhat resembles 'western red cedar', but is a little heavier and brighter in colour. The grain is straight, and the texture varies from fine and even to rather coarse. The wood is non-resinous, non-tainting and weighs about 420 kg/m^3.

Drying
No information available, but it is said to be without strong warping tendencies, and to hold its shape well.

Strength
The timber is lighter in weight, and slightly weaker in all strength properties by comparison with European redwood.

Durability
Durable.

Working qualities
Works easily, but due to its splintering tendencies, and soft character, care is needed in drilling, mortising and routing operations, and in planing and moulding. Sharp cutting edges are essential and waste removal must be efficient in order to reduce chip-bruising.

Uses
Its durability makes it ideal for wooden pipes, flumes, tanks, vats, shingles and exterior cladding for buildings. It is also used for coffins, posts and for interior trim. It has been used for plywood, and its thick bark is utilized for fibre board and filtering equipment.

SPRUCE

The Pinaceae family includes a number of species of the genus *Picea*. These produce spruce, whose timber features a creamy-white to yellowish-brown colour, relatively inconspicuous and small resin ducts. and not very conspicuous late-wood. The following are the principal species found in North America.

EASTERN CANADIAN SPRUCE

Picea spp. principally *P. glauca* Voss.

Other names
white spruce (Canada and USA); Quebec, St. John, New Brunswick, Nova Scotia, and maritime spruce (UK).

Distrubution
One of the most widely distributed trees, it occurs from Alaska to Newfoundland, and southwards to northern British Columbia. Its southern extremities are Minnesota, Wisconsin and Michigan, eastwards to New York State.

The tree
P. glauca attains a height of 15m to 24m and a diameter of 0.5m on average although on favourable sites it may be 30m tall with a diameter of 1.2m.

The timber
There is no difference by colour between sapwood and heartwood, the wood being almost white to pale yellowish brown, closely resembling European whitewood. It is straight-grained and lustrous, without taste or odour, and only slightly resinous. The wood weighs about 416 kg/m^3 when dried, but since a proportion of other species may be included in shipments, this weight is conservative and the average weight could be a little higher. See concluding notes.

Drying
Dries fairly easily, without undue degrade.

Strength
For structural purposes, the general strength properties are similar to those of European redwood of similar grade.

Durability
Non-durable.

Working qualities
Works very easily, but knots can sometimes be troublesome. With sharp cutting edges the wood can be finished cleanly. It can be stained, polished or painted, takes nails and screws well, and can be glued satisfactorily.

Uses
Light and medium construction, paddles and oars, ladder stock and scaffold boards, butter boxes, kitchen cabinets, and from selected stock, for piano sounding boards. It is also used extensively for the production of pulp for paper and rayon and cellophane.

The timber is generally marketed as Canadian spruce, and while the bulk of shipments contain mostly timber of *Picea glauca*, they may contain some red spruce, *P. rubens* Sarg. and black spruce, *P. mariana* B.S.P., and since balsam fir grows with black spruce, this species may also be included. A description of balsam fir is included elsewhere in this booklet, but the following notes summarize the characteristics of black and red spruce.

BLACK SPRUCE

Picea mariana B.S.P.

General characteristics
A slow-growing tree also known as swamp or water spruce, comparatively small, sometimes no more than 12m high, but usually 15m to 18m high with a diameter of 0.3m. Similar to eastern Canadian spruce in appearance, but a little heavier, about 480 kg/m^3 when dried, and rather harder and stronger. On account of its size it is not so important a timber species as *P. glauca*, but is a valuable pulpwood, and is also used for mining props.

RED SPRUCE

Picea rubens Sarg.

General characteristics
Sometimes called yellow spruce, it grows to a height of 18m to 24m with a diameter of about 0.5m. Similar to eastern Canadian spruce in appearance, but with rather more prominent latewood bands, giving a rather more prominent figure. Weighs about 448 kg/m^3 when dried. It is also a valuable pulpwood.

ENGELMANN SPRUCE

Picea engelmannii Engelm.

Other names
mountain spruce, Rocky Mountain spruce.

Distribution
It occurs throughout the interior mountain region of British Columbia and on the eastern slope of the Rocky Mountains. It also extends into the USA to the Sacramento Mountains and eastwards to the eastern slopes of the Cascade Mountains in Oregon and Washington.

The tree
It is usually from 24m to 36m in height with a diameter of 0.75m but may be larger on favourable sites.

The timber
The timber is similar to eastern Canadian spruce, being light in colour, and with a straight grain, but due to the size of the tree, a higher proportion of clear timber is usually produced. It weighs about 450 kg/m³ when dried.

Drying
Dries easily and well.

Strength
Although varying in mechanical properties according to growth conditions, on average it compares favourably with Sitka spruce, although a little softer and therefore rather less resistant to impact.

Durability
Non-durable.

Working qualities
Works easily and well, but cutting edges must be kept sharpened in order to obtain a really smooth finish. It can be nailed, screwed and glued satisfactorily, and takes the usual finishing treatments without difficulty.

Uses
Interior joinery, carpentry, building, plywood, piano sounding boards, oars and paddles.

SITKA SPRUCE

Picea sitchensis Carr.

Other names
silver spruce, tideland spruce, Menzies spruce.

Distribution
It occurs throughout the coastal belt of British Columbia, but attains its best development on the Queen Charlotte Islands. It occurs over the border through Washington and into California, generally in the coastal strip.

The tree
It attains a height of up to 60m with a diameter of 1m to 2m above the enlarged or buttressed base.

The timber
There is little difference in colour between sapwood and heart-wood, the wood generally being a creamy white, but the heart-wood usually has a pinkish tinge. It usually has a very straight grain, but occasionally this may be spiral, while the texture is medium but dependent on the rate of growth, although on average this is usually fairly slow and even. The wood is non-resinous, without odour and therefore non-tainting, light in weight, about 450 kg/m^3 when dried, and showing a silvery lustre on planed surfaces.

Drying
Dries rapidly and quite well, but care is needed if warping, splitting and loosening of knots is to be kept to a reasonable level.

Strength
Its strength to weight ratio is high, and compared with European redwood (*Pinus sylvestris*), it is some 25 per cent stiffer, and is about equal in bending strength, hardness and resistance to splitting.

Durability
Non-durable.

Working qualities
It is easily worked, and provided cutting edges are kept sharp-ened, finishes very cleanly. It can be nailed, screwed, glued, stained, polished and painted satisfactorily.

Uses
Gliders, sail-planes, oars and racing sculls, interior joinery, building and for boxes.

WESTERN WHITE SPRUCE

Picea glauca Voss. var. *glauce albertiana* Sarg.

Distribution
It occurs from Manitoba westwards towards the Pacific coast and northwards into Alaska, and spreads south to the Rocky Mountains and USA.

General characteristics
The wood is similar to eastern Canadian spruce, but the texture is more even and finer, and due to the size of the tree and the growth conditions, there are often fewer defects. The wood weighs about 430 kg/m^3 when dried.

It works well and is used for joinery, building construction, scaffold planks and plywood.

USE GUIDE FOR NORTH AMERICAN TIMBERS

AGRICULTURAL IMPLEMENTS AND EQUIPMENT

basswood (beehives)
'cedar, western red' (beehives, greenhouses etc.)
'cedar yellow'
coffee tree, Kentucky
cypress
elm, rock
elm, slippery
elm, white
hornbeam, hop
larch, tamarack
larch, western
maple
oak, live
oak, white

BOAT AND SHIP CONSTRUCTION

Decking
'fir, Douglas'
larch, tamarack
larch, western
pine, pitch
all edge-grain.

For canvas/plastic covered decks
'cedar, Port Orford'
'cedar, western red'
pine, lodgepole
pine, sugar
pine, western white.

Framing
ash, tough white
elm, rock
oak, live
oak, white

Keels and stems
oak, live
oak, white
pine, pitch

Masts and spars
'fir, Douglas' (when selected)
pine, pitch (when selected)
spruce, Sitka (when selected)

Oars and paddles

'cedar, Port Orford'
spruce, Canadian (when selected)
spruce, Sitka

Planking
'cedar, yellow'
elm, rock
'fir, Douglas'
larch, tamarack
larch, western
pine, various, (when selected)

Boat and ship construction (cont.)

Superstructures, cabins, fitments
butternut
'cedar, pencil'
cherry
plane

sassafras
walnut
whitewood

BOXES, CRATES AND CONTAINERS

basswood
birch, paper
buckeye
butternut
elm
fir, alpine
fir, amabilis
fir, grand
fir, noble
gum, red

hackberry
hemlock, eastern
larch, tamarack
pine, lodgepole
pine, Ponderosa
pine, sugar
sassafras
spruce
willow, black

CONSTRUCTION

Heavy/Medium
'cedar, pencil'
cypress
elm, rock
'fir, Douglas'

larch, western
oak, red
oak, white
pine, jack
pine, pitch

Light
'cedar, incense'
'cedar, Port Orford'
'cedar, western red'
'cedar, yellow'
fir, alpine
fir, amabilis
fir, balsam
fir, grand
fir, noble
hackberry
hemlock, eastern
hemlock, western

magnolia
pine, lodgepole
pine, pitch (low density)
pine, Ponderosa
pine, red
pine, sugar
pine, western white
pine, yellow
plane
spruce
tupelo
whitewood

COOPERAGE

basswood (heads)
buckeye (heads)
beech (slack)
birch, yellow (slack)
cypress (tight)
elm, slippery, (slack)
elm, white (slack)

'fir, Douglas' (slack and tight)
hackberry (slack)
oak, red (slack)
oak, white (tight)
sassafras (slack)

DOORS

birch, yellow
'cedar, pencil'
'cedar, yellow'
'fir, Douglas' (edge-grain)
fir, grand
fir, noble
hemlock, western (edge-grain)
magnolia
maple
oak, white

pine, pitch
pine, Ponderosa (sapwood ; treated for ext. use)
pine, red
pine, sugar
pine, western white
pine, yellow
plane
whitewood

FANCY GOODS

apple
butternut (stained)
cherry
holly

maple
osage orange
plane
walnut

FLOORING

beech
birch, yellow
'fir, Douglas' (edge-grain)
hemlock, western
larch, western
maple

oak, red
oak, white
pine, pitch (edge-grain)
pines, various
tupelo

233

FURNITURE AND CABINET-MAKING

beech
birch, yellow
buckeye (interiors)
'cedar, pencil'
'cedar, Port Orford'
'cedar, yellow'
cherry
chestnut
elm, rock (chair rockers)
elm, slippery
elm, white

hackberry
hickory/pecan (chairs)
maple
oak, red
oak, white
pine, Ponderosa (sapwood)
pine, western white
pine, yellow
poplar/cottonwood
(interiors)
sassafras

JOINERY

High-class
ash, soft white
basswood
beech
birch, yellow
butternut
'cedar, pencil'
'cedar, yellow'
cherry
chestnut
cypress
elm, slippery
elm, white

'fir, Douglas'
hackberry
hemlock, western
magnolia
maple
oak, red
oak, white
pine, pitch
pine, Ponderosa (sapwood)
pine, sugar
pine, western white
pine, yellow
plane

Utility
ash, black
ash, soft white
basswood
beech
buckeye
butternut
'cedar, incense'
'cedar, Port Orford'
'cedar, western red'
coffee tree
fir, alpine
fir, amabilis

fir, balsam
fir, grand
fir, noble
gum, red
hemlock, eastern
larch, western
pine, Ponderosa
pine, red
pine, sugar
poplar/cottonwood
spruce
tupelo
whitewood

MARINE PILING AND CONSTRUCTION

Under water

(a) Teredo infested waters

'fir, Douglas'	pine, lodgepole
pine, jack	pine, red

all pressure treated with preservative

(b) Non-teredo waters in addition to above

'cedar, incense'	'cedar, yellow'
'cedar, Port Orford'	larch, western
'cedar, pencil'	pine, pitch
'cedar, western red'	

Above water

(a) docks, wharves, bridges, etc.

coffee tree	hemlock, western
elm, rock	pine, jack
elm, slippery	pine, pitch
elm, white	pine, red
'fir, Douglas'	

(b) Decking

'fir, Douglas' (edge-grain)
hemlock, eastern (rough bridge planks)
hemlock, western (temporary work)
oak, white
pitch pine, (edge-grain)

STAIR TREADS

maple, hard	oak, white (quarter-sawn)

TOOL HANDLES

Striking

ash, tough white	hickory/pecan

Non-striking

ash, green	beech
	hornbeam, hop

TURNERY

alder, red	dogwood
apple	hickory/pecan
basswood	maple
beech	oak
birch, paper	persimmon
birch, yellow	pine, Ponderosa (sapwood)
cherry	walnut

VATS, TANKS, SILOS, ETC.

cypress	pine, jack (silos)
'fir, Douglas'	pine, red (silos)
larch, tamarack	sequoia
larch, western	

VEHICLE BODIES

ash, tough white	hickory/pecan
beech	hornbeam, hop
cypress	oak, live
elm, rock (bent work)	oak, red
hackberry	oak, white
hemlock, western	poplar/cottonwood

VENEER AND PLYWOOD

Corestock

alder	basswood
	poplar/cottonwood

Decorative

alder (selected with natural defects)	'cedar, yellow'
	maple
'cedar, pencil' (selected with natural defects)	oak, white
	plane
	walnut

Utility (plywood, chip baskets, small laminated articles, etc.)

alder	larch, western
basswood	maple
birch, paper	oak, red
birch, yellow	pine, western white
'fir, Douglas'	poplar/cottonwood
fir, noble (selected)	sequoia
gum, red	whitewood
hemlock, western	

AMENABILITY OF HEARTWOOD TO PRESERVATIVE TREATMENT

Extremely resistant
aspen
cedar, pencil

chestnut
oak
poplar, Canadian

Resistant
'cedar, incense'
'cedar, northern white'
'cedar, southern white'
'cedar, western red'
'cedar, yellow'
cottonwood, eastern
cypress
elm, rock
'fir, Douglas'
fir, alpine
fir, amabilis
fir, balsam
fir, grand
fir, noble

hemlock, eastern
hemlock, western
larch, tamarack
larch, western
maple
pine, lodgepole
pine, pitch
spruce, east Canadian
spruce, black
spruce, red
spruce, Engelmann
spruce, Sitka
spruce, western white
walnut
willow, black

Moderately resistant
ash
birch, paper
birch, yellow
'cedar, Port Orford'
cottonwood, black
elm, slippery
elm, white
hackberry
hickory/pecan

hornbeam, hop
magnolia
pine, jack
pine, ponderosa
pine, red
pine, sugar
pine, western white
pine, yellow
sequoia

Permeable
alder, red
basswood

beech
buckeye

The above classification refers to the ease with which a timber absorbs preservatives under both open-tank (non-pressure) and pressure treatments. Sapwood, although nearly always perishable, is usually much more permeable than heartwood, accordingly, the above classification refers to the relative resistance of heartwood to penetration.

Extremely resistant
Timbers that absorb only a small amount of preservative even under long pressure treatments. They cannot be penetrated to an appreciable depth laterally, and only to a very small extent longitudinally.

Resistant
Timbers difficult to impregnate under pressure and require a long period of treatment. It is often difficult to penetrate them laterally more than about 3mm to 6mm.
Incising is often used to obtain better treatment.

Moderately resistant
Timbers that are fairly easy to treat, and it is usually possible to obtain a lateral penetration of the order of 6mm to 18mm in about 2–3 hours under pressure, or a penetration of a large proportion of the vessels.

Permeable
Timbers that can be penetrated completely under pressure without difficulty, and can usually be heavily impregnated by the open-tank process.

TERMITE RESISTANCE

Termites are by no means restricted to tropical countries; they are serious pests in temperate regions also. Termites have always been present in the USA but are mainly absent from Canada. Termites of two distinct types occur in the USA ie those subterranean in habit and the non-subterranean or dry-wood termites. Subterranean termites are widely distributed throughout the USA and damage buildings in nearly every State. They can seriously and structurally weaken buildings in a short period of time.

Non-subterranean termites never burrow in the earth but fly to and attack wood directly. These dry-wood termites are not widely distributed, and their damage to buildings occurs only in that area of country south of a half-moon line drawn from Norfolk, Virginia to San Francisco in California.
Most serious damage to buildings due to termite attack occurs throughout the eastern USA, the Gulf States, the south-west, the central west and the Pacific Coast.

Since few timber species throughout the world are more than highly resistant to termite attack, and most of these would need to be imported, the USA generally regards protection of timber to be more practical where native commercial timbers are impregnated with standard chemical wood preservatives, coupled with Building Codes which provide for termite protection within the building design.

In tests carried out in the USA Californian redwood, 'incense cedar', yellow cypress, 'western red cedar' and a few *Juniperus* spp. have indicated their heartwood to be fairly resistant to attack, as was also the case with pitch pine stakes taken from the butts of logs which contained a high proportion of resin, locally called fatwood.

American building regulations and codes contain mandatory sections on termite protection of both foundation timbers and interior and exterior woodwork, and incorporate preservative treatments recommended by the American Wood-Preservers' Association.

4
AUSTRALASIA

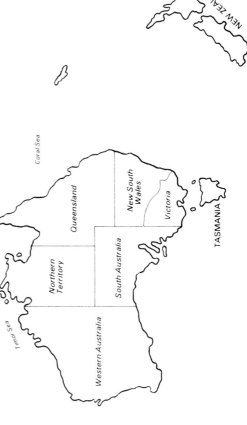

Pacific Ocean

SOLOMON ISLANDS

Coral Sea

IRIAN
JAYA

PAPUA
NEW
GUINEA

SOUTH
MOLUCCAS

Timor Sea

Queensland

New South
Wales

Victoria

TASMANIA

Northern
Territory

South Australia

Western Australia

Indian Ocean

NEW ZEALAND

INTRODUCTION

The geographical scope of this chapter is confined to Australia and the adjoining islands.

Australia

Although there are indications that Australia was at one time united with Asia through Malaysia, this conjunction was so remote that the unbroken isolation of Australia from a period long before historic times is the key of its whole development, and is strongly marked in its indigenous flora. Forms of vegetable life survive in Australia which have become extinct elsewhere, and this can be attributed only to the absence of invasion by, and competition from, external forms of vegetable life at least until the close of the 18th century and the beginning of European colonisation.

The fact that the soil and the climate were suited to other species has been proved by the fact that products and plants of the rest of the world, since introduced, have flourished so greatly that they have reduced, or even destroyed, aboriginal forms. Natural forests at the present time cover only about 6 per cent of the land area of Australia, with about 4 per cent of the forests being coniferous, 10 per cent or so being of temperate hardwoods, and the remainder of tropical hardwoods.

Conifers occur in New South Wales, Queensland and Tasmania mainly, and temperate hardwoods principally in Tasmania. Tropical hardwoods occur in all the states except Tasmania. The indigenous tree species are different from those found in other parts of the world. There are over 70 species of commercial Eucalyptus, and many Acacias. Many coniferous species have been introduced into Australia and Tasmania, and hardwoods are imported from elsewhere.

Australia lies wholly south of the equator, and its climate is partly temperate and partly sub-tropical. Tasmania is the most temperate area, with a climate similar to that of Eire. Queensland and New South Wales, southwards to Victoria, is the principal area of Australia with water supply from rainfall being in excess of evaporation.

New Zealand

In New Zealand about 25 per cent of the land area is forested, with

65 per cent or more coniferous, and the remainder temperate hardwoods, but much of the present timber used comes from planted forests, in particular radiata pine, since no true pines are indigenous to the country.

The two large islands, North and South, are in striking contrast physically. South Island consists of a great mountain range, the Southern Alps, with summer pastures, alpine lakes, glaciers and snowfields. The western slopes almost reach the shore and are clothed with fern forests.

North Island consists of a highland reaching from Mount Egmont in the south-west, to East Cape in the north-east, and two peninsulas. The first of these is mountainous, and reaches Cook Strait, the second is a lowland terminating in the north-west in the North Cape.

The climate is equable, and typically insular. North Island is warmer than South Island, while rainfall is sufficient, exceeding 880mm everywhere in North Island. In South Island the west coast is very wet, with an annual precipitation of over 2500mm at Hokitika, while the eastern plains are dry, the Canterbury Plains having less than 760mm.

The New Zealand flora is essentially of the forest type; tree ferns grow in great profusion in Westland in South Island. The kauri of the north, rimu, and similar trees are due to the heavy rains, while the beeches of South Island are a mountain type. For many years now the New Zealand Forest Service and some private interests have concentrated on planting extensive areas of conifers, including radiata pine, as a principal species, but also lodgepole, ponderosa and Corsican pine and a small amount of Douglas fir.

The production of timber from these introduced pines has risen from 0.019 million m^3 in 1926 to about 1.9 million m^3 at the present time. Native softwoods like rimu and matai are presently holding their 1926 levels of production of about 0.25 and 0.019 million m^3 respectively, and may fall lower during the next decade.

Papua New Guinea
This island of the Pacific, physically belonging to the festoon of islands which runs parallel to the east coast of Australia, after various political changes is now Indonesian in the west, which part

of the island is now known as Irian Jaya, while the eastern part, incorporating Papua, is self-administered and is now known as Papua New Guinea.

Much of Papua New Guinea is covered by primeval forest to the extent of some 80 per cent of the land area, and a very large number of tree species occurs. Some of the timbers long ago established themselves on the Australian timber market, but other useful timbers are relatively unknown. There is now a mounting interest in marketing more of Papua New Guinea's large variety of timbers, and CSIRO, Australia have for some years now been testing and evaluating many PNG timbers. In 1976 TRADA was approached by the Commonwealth Secretary (CFTC) on behalf of the Government of Papua New Guinea to assist them in the marketing of their timber and some 28 selected species were evaluated.

British Solomon Islands Protectorate
The Solomon Islands are an archipelago in the Pacific. Most of the islands are mountainous and fringed with coral reefs. The forests yield many fine timbers of the Papua New Guinea and Malaysian type. The commercial use of Solomon Islands timber is as yet in its infancy, but both the BSIP Forestry Department and CSIRO are undertaking extensive evaluation of the Solomons timbers, and increasing quantities of some species have for some time now been appearing in consumer markets.

Further references
Most of the important species that have been introduced into Australia and New Zealand from elsewhere have been excluded from the text. Since many of these species have come from North America, information on these will be found in the previous chapter. Reference should also be made to Timbers of the World, Volume 1, Chapter 4, 'South-east Asia' for information on certain hardwoods which occur throughout Malaysia and are also found in Papua New Guinea and the Solomons.

Trade names of timbers given in the text follow closely those given in Australian Standard AS 02 and British Standard BS 881 and 589.

A guide to present and potential uses of the timbers is provided, together with notes on termite resistance and amenability of heartwood to preservative treatment.

PART I HARDWOODS

AMBEROI

Pterocymbium beccarii   Family : Sterculiaceae

Other names
por-lekeng (Thailand) ; kelumbuk (Indonesia).

General characteristics
A soft, light-weight wood, weighing about 360 kg/m³ when dry. It is whitish to cream-coloured, with a straight grain and moderately coarse texture. The conspicuous rays, typical of the Sterculiaceae timbers, give a fleck figure on quarter-sawn surfaces. The timber is prone to fungal staining and must be converted and dried as soon after felling as possible, or it should be anti-stain treated. The timber has good machining and finishing properties, is perishable but permeable, and is suitable for plywood manufacture and general interior utilitarian use. It is a single species found scattered in the forests of Papua New Guinea.

BLACK BEAN

Castanospermum australe A. Cunn.   Family : Leguminosae

Other names
Moreton Bay bean, Moreton Bay chestnut, beantree.

Distribution
New South Wales and Queensland.

The tree
A tree of the moist scrub forest, it attains a height·of 40m and a diameter of about 1.0m.

The timber
A handsome wood of a chocolate-brown colour, figured with greyish-brown streaks due to parenchyma tissue surrounding the large pores. The grain is generally straight, but may be slightly interlocked, and the texture rather coarse. It weighs 720 kg/m³ when dried.

Drying

Difficult to dry, extreme care being required during air drying to avoid inducing stresses leading to collapse, honeycomb and splitting during kiln drying. The marked tendency to degrade is most pronounced when drying from the green, accordingly, very slow air drying, prior to kilning is recommended. The timber does not respond well to reconditioning treatments.

Strength

No strength data are available.

Durability

Durable.

Working qualities

The wood works reasonably well with little dulling effect on cutting edges. The relatively soft patches of lighter-coloured tissue tend to crumble under blunt knife edges during planing and moulding, but the wood can be finished smoothly. It takes an excellent polish, and it has good, though sometimes variable gluing qualities.

Uses

Decorative veneer, high-class furniture, cabinets and joinery.

BLACKBUTT

Eucalyptus spp.   Family: Myrtaceae

Various species of *Eucalyptus* produce Australian blackbutt as follows,
E. pilularis Sm. is the most important, it is known as blackbutt, and is common to New South Wales and Queensland.
E. patens Benth. is an important species known as Western Australian blackbutt, or alternatively as yarri.
E. andrewsii Maid. and *E. campanulata* R. T. Bak. and H. G. Sm. produces New England blackbutt, otherwise known as New England ash, or New England peppermint. These occur also in New South Wales and Queensland.
E. dundasii Maid. produces dundas blackbutt, also found in western Australia.

The tree
The various species on average attain a height of 45m and a diameter of about 1.0m.

The timber
The enormous varieties of *Eucalyptus* found in Australia are, for convenience, divided into two main groups, those with definitely coloured woods, including dark-red, red, dark-brown, etc and those with pale or lightly-coloured woods, including light-brown, brown, yellow, white, or faintly coloured. The blackbutts fall within this latter group, and in general they are light-brown to brown in colour, with a narrow, lighter-coloured sapwood. The heartwood often has a pinkish tinge, and small gum veins scattered in the wood are a typical feature. The grain varies from straight to occasionally interlocked or wavy, and the texture is moderately fine. The different species vary in weight from 850 kg/m^3 to 900 kg/m^3 when dried.

Drying
Requires care in drying in order to avoid the tendency to surface check.

Strength
The strength of blackbutt from New South Wales and Queensland, ie *E. pilularis* is similar to that of karri, except that it is slightly less hard. Western Australian blackbutt, *E. patens* is some 30 per cent weaker in general strength properties and is less tough and hard. Both types are more easy to split than karri.

Durability
Durable.

Working qualities
Fairly hard to work, generally without undue blunting of cutting edges. It can usually be finished to a smooth surface without undue difficulty, but a reduction of cutting angle to 15° is often necessary when curly or wavy grain is present. It can be glued and polished satisfactorily, but is hard to nail.

Uses
General construction, bridge decking, flooring, sleepers, joists, posts and rails.

BLACKWOOD, AUSTRALIAN

Acacia melanoxylon R. Br.   Family: Leguminosae

Other names
black wattle.

Distribution
Occurs in the mountain districts of New South Wales, Queensland, South Australia and Victoria, and is also found in Tasmania.

The tree
A medium-sized tree 18m to 24m in height, with a diameter of 1.0m to 1.5m.

The timber
The heartwood ranges from a lustrous golden-brown to reddish-brown or dark brown, with fairly regular dark brown zones marking the growth rings. The grain is usually straight, but may be interlocked or wavy, and the texture is medium and even. Wavy grain often produces a beautiful fiddle-back figure. The wood weighs about 670 kg/m^3 when dried.

Drying
Dries fairly easily and without undue degrade, although there is some tendency to cupping; final conditioning in kiln drying will help overcome this.

Strength
Similar to Western Australian blackbutt in most strength categories, but is considerably tougher.

Durability
Durable.

Working qualities
Works fairly easily, but cutting edges must be kept sharpened for end grain working. A reduction of cutting angle to 20° is usually beneficial in planing and moulding, particularly when curly grain is present. The wood can be screwed and nailed well, but gluing properties are often variable. It takes an excellent polish.

Uses

A highly decorative wood, it is used for fine furniture, fittings for banks, offices and shops, billiard tables, gun stocks and for sliced decorative veneer.

BLUE GUM

Eucalyptus stjohnii (R. T. Bak.)   Family: Myrtaceae
R. T. Bak., syn *E. bicostata* Maid. et al.,
and *E. globulus* Labill.

Other names

Southern blue gum (BSI standard name) ; Tasmanian blue gum, formerly Southern blue gum (Australian standard name); eurabbi (Australia).

General characteristics

The general appearance and properties of these species is similar. The pale-coloured sapwood is generally about 38mm wide, and the heartwood is light brown or light yellowish-brown in colour. The grain is usually interlocked, the texture is coarse, and the wood weighs about 830 kg/m^3 when dried.

Strength properties compare favourably with those of karri, the wood is durable, and has a high resistance to attack by marine borers.

It needs care in drying, since it is prone to surface checking and collapse, and surface cracks may penetrate deeply in thick stock.

Working qualities

Works fairly well, but it is rather difficult to obtain a smooth surface in planing operations unless the cutting angle is reduced to about 20°. It takes nails and screws reasonably well.

Uses

Constructional work, wharf decking, waggon building, boat building, bridge building, felloes, shafts and posts. It is especially valuable for piling since it can be obtained in large dimensions, and is reputed to enjoy almost complete immunity from *Teredo* attack. It should be noted that this reference has usually been made in respect of *E. globulus* from Tasmania and Victoria; *E. stjohnii* also occurs in Victoria and New South

Wales, and it is probable it likewise possesses similar resistance to marine borers.

A further type of blue gum occurs in New South Wales and Queensland, produced from *E. saligna* Sm. The Australian standard name for this timber is Sydney blue gum, the British standard name being saligna gum. BSI also include the timber of *E. grandis* Hill ex Maio in this designation, while Australian sources give it the standard name of rose gum. Both species occur in the same areas, but there would seem to be sufficient difference between their appearance and properties to merit separation. The following is a description of each species.

Saligna gum or Sydney blue gum, (*E. saligna* Sm.)

General characteristics
Sapwood about 50mm wide, pale yellow in colour, fairly well-defined from the light rose-brown heartwood. The grain is usually interlocked, occasionally straight, and the texture is rather coarse. The wood weighs about 920 kg/m³ when dried. The strength properties are similar to those of karri. The wood is moderately durable.

Uses
General construction, flooring (light domestic), weather-boards, boat building, waggon construction, fencing and for plywood, for which purpose the veneer needs careful drying.

Rose gum or flooded gum. (*E. grandis* Hill ex Maio.)

General characteristics
The sapwood is light red in colour, the heartwood dark red. The grain is usually interlocked, and the texture is fine; the wood weighs about 705 kg/m³ when dried. It has similar strength to that of jarrah. The sapwood is said to be non-susceptible to Lyctus attack.

Uses
Classified as being non-durable, it is used for construction, sleepers, posts, fencing, cases and weather-boards when treated for severe exposure.

BRUSH BOX

Tristania conferta R. Br.   Family : Myrtaceae

Other names
pink box.

Distribution
A common tree of Australia, particularly in New South Wales, Queensland and the Northern Territories.

The tree
Grows to about 36m in height with a diameter up to 2m. The bole is usually long and clean above the slight buttress.

The timber
The wood varies from brown to reddish-brown in colour, sometimes with a yellowish tinge, but turning grey after exposure. The grain is generally interlocked, and the texture is fine and even. The wood is hard and heavy, and weighs about 910 kg/m³ when dried.

Drying
A difficult timber to dry. It has a marked tendency to warp and check, and some collapse is liable when drying from the green. Needs to be air dried slowly by the use of thin sticks, prior to kiln drying and final reconditioning.

Strength
The timber is said to have similar strength properties to those of African opepe, and under rough usage, to bruise instead of splitting.

Durability
Moderately durable.

Working qualities
Fairly hard to work and machine, and although straight-grained material finishes quite well in planing, the general run of interlocked or curly grain requires a reduction of cutting angle to about 20° in order to obtain a reasonable finish. It is rather difficult to nail, holds screws firmly, and takes stain and polish satisfactorily, when this is a requirement of use.

Uses

Mauls, mallets, handles, shuttles, turnery, flooring, wharf and bridge decking, lifting wedges and heavy construction.

CALOPHYLLUM SPECIES

The Guttiferae family includes a number of species of the genus *Calophyllum* occurring in Malaysia (eg bintangor), Australia, and in the various islands of the Pacific. The following are some of these.

Calophyllum inophyllum L. procudes beach calophyllum, otherwise known as satin touriga (Australia), found in Queensland, Northern Territory and in Papua New Guinea.

C. australianum F. Muell. produces blush touriga, and *C. tomentosum* Wight. syn. *C. alatum* Bedd. produces pink touriga, both found in Queensland and Papua New Guinea.

C. costatum F. M. Bail. produces red touriga found in Queensland, also known as calophyllum and satin mahogany.

C. kajewski and *C. vitiense* occur in the Solomon Islands, the first named being known as kokilo, buni, koilo or pagura bunu, while the timber of the latter species is called gwara gwaro, vivinjolo, kioli or mengeri. *C. kajewski* is also known in Australia as island cedar, and in Fiji as damanu.

Species referred to as beach calophyllum are those growing close to the waters edge, as opposed to those growing in inland rain forests, the former generally producing badly-shaped trees, while the latter are about 40m tall, with a clean bole of some 15m to 18m in length, and a diameter of 1.5m at breast height.

General characteristics

The sapwood of the various species is relatively wide, up to about 50mm and from pale to deep orange-brown in colour, while the heartwood varies from pinkish-brown to reddish-brown, the darker-coloured wood somewhat resembling mahogany, and tending to darken further on exposure. The timbers vary in weight from 560 kg/m^3 to 768 kg/m^3 when dried. The grain is generally straight, and the texture medium coarse. The wood of the various species is moderately durable, with strength properties equalling, and sometimes exceeding those of European oak.

253

Uses

Papua New Guinea and Australian sources give the following uses, sawn construction timber, cross-arms, light framing, piles, posts and poles, cladding, decking, flooring, joinery, furniture, turnery, plywood, panelling, mouldings and shelving. *Calophyllum* is presently one of the most important commercial species of the Solomon Islands, and large quantities are exported each year, much in the form of logs to Japan for rotary peeling and slicing for veneer which is used for plywood, and in decorative form for pianos and television cabinets.

CAMPNOSPERMA SPECIES

The genus *Campnosperma*, of the family Anacardiaceae, contains several species which produce terentang of Malaysia. A further species, *C. brevipetiolata*, occurs in Papua New Guinea and the Solomon Islands, and in this latter area, this species figures in current provenance trials, aimed at the establishment and development of plantation stock.

C. brevipetiolata produces campnosperma or siruga of Papua New Guinea, and karimari, noteniga, kete kete, or solo, of the Solomons, and also sometimes erroneously called Solomon Islands maple.

The tree

The tree is fairly widely distributed in the Solomons and Papua New Guinea, and attains a height of 39m and a diameter above the slightly buttressed base of about 1.0m or rather more. Although some specimens are badly misshapen, good trees, with a clear stem of some 20m are available.

The timber

There is generally no difference by colour between sapwood and heartwood, the wood being pale pink when freshly sawn, turning a greyish-brown on exposure, occasionally appearing mauve-grey. The wood is rather plain in appearance, but tends to show a minor ray fleck figure on quarter-sawn surfaces. The grain may be straight, but is more usually interlocked, occasionally spiral, and the texture is fine and even. The wood weighs from 420 kg/m³ to 560 kg/m³ when dried.

Drying
Dries rapidly, with a tendency for the ends to split, and for staining to occur in high humidities.

Strength
A relatively soft and weak wood, unsuited for constructional purposes.

Working qualities
Works and machines easily, but is inclined to woolliness in planing. Takes nails, screws, and glue satisfactorily, and stains and polishes quite well.

Uses
Plywood, match boxes, packing cases and light framing. The wood is non-durable.

'CEDAR, AUSTRALIAN'

Toona australis (F. Muell) Harms syn   Family: Meliaceae
Cedrela toona Roxb. var. *australis* C.DC.

Other names
red cedar.

Distribution
New South Wales, Queensland, and Papua New Guinea, and Irian Jaya.

The tree
In competition with other trees it forms a straight, cylindrical stem some 9m to 12m to the first branch, but in open situations it can be much shorter. The diameter varies from 1.0m to 1.5m.

The timber
The sapwood is pinkish or greyish-white, and the heartwood is light brick-red when first exposed, turning a rich reddish-brown with darker streaks. The wood has a spicy odour, is rather lustrous, has a straight grain and a moderately close, but somewhat uneven texture. It varies in weight, but is generally about 450 kg/m^3 when dried.

Drying
Dries rapidly and fairly well, but care is needed to avoid cupping and warping of thin stock, and surface checking and collapse in thick material. Shrinkage in drying from the green to 12 per cent moisture content is 2.1 per cent radially, and 4.3 per cent tangentially.

Strength
A relatively weak wood.

Durability
Moderately durable.

Working qualities
The timber saws and works easily, but is inclined to be woolly. Quarter-sawn material may prove difficult to obtain a smooth finish, but with care a good finish is possible. The wood stains, polishes and glues satisfactorily.

Uses
Furniture, interior joinery, doors, linings, cigar boxes, boat building, masts oars, cabins.

CELTIS SPECIES

The Ulmaceae family includes several species of the genus *Celtis*, occurring in Australia, Papua New Guinea, and Solomon Islands.

Celtis philippinensis Bl. produces celtis of Queensland, western Australia, Northern Territory, Papua New Guinea and the Solomons. This is also called hard celtis in Papua New Guinea. *C. nymannii* and *C. kajewski* occur in Papua New Guinea, where it is known as light celtis, while these two species along with *C. latifolia*, also occur in the Solomons, where they are known as lae lae, lailai, skatuku, takupi or lausi.

C. paniculata (Endl.) Planch. produces Australian silky celtis.

General characteristics
A pale yellowish-brown timber with no clear distinction by colour between sapwood and heartwood. The wood has a slight silky lustre, the grain varies from straight to interlocked, and the texture is fine in *C. kajewski*, and rather coarse in

C. philippinensis. The weight of the wood varies according to species and locality, Papua New Guinea wood of *C. philippinensis* is given as from 620 to 800 kg/m³ and that of *C. nymannii* and *C. kajewski*, as 570 kg/m³ when dried. Celtis is non-durable and the sapwood is subject to blue-stain.

The wood varies in its working and machining properties; straight-grained material planes without undue difficulty, but a reduction of cutting angle to 15° is usually necessary when planing or moulding material with interlocked grain, particularly on quarter-sawn surfaces.

The wood can be stained, polished and glued satisfactorily, but requires to be pre-bored for nailing.

Uses
The heavier wood (hard celtis) is used for sawn constructional timber, cross arms and for posts and poles, flooring and decking, while both types are used for furniture, joinery, interior trim and plywood.

COACHWOOD

Ceratopetalum apelatum D.Don.   Family: Cunonaceae

Other names
scented satinwood.

Distribution
New South Wales and Queensland.

The tree
A medium-sized tree with a straight stem, some 18m to 24m tall, and a diameter of 0.5m to 0.75m.

The timber
The sapwood is light brown to pinkish-brown in colour, not well-defined from the slightly darker heartwood, and not unlike New Zealand silver beech in general appearance. The numerous fine rays produce an attractive fleck figure on quarter-sawn surfaces, and the wood has a pleasant odour. The grain is generally straight and the texture fine and even. It weighs about 630 kg/m³ when dried.

Drying
Dries fairly rapidly, but with a tendency to split and warp.

Strength
Although somewhat softer than European beech, its strength properties are similar.

Durability
Non-durable.

Working qualities
Works fairly easily, and gives a smooth, clean finish in planing and moulding. There is a slight tendency for the wood to chip at the exit of tools in drilling and mortising, and it tends to split when nailed. The wood can be stained and takes an excellent polish.

Uses
The delicate figure, fine texture, and smooth finish renders selected stock ideal for furniture and cabinet making. It is also used for panelling although there is hardly sufficient contrast and variation in its appearance to provide more than a fairly uniform impression, without visual impact. It is favoured for mouldings, flooring, gun stocks, skirtings, bobbins, shoe heels, sporting goods, boat building and for plywood and corestock.

COCONUT PALM

Cocos nucifera   Family: Palmaceae

Although palm trees belong to a different plant order from those which produce hardwoods (Dicotyledonae), and softwoods (Coniferae), nevertheless, they are of economic importance, and for that reason it is thought expedient to introduce at least one species into this publication.
Palm trees belong to the Monocoryledonae (mono, one; cotyledon, seed leaf), a plant order characterized by the fact that only one leaf appears first when the seed germinates. The leaves that follow do not usually have a network of branching veins, and there is no clear distinction of bark, wood and pith, in the stem of the tree.
The coconut palm is one of the world's most important econ-

omic plants, indispensible in the daily life of the native population of the Pacific area and other tropical areas, since it is the
source of various products such as textile fibre, vegetable fat,
oil cake, sugar and copra, while the woody stem is used for
structural and other purposes.

The trees are of slender habit, with a slightly swollen base,
attaining a height of about 15m. The large, pinnate leaves are
borne in a cluster at the tip of the stem.

The structure of a palm stem differs from that of the Dicoty-
ledons. There is no proper pith, but a parenchymatous ground
tissue, light-brown in colour, in which numerous black-
coloured vascular bundles are scattered. On end-grain these
bundles appear to be scattered throughout the stem, although
they are more numerous in the peripheral part. On longitudinal
surfaces, the wood is therefore light-brown in colour with
black streaks, the lighter-coloured wood being relatively soft
and fibrous, the darker-coloured streaks being quite hard.

Coconut palm wood weighs about 440 kg/m³ when dried, and
by comparison with western red cedar (*Thuja plicata*) is about
20 per cent weaker in modulus of rupture, 15 per cent weaker in
compression along the grain, 25 per cent weaker in shear, but is
about equal to that timber in modulus of elasticity, about twice
as hard on side grain, and some three times as tough.

Uses

Coconut palm is used in the round for piling, particularly around
wharves, for temporary construction of all classes and for fancy
items and walking sticks.

ENDOSPERMUM

Endospermum spp.   Family : Euphorbiaceae

Endospermum myrmecophilum L. S. Sm. produces Australian
endospermum, or toywood, found in Queensland, while
E. medullosum produces similar timber found in Papua New
Guinea, and known as New Guinea basswood, and in the
Solomon Islands where it is known variously as endospermum,
sasa and hongopo, and in Fiji where it is called kauvula.

The tree

Mature trees, grown under favourable conditions, attain a

259

height of 33m with a diameter above the buttressed base of about 0.75m. Some specimens are of poor form, but clear boles of some 18m can be found.

The timber
The wood is creamy-white to pale yellow in colour, assuming a straw colour after exposure. The grain may be straight, but is sometimes interlocked, or wavy, and the texture is medium coarse, but even. The wood is soft and light in weight, about 400 to 480 kg/m³ when dried.

Drying
Dries readily and well. The shrinkage is recorded as low, some 3.2 per cent tangentially, and 1.3 per cent radially.

Strength
A soft, weak wood, unsuited to construction.

Durability
Non-durable.

Working qualities
Easy to saw and machine, but inclined to woolliness. It is capable of a good, smooth finish, but the variable grain may cause some difficulty in planing and moulding. It takes nails and screws well, and can be glued, stained, polished or painted satisfactorily.

Uses
Light framing, lining, joinery, flooring, turnery, plywood, furniture and cabinets from selected stock.

ERIMA

Octomeles sumatrana Miq.   Family : Datiscaceae

Other names
ilimo (PNG) ; binuang (Malaysia).

General characteristics
The timber is soft, variable in colour, ranging from pale brown to grey or yellow-brown, sometimes with a purple tinge, with

an interlocked grain giving a ribbon figure on quarter-sawn surfaces. The texture is moderately coarse to coarse, and the wood weighs 400 kg/m³ when dry.

The wood is of the utility type, working and machining moderately well with a tendency to woolliness in planing. It glues and polishes satisfactorily, but has rather poor nailing properties. The wood is perishable but permeable, and is suitable for interior light construction, carpentry, boxes and crates, core stock and backing veneer for plywood.

FLINDERSIA SPECIES

Family : Rutaceae

Various species of *Flindersia* produce commercial timbers found in Australia and Papua New Guinea, and having common names such as ash and maple but being unrelated to these timbers. The following list gives some of these, the Australian standard name being given first.

Flindersia australis R. Br. produces Crow's ash, flindosy or teak ; found in New South Wales and Queensland.

F. acuminata C. T. White, produces silver silkwood, silver maple or Putt's pine ; found in Queensland.

F. bennettiana F. Muell. ex Benth. produces Bennett's ash ; found in New South Wales and Queensland.

F. bourjotiana F. Muell. produces Queensland silver ash.

F. schottiana F. Muell. produces southern silver ash, also known as bumpy ash or cudgerie ; found in New South Wales, Queensland and Papua New Guinea.

F. pubescens F. M. Bail. syn. *F. scottiana* var. *pubescens*. produces northern silver ash of New South Wales and Queensland.

F. collina F. M. Bail. produces leopard ash, otherwise known as leopardwood, leatherwood or broad-leaved leopard-tree ; found in New South Wales and Queensland.

F. xanthoxyla (A. Cunn. ex Hook.) Domin. syn. *F. oxleyana* F. Muell. produces yellowwood of New South Wales and Queensland, also known as long-jack and yellowwood ash.

Largely, all the above species have utilitarian uses, ranging from furniture to joinery to vehicle bodies, but in the main they are of less importance than the two or three species which furnish the well-known Queensland maple. These are described below.

Flindersia brayleyana F. Muell. and *F. pimenteliana* F. Muell. both occur in Queensland, producing Queensland maple, otherwise known as maple and maple silkwood.

F. pimenteliana also occurs in Papua New Guinea, along with *F. laevicarpa* var. *heterophylla*, where their timber is known as scented maple.

The tree
The trees are usually about 30m tall, with a diameter of 0.75m or a little more.

The timber
The term maple is rather misleading since the timber does not resemble, nor is it related to the Aceraceae family which produces commercial maple, in fact the wood rather resembles the plainer types of African mahogany. The two principal species vary slightly in appearance and character, as follows:

F. brayleyana is light brown, brownish-pink, or flesh-pink in colour, lustrous, and with an attractive stripe figure when quarter-sawn. The grain is interlocked, curly or wavy, and the texture medium and even. It weighs about 560 kg/m^3 when dried.

F. pimenteliana is a pinkish coloured wood, which darkens eventually to a light brown shade. It is a little lighter in weight, about 544 kg/m^3 when dried.

F. laevicarpa, the principal Papua New Guinea species is heavier, weighing about 690 kg/m^3.

Drying
The species have varying drying properties, and where it is possible to dry these separately, this can be beneficial. Generally speaking, they all require much care, since there is a pronounced tendency for distortion to occur, and for wide boards to cup, while there is also a tendency for collapse. Australian sources give the following shrinkage values in drying from the green to 12 per cent moisture content,

F. brayleyana; high, ie 6.5 to 8 per cent tangentially, 4 to 5 per cent radially.

F. pimenteliana; medium, ie 5 to 6.5 per cent tangentially, 3 to 4 per cent radially.

F. laevicarpa; high, ie 7.6 per cent tangentially, 3.1 per cent radially.
From all accounts it seems that the timber of *F. pimenteliana* dries with less trouble than the others, but reconditioning treatment is usually advisable in all cases, when warping tendencies can usually be corrected.

Strength
In general, the strength of these species is similar to those of European oak.

Durability
Moderately durable.

Working qualities
They all work and machine fairly readily, with only a moderate blunting effect on cutters. There is a distinct tendency for the grain to pick up during planing and moulding, particularly on quarter-sawn surfaces, due to the interlocked grain, but a reduction of cutting angle to 20° helps to overcome this. The wood can be glued, stained and polished satisfactorily and it takes nails and screws well.

Uses
Furniture, high-class joinery, vehicle bodies, rifle-stocks, printing blocks, interior fittings, mouldings, boat fittings, oars, veneer and plywood.
The principal Papua New Guinea species, *F. laevicarpa*, is used for similar purposes, and more specifically, for light framing and sawn construction timber, exterior cladding, and for doors, hand-rails and newel posts. This species is considered slightly more durable than the others, being classified as moderately durable to durable.

HOPEA SPECIES

Family: Dipterocarpaceae

The following species of *Hopea* occur in Papua New Guinea.
Hopea papuana produces light Hopea, which corresponds approximately to merawan of Malaysia.

H. parvifolia and *H. iriana* produce heavy Hopea, which corresponds approximately to giam (Malaysia) and selangan batu (Sabah).

Light Hopea has a light yellow sapwood distinct from the pale yellow brown to dark brown heartwood. The grain is shallowly interlocked, and the texture is moderately fine and even. Vertical resin canals produce greyish narrow streaks on longitudinal surfaces; the wood weighs about 700 kg/m^3 when dry. Dries slowly, and requires care to ensure against surface checking.

The wood is rather hard to work, but is capable of a smooth finish, usually when the cutting angle is reduced to 20°. It glues, nails, stains and polishes satisfactorily.

Light Hopea has similar strength to kapur (*Dryobalanops*), is classified as durable, and is used for joinery, light construction and for furniture.

Heavy Hopea has a sapwood not very distinct from the heartwood which is yellowish-brown, often with a greenish tinge, darkening on exposure to a dark tan-brown. The grain may be interlocked, but more often it is spiral or wavy, while the texture is fine and even. Resin canals are present, and the timber is hard and heavy, weighing about 990 kg/m^3 when dry.

It dries slowly with a tendency to surface check, and is hard to work due to its hard, and horny nature. Grain irregularities can give rise to tearing during planing, but with care the wood can be finished smoothly. It can be stained and polished reasonably well. Because of its very durable rating and its high strength, the timber is used for structural work, sleepers, boats, flooring and textile rollers.

IRONBARK

Eucalyptus spp.   Family: Myrtaceae

A large number of species of *Eucalyptus* make up the ironbarks of Australia. Those species making up the red and grey ironbarks are probably the most important, and are described here. *Eucalyptus crebra* F. Muell. and *E. sideroxylon* A. Cunn. ex Woolls. produce red ironbark,

E. drepanophylla F. Muell. ex Benth., *E. paniculata* Sm. and *E. siderophloia* Benth. produce grey ironbark.

Other names
mugga, broad-leaved ironbark, narrow-leaved ironbark (red ironbark).

Distribution
New South Wales, Victoria and Queensland.

The tree
The trees of the various species are all of fairly good habit, but they vary in height and girth. On average they are 18m tall, but may reach 30m with an average diameter of 0.75m to 1.0m.

The timber
Red ironbark; the sapwood is yellow in colour and about 25mm wide, and the heartwood is dark red. The grain is usually interlocked, and the texture medium and even.
Grey ironbark; the sapwood is white or pale brown in colour, and up to 38mm wide, while the heartwood varies from reddish-brown to dark brown or chocolate colour. The grain is interlocked and the texture fine and uniform.
Both types are hard and heavy timbers, weighing about 1120 kg/m^3 when dried.

Drying
All these species are refractory and require great care in drying, especially in thick material. The timber is prone to checking, but quarter-sawn stock resists this tendency. Very mild drying conditions are essential.

Strength
All the species are hard, heavy and strong, and compare favourably with the strength of greenheart, except in resistance to splitting, where ironbark is some 50 to 60 per cent inferior. It is a much harder type of timber than greenheart.

Durability
Very durable.

Working qualities
Very difficult to work with hand tools, and fairly difficult to machine. There is a considerable dulling effect on cutting edges,

and a tendency for wood to ride on planer cutters. A smooth finish can be obtained, but this is usually dependent on a reduction of cutting angle to about 15°. There is some evidence to suggest that red ironbark tends to finish more easily than the grey variety, since the former is usually preferred for flooring, and the latter for relatively rough decking. The various species accept the usual finishing treatments satisfactorily, but all are rather difficult to nail owing to their great hardness.

Uses
Red ironbark; commercially susceptible to *Lyctus* attack in sapwood; used for sleepers, bridge construction, fencing, waggon construction, heavy construction, house framing, flooring, sporting goods.

Grey ironbark; commercially non-susceptible to *Lyctus* attack in sapwood; used for sleepers, posts, piles, poles, wharf and bridge construction, deckings, heavy construction, framing, shafts, spokes and shipbuilding.

A further species of *Eucalyptus* produces a timber known as ironbark in Tasmania. This is *E. sieberi* L. Johnson syn. *E. sieberiana* F. Muell. The Australian standard name is silvertop ash, and apart from its alternative Tasmanian name, it is also known as coast ash in that area, and silvertop in Victoria.

The timber should not be confused with the commercial iron-barks since it is much lighter in weight, about 672 kg/m^3 when dried, and is a brown colour, often with a pink tint. It has an interlocked grain, a moderately open texture, and gum veins are usually present. It is used for general construction, bridges, wharves, etc and for furniture, joinery, fence posts, boxes and cases and for chemical pulp.

JARRAH

Eucalyptus marginata Sm.   Family : Myrtaceae

Distribution
Occurs in the coastal belt of Western Australia.

The tree
A large tree, 30m to 45m in height, with a clear bole some 12m to 18m long, and a diameter of 1.0m to 1.5m.

The timber
The sapwood is narrow, and pale in colour, and the heartwood is light red to dark red, darkening to a uniform red-brown mahogany shade. Gum veins or pockets may be present, and in some logs there may be small, dark markings caused by the fungus *Fistulina hepatica*. These may enhance the decorative value of the timber. The grain is usually fairly straight, but may be wavy or interlocked, and the texture is medium coarse, but even. The wood weighs about 820 kg/m^3 when dried.

Drying
With care, jarrah air dries and kiln dries very well, but there is some tendency to warping and to surface checking, warping of wide pieces, when it does occur, being generally unresponsive to reconditioning treatment. Partial air drying prior to kiln drying usually gives the best results.

Strength
By comparison with European oak, jarrah is some 10 to 20 per cent superior in all strength categories except in resistance to splitting, where it is not quite as resistant. It is also a much harder timber than oak.

Durability
Very durable.

Working qualities
Rather difficult to work with hand tools, and fairly hard to machine. It has a moderate dulling effect on cutting edges, and tends to pick up in planing, particularly on quarter-sawn surfaces, or when wavy or interlocked grain is present. A reduction of cutting angle to 15° is advisable when a smooth planed surface is required. The timber glues satisfactorily, and holds screws well, but it is rather hard to nail. It takes a high polish.

Uses
Wharf and bridge construction, decking for piers, flooring, piles, interior fittings, furniture. sleepers, shingles, weatherboards, rafters, joists, veneer, shipbuilding, keel blocks, chemical vats, filter presses, sea defences, groynes.

KAMARERE

Eucalyptus deglupta   Family : Myrtaceae

This is a further tree species currently undergoing provenance trials in the Solomons, employing both indigenous plants and specimens from Papua New Guinea.

General characteristics
The sapwood is white, and the heartwood is reddish-brown or golden-brown in colour. The grain is usually interlocked, seldom straight, while the texture is medium. The wood weighs about 690 kg/m³ when dried, and shrinkage is said to be 3 per cent radially, and 5.1 per cent tangentially.
The timber has good strength properties, comparing favourably with those of *Calophyllum* spp, and is classified as being moderately durable.

Uses
Papua New Guinea sources suggest the following uses ; structural and engineering ; sawn construction timber, sleepers, heavy decking, piles, poles, posts and light framing. Non-structural ; cladding, flooring, joinery, lining, interior trim, furniture, cabinets, moulding, panelling and plywood.

KARRI

Eucalyptus diversicolor F. Muell.   Family : Myrtaceae

Distribution
Western Australia.

The tree
A large tree, attaining a height of 45m to 60m and a diameter of 2m to 3m.

The timber
Karri closely resembles jarrah in structure and appearance, the heartwood being reddish-brown darkening to a rather more uniform brown than jarrah. The burning splinter test is generally useful in separating the two timbers. When a small splinter of

dry heartwood is burned the embers continue to glow after the flame is extinguished. With karri, a thick white ash is formed, while jarrah burns to a black, ashless charcoal. Karri is slightly heavier than jarrah, and weighs about 900 kg/m³ when dried.

Drying
The timber requires great care in drying; it is prone to checking, and under adverse drying conditions, the cracks can extend well into the wood. Thin stock is more liable to warping than with jarrah. Partial air drying prior to kiln drying produces the best results.

Strength
A hard, strong timber, which compared with European oak is some 40 to 50 per cent stronger in bending, in compression along the grain and in shear, and is about twice as stiff. It is about 30 per cent more difficult to split than oak, and in shock resistance is more comparable to European ash.

Durability
Moderately durable.

Working qualities
Difficult to work with hand tools, and fairly difficult to machine. It has a slightly higher blunting effect on cutting edges than jarrah, and like that timber finishes better when the cutting angle is reduced to about 15°. It can be glued, screwed, stained and polished satisfactorily, but is hard to nail.

Uses
Wharf and bridge construction, superstructures, agricultural implements, shipbuilding, flooring, joists, furniture, interior trim and plywood, in which respect care is needed to avoid excessive buckling of the veneer during its drying.

KWILA

Intsia bijuga (Colebr.) O. Ktze.   Family: Leguminosae

Other names
hintzy (Madagascar); ipil (Philippines); kwila (PNG and New Britain).

Note : *Intsia bijuga* is found in Madagascar, the Philippines and south-west Pacific islands, including Papua New Guinea. A further species, *Intsia palembanica* Miq. occurs principally in Malaysia and Indonesia and produces merbau. This latter species is also found in small quantities in Papua New Guinea and may be mixed with *I. bijuga* in commercial kwila. There is no essential difference between the timber of both species.

General characteristics
The fairly wide sapwood is a pale yellow colour and is sharply defined from the heartwood which varies from brown with an orange cast to dark reddish-brown. The cells often contain yellow or dark-coloured deposits. The grain is interlocked and often wavy, and the texture is coarse but even. It weighs from 750–830 kg/m³ when dry. The timber dries slowly and well, but if hurried tends to check, with end splitting. It works and machines reasonably well ; there is a tendency for the grain to tear out in planing and a reduction in cutting angle to 20° is helpful. The wood tends to split in nailing, but it holds screws well ; it can be glued, stained and polished. The yellow deposits are soluble in water, and the dye thus produced can spoil textiles or fair faced concrete if these are in contact with the wood in exposed situations.

The wood is durable and is used for heavy construction, flooring, sleepers and agricultural implements.

LABULA

Anthocephalus chinensis syn *A. cadamba*   Family : Rubiaceae

Other names
kadam (UK, USA, France, Germany, Burma) ; kelampayon (Malaysia).

General characteristics
Labula is a rather plain, general utility timber of a cream colour with a yellowish tinge, a straight grain, and moderately fine and even texture. It dries easily and well, has good machining and finishing properties, and weighs about 430 kg/m³ when dry. It occurs in Papua New Guinea in reasonable quantities, and is suitable for joinery, plywood, light construction for interior application. The wood is non-durable, but can be preservative treated.

MALAS

Homalium foetidum   Family : Flacourtiaceae

Other names
aranga (UK) ; takaliu (Sabah).

General characteristics
The wood is red-brown, or purplish-red in colour, with no distinction between sapwood and heartwood. The grain is usually straight but may be interlocked, and the texture is fine or moderately fine. The wood weighs about 850 kg/m³ when dry. The timber is difficult to dry and requires care to avoid checking and splitting. It works reasonably well, and is used for sports goods, marine construction, piling and agricultural implements.
The timber is in moderate supply in Papua New Guinea.

MELIACEAE

The Meliaceae family, which produces true mahogany, also contains a few genera which produce mahogany type of timber. Two of these, *Aglaia* spp. and *Amoora* spp. occur throughout the Pacific islands, and frequently are marketed under the collective name of meliaceae, or as the particular local name applicable to either genera, eg *Aglaia* spp. ayabala, fangeri, ulukwala (Solomons) ; aglaia, red bean (Papua New Guinea) ; rose kamala (Australia).
Amoora spp. amoora, mawa, maota, maoa (Solomons).

General characteristics
Aglaia spp. is a comparatively small tree, producing a clear bole of about 9m and a diameter of about 0.9m.
The heartwood is reddish-brown in colour, clearly defined from the straw-coloured sapwood which is from 38mm to 75mm wide. The wood weighs about 720 to 830 kg/m³ when dried. It is moderately durable.

Uses
Papua New Guinea suggests its use for sawn construction timber, heavy decking, and for posts, poles and piles, and also

for flooring, joinery, furniture, sliced and peeled veneer and turnery.

Amoora spp. usually produces a clear bole of some 6m in length, and a diameter of 0.5m.

The heartwood is red or wine-red when freshly cut, turning a deep reddish-brown on exposure, the sapwood is light red in colour. The grain varies from straight to interlocked, and the texture is rather coarse. The wood weighs about 608 kg/m^3 when dried. It is moderately durable.

Uses
Canoes, boat knees, paddles, light construction, furniture and joinery.

NORTHERN RATA

Metrosideros robusta   Family : Myrtaceae

Distribution
New Zealand.

General characteristics
The wood is a pale chocolate-brown colour, with a straight grain, and a fine, even texture. It weighs about 880 kg/m^3 when dried, is said to have a high to very high shrinkage potential, but is hard and strong, with strength properties similar to those of karri.

Uses
A durable timber, it is used for bridge and wharf construction, shipbuilding, vehicle bodies, sleepers, cross arms, hockey sticks, tool handles, fencing and agricultural implements.

A further species, *M. queenslandica* occurs in Queensland, where it is known as pink myrtle or myrtle satinash.

NOTHOFAGUS SPECIES

The Fagaceae family includes the genus *Fagus*, whose various species produce beech of the Northern hemisphere, and various species of *Nothofagus*, whose trees produce timber bearing a superficial resemblance to that of *Fagus sylvatica* (European

beech), but sometimes being known under widely differing commercial names, eg coigue and rauli from Chile, or myrtle from Australia; also known as beech of the Southern hemisphere.
The following describes the principal Australasian species.

'SILVER BEECH'
Nothofagus menziesii Oerst. principally, but also *N. fusca* (Hook f.) Oerst. and *N. truncata* (Col) Cockayne.

Other names
'Southland beech' (*N. menziesii*); 'red beech' (*N. fusca*); 'hard beech' (*N. truncata*).

Distribution
North and South Islands of New Zealand.

The tree
'Silver beech' attains a height of 30m and a diameter of 0.6m to 1.5m.

The timber
'Silver beech' (*N. menziesii*) is a uniform pinkish-brown or pale salmon colour, generally with a narrow, slightly lighter-coloured sapwood, and a zone of false heartwood separating the sapwood from the heartwood or true-wood. This intermediate zone for practical purposes is regarded as sapwood. The wood is similar to European beech by colour, but both 'red' and 'hard beech' are darker, especially the true-wood, but all lack the large rays so characteristic of European beech, and in consequence, quarter-sawn surfaces are relatively without feature. The timber is usually straight-grained, with a fine, even texture. The weight of the separate species varies, and especially so as the location varies from north to south, timber from North Island being usually heavier and harder than that from South Island. Accordingly, 'silver beech' varies from 545 to 740 kg/m^3 when dried, while 'red beech' is about 710 kg/m^3 and 'hard beech' about 770 kg/m^3.

Drying
The timber dries fairly easily, but it appears reluctant to give up its moisture from the centre, and therefore requires care. It

tends to split at the ends of boards if the drying is hurried, but due to the lack of large rays, surface checking and distortion are not usually serious problems.

Strength
Although similar to European beech in shock resistance, it is about 30 per cent inferior in hardness and shear, and some 15 to 20 per cent inferior in other strength categories.

Durability
'Silver beech' is non-durable, 'red' and 'hard beech', durable.

Working qualities
All these species are milder to work and machine than European beech, and in general they finish smoothly in planing and moulding, but a reduction of cutting angle to 20° may be necessary when curly grain is present. The dulling effect on cutting edges is relatively mild with 'silver' and 'red beech', but may be more severe when machining 'hard beech' due to silica in the ray cells. It can be stained and polished and nails and screws reasonably well.

Uses
'Silver beech' is used for furniture, flooring, turnery, boxes, cheese crates, motor-body work, toys and tool handles. 'Red' and 'hard beech' have similar uses, and all three types are classified as Group III timbers according to New Zealand Standard 3631 : 1971 where, according to grade, they are recommended for such purposes as Board Grade, suitable for painting, 1st class framing (Building Grade A), and rough and temporary use (Commons Grade).

Note : Although some 84 per cent of the South Island forest is predominantly 'beech', the timber tends to be over-mature with a high proportion of defects. Recent plans to develop parts of the forests for pulp production have encountered opposition from conservationist groups. At present only 20 000 m³ of 'beech' are produced annually.

'TASMANIAN MYRTLE'
Nothofagus cunninghamii Oerst.

Other names
'myrtle beech', 'myrtle', 'Tasmanian beech'.

Distribution
Tasmania and Victoria.

The tree
Usually from 15m to 30m tall, but may reach 60m with a clear bole up to 12m and a diameter of about 1.0m.

The timber
The timber is similar to New Zealand 'silver beech' but is heavier, weighing about 740 kg/m^3. The sapwood is narrow and whitish, and the heartwood varies from pink to reddish-brown, with an intermediate zone of lighter colour. The grain is straight or slightly interlocked, occasionally wavy, and the texture is very fine and uniform. Large rays are lacking.

Drying
This timber has very variable drying characteristics. Timber containing a high proportion of dark-coloured wood (true-wood) is liable to internal honeycombing and severe surface checking if the drying is forced, but the lighter coloured wood, containing as a rule a higher proportion of false heartwood, dries without excessive degrade. Much care is therefore needed in kiln drying, either to separate the two classes of wood and to dry them separately, or to air dry the stock to fibre saturation point, about 30 per cent moisture content, prior to kilning.

Strength
By comparison with 'silver beech', 'Tasmanian myrtle' is some 40 per cent harder on side grain, and about 12 per cent superior in bending, compression along the grain and in shear strength, but about equal to that timber in stiffness and toughness.

Durability
Non-durable.

Working qualities

Works and machines fairly readily, being comparable to European beech in most respects. It planes and moulds to a good smooth finish, glues, stains and polishes satisfactorily and takes nails and screws quite well.

Uses

Furniture, cabinets, joinery, flooring, parquetry, shoe heels, brush backs, bobbins, handles, interior trim, panelling, bridge and wharf decking, plywood and bent work.

Other species of *Nothofagus* occur in Australasia, producing timber of commercial importance. These include *N. gunnii* (Hook f.) Oerst. producing 'tanglefoot beech' of Tasmania, *N. moorei* Maid. which is found in New South Wales and Queensland, with the standard name of 'negro-head beech', otherwise known as 'Antarctic beech', and *N. carrii*, *N. grandis*, and *N. perryi*, all of which occur in Papua New Guinea where it is known as 'New Guinea beech'.

The timber of these species is reddish in colour, and *N. moorei* especially is very similar to Chilean roble (*N. obliqua*). The timber is used for furniture, flooring, boat decking and agricultural implements.

Other timbers known in Australia as 'beech', fall outside the true classification ie *Fagus* and *Nothofagus* (Fagaceae), although their appearance and uses may be similar to beech. These include *Citronella moorei* (F. Muell ex Benth.) Howard. syn *Villaresia moorei* F. Muell ex Benth, which produces 'silky beech' of New South Wales and Queensland, otherwise known as churnwood, corduroy and soapbox, and *Citronella smythii* F. Muell, which produces 'northern silky beech' of Queensland, otherwise known as soapbox and 'white oak'.

Both of these species belong to the Olacaceae family, which is closely related to the holly family (Aquifoliacae). The timber is light brown in colour, a little lighter in weight than 'Tasmanian myrtle' but with similar strength and uses.

'NEW GUINEA WALNUT'

Dracontomelum spp.   Family : Anacardiaceae

Other names

Pacific or Papua walnut (UK) ; loup or lup (Papua New Guinea).

Distribution
Papua New Guinea and neighbouring islands.

The timber
'New Guinea Walnut' resembles the more lightly-coloured type of wood of 'Queensland walnut', being a distinctive yellowish-brown colour, with a pinkish or reddish tinge. It lacks the sour smell characteristic of fresh-cut 'Queensland walnut', and also differs from that timber in that the abundant tyloses are thin-walled, and the irregularly spaced, tangential lines of paren-chyma, typical in 'Queensland walnut', are absent from the Papua New Guinea wood.
The grain is more or less interlocked and sometimes wavy, producing a broken stripe figure on quarter-sawn surfaces, while the texture is medium and even. The wood weighs about 750 kg/m^3 when dried.

Drying
Dries quite well, with a slight tendency to warp in the thinner sizes, and to check if the drying is hurried. Shrinkage from the green to 12 per cent moisture content is 4.6 per cent tangentially and 2.1 per cent radially.

Strength
A timber of moderate strength, unsuitable for engineering uses.

Durability
Moderately durable.

Working qualities
Works and machines readily with a moderate blunting effect on cutting edges. The wood is capable of a smooth finish, but the interlocked grain tends to tear and pick up on quarter-sawn surfaces and a reduction of cutting angle to 20° is usually beneficial. The wood takes nails and screws well, and glues, stains and polishes, satisfactorily.

Uses
Light framing, exterior cladding, joinery, linings, flooring, interior trim, mouldings, turnery, furniture, cabinets, shop fitting, and veneer from selected stock.

PNG 'OAK'

Castanopsis acuminatissima   Family : Fagaceae

Other names
Indonesian chestnut (UK, USA) ; gunung (France) ; berangan (Malaysia).

General characteristics
This timber is neither a true oak (*Quercus*), nor a sweet chestnut (*Castanea*), but is related to both. The wood is a pale brown colour, not unlike a coarse sweet chestnut, but with slightly larger rays giving a small fleck figure on quarter-sawn surfaces. The grain varies from straight to interlocked, and the wood weighs about 630 kg/m^3 when dry. It dries reasonably well, but with a tendency to surface check, has quite good machining properties, glues well, and is suitable for construction, joinery, flooring, furniture, plywood and sliced veneer.
Castanopsis occurs in rather limited amounts in Papua New Guinea and may be mixed with *Lithocarpus perclusa* and different species of *Pasania* under the general description of PNG 'oak'.

PALAQUIUM SPECIES

The Sapotaceae family contains a large number of species of *Palaquium* found in south east Asia and the various islands of the Pacific, while one species occurs in Australia. In general, the various species have similar characteristics, and are often mixed, occasionally with the addition of one or two other, and similar genera. *Palaquium* from the Pacific area corresponds closely to the timber shipped from Malaysia under the trade name nyatoh. The following is a guide to the principal species from the Pacific area.
Palaquium galactoxylum (F. Muell.) H. J. Lam. syn. *Lucuma galactoxylon* F. Muell. is found in Queensland, where it is known as Cairns pencil cedar or moordooke.
P. galactoxylum, *P. firmum*, *P. erythrospermum*, and others, occur in the Solomons, where the timber is known as bubungu, paloto and aisulu.
P. stehlini occurs in Western Samoa, where it is known as gasu.

278

Palaquium species also occur in Papua New Guinea, where they are grouped under the general name of pencil cedar.

The tree
The trees grow from 21m to 33m in height, producing clear boles of 18m or more, with a diameter of about 1.0m.

The timber
The sapwood is yellowish-grey to pinkish-brown in colour, and may be wide, varying usually from 50mm to 100mm in width, while the heartwood is a warm pinkish-brown, sometimes with darker streaks. The wood tends to darken in colour after exposure to a reddish-brown. The grain varies from straight to interlocked, and the texture is medium fine and even. The weight of the various species varies considerably, the average being about 680 kg/m³ when dried. Papua New Guinea species are given as from 460 to 570 kg/m³ while in Fiji it is the practice to group the various species into two classes, medium density = 560 kg/m³; heavy density = 880 kg/m³ *P. firmum* is said to vary from 544 to 640 kg/m³ when dried.

Drying
The wood dries at a moderate rate, with only a slight tendency to distortion, and a moderate tendency for surface checks to develop, but more so in the vicinity of knots.

Strength
The heavier species have strength properties similar to those of the closely related makoré of Africa (*Tieghemella heckelii*), the lighter weight species having strength more akin to those of African abura or agba.

Durability
Non-durable to moderately durable.

Working qualities
The working properties vary according to density, type of grain, and amount of silica present, but on the whole, the wood works reasonably well and is capable of a smooth finish, although a reduction of cutting angle to 20° may be necessary in order to avoid tearing out on quarter-sawn surfaces. The

wood gives good results in staining and polishing, and it glues well, but tends to split in nailing.

Uses
The heavy species are suitable for sawn construction timbers, the medium weight species for flooring, joinery, furniture, panelling, turnery, interior trim, mouldings, windows, plywood and decorative veneer from selected logs.

PEPPERMINT

Eucalyptus spp.   Family: Myrtaceae

A number of species of *Eucalyptus* are marketed in Australia and Tasmania as peppermint, either singly, or in a combination of two or three species. The following briefly describes a few of the more important of these.

E. piperita Sm. including *E. urceolaris* Maid. and Bl. produce Sydney peppermint found abundantly in New South Wales. This is a light brown coloured wood, with pink tints, often containing numerous gum veins; generally with interlocked grain, and fairly close texture. The weight varies from 560 to 720 kg/m^3 when dried.

E. amygdalina Labill. syn. *E. salicifolia* Cav. produces black peppermint, found widely scattered in Tasmania.

This is also light brown in colour with a pink tint; gum veins are common, and the timber is fissile. The grain is usually straight, but may be interlocked, and the texture is more or less open. It is a little lighter in weight than Sydney peppermint, about 590 kg/m^3 when dried.

E. dives Schau. produces broad-leaved peppermint found in New South Wales and Victoria. This is a brown-coloured, fissile timber, of rather poor quality, with numerous gum veins and interlocked grain, and fairly close texture. The logs are frequently unsound in the heart, but sound wood weighs about 640 kg/m^3 when dried.

Uses
Depending on quality, these and other species are used for similar purposes as stringybark, general construction, furniture vehicle bodies and building purposes.

PLANCHONELLA SPECIES

The Sapotaceae family includes a number of species of *Planchonella*, found in Australia and the Pacific Islands. There is some confusion at the present time over the commercial classification of these timbers since they appear to vary considerably in weight, according to locality, and in their suitability for specific uses.

In Papua New Guinea, the principal species are divided into two types, as follows,

Planchonella torricellensis ; red planchonella, weight about 590 kg/m³ when dried. Sapwood susceptible to *Lyctus* attack.

P. kaernbachiana ; white planchonella, weight about 530 kg/m³ when dried. Sapwood non-susceptible to *Lyctus* attack.

Suggestions for the separation of the Solomons species are on the basis of weight, ie heavy planchonella, 880 to 1040 kg/m³ when dried, and light planchonella, 480 to 640 kg/m³ when dried.

Heavy planchonella; Three principal species are considered here, *P. obovata, P. costata,* and *P. sessiliflora.*

P. obovata ; known as tata, tala or riru, in the Solomons, and as yellow northern boxwood, black ash or yellow teak, in Australia, where it also occurs. The sapwood is some 75mm wide, straw-coloured, and the heartwood is pinkish-brown. It has a straight grain, and a fine texture, and weighs about 880 kg/m³ when dried. Suggested for use in general construction.

P. costata; ; known as riru, or arimanu in the Solomons. The wood is straw-coloured, with no clear distinction between sapwood and heartwood, which may however, contain darker streaks of colour. Weight unknown, but the wood is reputed to be hard and heavy, and to be suitable for heavy constructional work.

P. sessiliflora ; known as raumuga in the Solomons. The heartwood is reddish-brown, and only slightly darker than the sapwood. The wood is said to be fairly hard and fairly heavy, and suitable for medium construction work.

Light planchonella ; The principal species making up this group is *P. thyrsoidea,* known as keta, tete, sesele and verure in the Solomons. Both sapwood and heartwood are straw-coloured, and the wood is light in weight, from 400 to 480 kg/m³ when dried. It produces good veneer core-stock.

Durability

There would appear to be some uncertainty regarding durability of all these species. Papua New Guinea sources quote red and white planchonella as varying from non-durable to moderately durable.

Uses

Papua New Guinea suggested uses include, sawn construction timber, posts, piles and poles, light framing, for both types, with red planchonella being suitable for cladding, flooring, decking, joinery, mouldings, interior trim, furniture, cabinets, veneer and turnery, and white planchonella being suitable for cladding, lining, joinery, mouldings, interior trim, furniture, cabinets, veneer and core-stock, and turnery.

Some reservations must be made regarding the entire suitability of the various species for the suggested uses, eg red planchonella has a sapwood susceptible to *Lyctus* attack, but is classified as erratic, ie non-dependable in regard to penetration of heartwood by preservatives. On the other hand, white planchonella, is not only said to resist *Lyctus* attack, but further has a wide, easily penetrated (treatable) sapwood, with a reasonable treatment of heartwood. While, for use as cladding, for example, red planchonella could be treated sufficiently well to preclude *Lyctus* attack in the sapwood, the resistance to treatment of the heartwood, might not be sufficient to resist fungal attack, or other beetle attack, long term, and accordingly, white planchonella would offer distinct advantages.

'QUEENSLAND WALNUT'

Endiandra palmerstonii   Family : Lauraceae
C. T. White et W. D. Francis

Other names

'Australian walnut', 'walnut bean', oriental wood.

Distribution

A common tree of northern Queensland.

The tree

A large, buttressed tree, some 36m to 42m tall, with a diameter of 1.5m.

The timber

Although unrelated to true walnut (*Juglans* spp.), the wood bears a striking resemblance to European walnut, except that it is often more prominently striped. The wood varies considerably in colour, from light brown to dark brown, frequently streaked with pinkish, greyish-green or blackish colour. Silica in the form of irregular crystalline aggregates is usually present in the ray tissue, and the wood has an unpleasant odour when freshly cut, but this disappears after drying. The grain is generally interlocked and often wavy, and this, combined with a natural lustre and variegated colour of the wood, produces a very attractive figure, particularly on quarter-sawn surfaces. The wood weighs about 690 kg/m^3 when dried, which is a little heavier than European walnut.

Drying

The timber tends to dry rapidly with a distinct inclination to split at the ends of pieces, and end-coating is therefore valuable. There is a tendency for thin stock to cup, and thick stock to collapse if drying is hurried. The timber generally responds well to reconditioning treatment, and quarter-sawing is said to reduce end splitting.

Strength

A much stronger timber than European walnut, comparing more closely to European oak in general strength properties.

Durability

Non-durable.

Working qualities

A rather difficult timber to saw and machine generally, requiring the use of tipped saws and high quality high-speed cutters and a reduction of cutting angle to 20° in order to overcome the severe dulling effect on cutting edges, and to produce a good finish. The timber takes an excellent polish, and can be screwed and glued satisfactorily.

Uses

'Queensland walnut' is used for high-class furniture, cabinets, panelling and flooring, and in shop fitting and for decorative veneer.

283

RED RIVER GUM

Eucalyptus camaldulensis Dehnh. syn.   Family: Myrtaceae
E. rostrata Schlecht

Other names
Murray red gum, blue gum (Queensland), red gum.

Distribution
New South Wales, Queensland, South Australia, Victoria, Western Australia and the Northern Territory.

General characteristics
The timber varies in colour according to age and locality of growth, through various shades of red. The grain is interlocked, often wavy producing a fiddle-back figure on quarter-sawn surfaces, and a close texture. Gum pockets are frequent. The wood is very durable, and weighs about 825 kg/m^3 when dried. It is rather hard to work.

Uses
Its good strength, high natural durability, and reputed high resistance to termites and marine borers, render it ideal for piling, shipbuilding, mining timbers, constructional purposes, and for weatherboards. It is also used for flooring, paving blocks and stair treads.

'SHE-OAK'

Casuarina spp.   Family: Casuarinaceae

A large number of species of *Casuarina* occur in Australasia and the Pacific islands. Although unrelated to the true oaks (*Quercus* spp.), their timber bears some resemblance to oak, and particularly to the evergreen oak (*Quercus ilex*). The name 'she-oak' is derived from the sound of the wind when passing through the branches. Another common name is 'forest oak'.

General characteristics
The western Australian *C. fraserana* Miq. is a light reddish-yellow-coloured wood, fairly well defined from the light brown sapwood. The wood is lustrous, and mottled with a figure

284

produced by the larger of the two types of ray. The grain is fairly straight, and the texture fine, and open. The wood weighs about 720 kg/m³ when dried.

The 'rose she-oak', *C. torulosa* Ait. of New South Wales and Queensland has a light brown sapwood, sharply defined from the heartwood which ranges in colour from light red, brick-red, to dark red, the rays, of two sizes, one extremely fine, the other exceptionally prominent, produces an attractive broad flake figure, darker in colour to the background, on radial surfaces. The grain is straight, the wood fissile, and the texture fine and even. The wood weighs about 929 kg/m³ when dried.

The various species vary considerably in depth of colour and grain pattern, but they are very attractive woods, requiring much care in drying, but suitable for decorative cabinet-work, turnery, veneer, wooden hand-screws, shingles and cooperage.

'SILKY OAK'

Grevillea spp. and *Cardwellia* spp.   Family : Proteaceae

A number of different genera and species produce the silky oaks of Australia and New Zealand, but the principal species are,

Grevillea robusta A. Cunn. which produces southern silky oak (Australian standard name), or grevillea (British standard name), this latter name being adopted in the UK since present-day supplies originate from East Africa, where the tree has been introduced for shade purposes, and where it is better known under that name.

The tree is native to New South Wales and Queensland.

Cardwellia sublimis F. Muell. produces northern silky oak (Australian standard name), or bull oak. The British standard name is Australian silky oak.

The tree is native to Queensland.

General characteristics

The timber of both species is pinkish or reddish-brown, rather like American red oak, and toning down to brown with age. *Cardwellia* heartwood is generally darker than that of *Grevillea* which tends more to pale pinkish-brown. There is sometimes a golden sheen to the wood, but the most prominent feature of either species is the large rays which produce a well-marked silver-grain figure.

The wood is straight-grained, except where the fibres pass round the rays, and the texture is coarse, but even.

The weight of *Grevillea* is 580 kg/m³ and that of *Cardwellia*, 550 kg/m³ when dried.

With care, both types dry reasonably well, but the timber does not part with its moisture very readily, and drying should not therefore be hurried.

The wood works easily, but with a tendency for the large rays to crumble slightly in cutting. Quarter-sawn material presents a problem in planing due to the grain tending to pick up on account of the rays, and a reduced cutting angle of 20° is usually beneficial. The timber can be nailed, screwed, glued and stained satisfactorily, and a reasonable polish can be obtained.

Uses
Furniture, cabinets and decorative items, panelling, shop fitting and veneer.

SOLOMONS PADAUK

Pterocarpus indicus Willd.   Family : Leguminosae

Other names
warara, linggi, liki (Solomons) ; rosewood (Papua New Guinea).

Distribution
Various species of *Pterocarpus* occur throughout southern and south east Asia, and in the Pacific islands. *Pterocarpus indicus*, and probably other species, produces the padauk of the area with which this booklet is concerned. Allied species are described in other booklets in the series.

The tree
The tree may reach 30m in height, with a diameter above the wide buttress of about 0.75m. It is fast-growing, but in general the trees are of poor form, and therefore of limited economic use. However, the attractive wood is highly prized locally.

The timber
The sapwood is whitish to pale yellow, from 38mm to 62mm wide, clearly defined from the heartwood, which varies from whitish to pale yellow, to golden brown to rich red, with prominent figuring, brought about by the combined effect of storied rays and other elements, terminal parenchyma, and grain irregularities, producing figured wood such as fiddle-back, ripple, mottle and curls. The grain may be straight, but more often is interlocked and wavy, and the texture is moderately coarse but even. The wood weighs about 610 kg/m^3 when dried.

Drying
The timber dries rather slowly but reasonably well, with little distortion, but with a tendency to splitting and checking, particularly in highly figured wood.

Strength
Straight-grained material has very good strength, but since this is not a general requirement of normal end use, it is of only relative importance. Compared with European beech, the timber is some 30 per cent inferior in hardness on side grain, and about 12 per cent less tough and resistant to shear.

Durability
Very durable.

Working qualities
Fairly easy to work and machine, with little dulling effect on cutting edges. A good finish is obtainable in planing and moulding straight-grained material, but otherwise the cutting angle should be reduced to 20° in order to obtain the best results. The timber can be nailed, screwed and glued satisfactorily, and takes an excellent polish. Although similar in appearance to the allied muninga (*Pterocarpus angolensis*) of Africa, the pores in Solomons padauk are smaller, and there is usually less filling required in polishing. The wood turns well and can be sliced for veneer.

Uses
Veneer, turnery, rifle butts, panelling, flooring, boat building, furniture and cabinet making. The name amboyna is used to describe burr-figured wood.

SPONDIAS

Spondias dulcis   Family: Anacardiaceae

General characteristics
Spondias occurs in Papua New Guinea and is a light-weight wood weighing about 360 kg/m^3 when dry. There may be no difference in colour between sapwood and heartwood, the wood being a greyish-brown colour, but sometimes the heartwood is a decided rose-pink colour. The grain is straight as a rule, but occasionally is interlocked, and the texture is moderately coarse but even.

The timber dries reasonably well, but is rather difficult to machine, the grain tending to tear and for woolliness to show in planing. The wood can be glued, but it has poor nailing qualities. Suitable for core stock and mouldings.

SPOTTED GUM

Eucalyptus maculata Hook. and   Family: Myrtaceae
E. citriodora Hook

Other names
spotted irongum; lemon-scented gum (*E. citriodora*).

Distribution
E. citriodora occurs in Queensland, *E. maculata* is found in New South Wales, Victoria and in Queensland.

The tree
These vary from 24m to 45m in height, and a diameter of about 1.0m.

The timber
The wide sapwood is usually white in colour, but that of the heartwood varies according to age and locality of growth. Some specimens are dark brown in colour, others vary from greyish-yellow to light brown or greyish-brown. The wood has a rather greasy nature, the grain is slightly interlocked, and the texture is even, but coarse. The wood is heavy, weighing about 1030 kg/m^3 when dried.

Drying
Rather difficult to dry if surface checking is to be kept to a minimum. There is also a tendency for slight collapse to occur, and which does not respond too well to reconditioning treatment.

Strength
Tests on *E. maculata* indicate that by comparison with European oak, spotted gum is about twice as strong in bending, and in compression along the grain, and in stiffness.

Durability
Moderately durable.

Working qualities
Although hard, it works with moderate ease in most hand and machine operations. A good finish can be obtained, but wavy grain tends to pick up in planing, and a cutting angle of 20° to 25° is usually beneficial. It takes screws and glues fairly well, but is hard to nail. It can be stained and polished with good results.

Uses
Bridge and general construction, flooring, handles, cross-arms for telegraph poles, railway waggons.

STRINGYBARK

Eucalyptus spp.   Family: Myrtaceae

A large number of species of *Eucalyptus* are marketed under the commercial name of stringybark. The following is a brief description of red, white and yellow stringybark.
Red stringybark; *E. macrorhyncha* F. Muell ex Benth. occurs in Victoria, New South Wales and South Australia.
This is a light pinkish-brown-coloured wood, with a close texture, weighing about 850 kg/m³ when dried. A durable wood, used for light construction, bridges and wharves, weatherboards, sleepers, posts, poles, fencing and cross-arms for telegraph poles.
White stringybark is the product of the following species,

E. eugenioides Sieb. ex Spr. syn. *E. wilkinsoniana* and including *E. acervula, E. laevopinea* and *E. wiburdii.*
E. globoidea Bl. syn. *E. scabra*, including *E. yangoura*, and *E. phaeotricha.*
These occur mainly in Queensland, Victoria and New South Wales, except *E. phaeotricha* which does not occur in Victoria, and is also known in Queensland as pink blackbutt. Other names for these species are Wilkinson's stringybark, and thin-leaved or small-leaved stringybark. The timber varies in colour, according to species and locality, ranging from pale pink to brown. The grain is generally straight, but may be interlocked, with a medium texture. Unlike red stringybark it is reputed to be non-susceptible to *Lyctus* attack. The wood weighs from 817 to 897 kg/m³ when dried, and is used for heavy and general construction, sleepers, poles and cross-arms.

Yellow stringybark is the product of *E. acmenioides* Schau. and *E. muellerana* Howitt, and is found in New South Wales, Queensland and Victoria. It is a yellowish or yellowish-brown wood, with a straight grain, sometimes interlocked, and a medium fine texture. It weighs from 850 kg/m³ to 950 kg/m³ when dried, and is a durable timber used for building construction, posts, piles, bridge and wharf construction and sleepers.

TALLOWWOOD

Eucalyptus microcorys F. Muell.   Family : Myrtaceae

Distribution
New South Wales and Queensland.

The tree
Attains a height of 30m to 45m and a diameter of up to 1.5m.

The timber
The sapwood is not well-defined, and the heartwood is light yellowish-brown to brown in colour. The grain is interlocked, and the texture even and medium coarse. Planed surfaces are mildly lustrous and slightly waxy or greasy, a feature that gives the timber its common name. The wood is heavy, weighing about 990 kg/m³ when dried.

Drying
A very refractory timber, prone to check severely, and requiring great care to avoid existing shakes from extending.

Strength
Apart from its resistance to splitting, which is rather poor, tallowwood is a very strong timber, almost twice as strong as European oak.

Durability
Very durable.

Working qualities
Bearing in mind its density and hardness, tallowwood is only moderately difficult to work by hand, while its resistance to cutting by machines is not too severe. Smooth surfaces can be obtained in planing, but the interlocked, and frequently wavy grain usually requires a reduction of cutting angle to 20° to help avoid the grain picking up. The wood turns quite well, but is rather difficult to stain, although it can be polished reasonably.

Uses
Flooring, where high resistance to wear is a requirement, wharf and bridge decking, piling, posts, structural work, cross-arms.

'TASMANIAN OAK'

Eucalyptus spp.   Family : Myrtaceae

The British standard name 'Tasmanian oak', has been adopted since it is commonly applied to certain species of *Eucalyptus* exported from Australia. It is however, botanically inappropriate, and the following trade descriptions, based on Australian nomenclature, are given for clarification.
Eucalyptus obliqua L'Herit. produces messmate (Australian standard name), otherwise known as messmate stringybark, brown-top stringybark, 'Australian oak', 'Tasmanian oak'.
This occurs in New South Wales, Queensland, South Australia, Victoria and Tasmania.
E. delegatensis R. T. Bak. syn. *E. gigantea* Hook f. produces

'alpine ash' (Australian standard name), otherwise known as white-top or gum-top stringybark, woollybutt, 'Australian oak', 'Tasmanian oak'.

This occurs in New South Wales, Victoria and Tasmania.

E. regnans F. Muell. produces mountain ash (Australian standard name), otherwise known as stringy gum, swamp gum, white mountain ash, Victorian ash, 'Australian oak', 'Tasmanian oak'.

This occurs in Victoria and Tasmania.

The tree

The trees can be very large, attaining a height of 60m to 90m and a diameter of 2m but exploitable trees are generally much smaller.

The timber

The timbers of the three species are similar in appearance and are generally difficult to separate, nor is it usually necessary to do this, however the following descriptions give a guide to their separate identification.

E. obliqua.

The wood is usually of a pale to light-brown colour, but some Tasmanian specimens are distinctly pink, and bordering on reddish-brown. The growth rings are quite distinct, due to the crowding of pores in the early-wood; usually of straight grain and fissile, and the texture is open to moderately open. Gum veins are common and the weight of the wood varies from 608 kg/m^3 to 880 kg/m^3 with an average after reconditioning, of 710 kg/m^3.

E. delegatensis.

The wood is pale brown in colour, but often with distinct pinkish tints, usually straight-grained, and of open texture. The growth-rings are generally distinct with a definite tendency for the pores to be clustered in the early-wood and practically absent from the late-wood. Gum veins generally less in evidence. The wood weighs between 560 kg/m^3 and 800 kg/m^3 with an average weight of 610 kg/m^3 after reconditioning.

E. regnans.

The wood varies in colour from almost white, to pale brown, but some specimens show a pink tinge. The grain is usually straight, but is sometimes interlocked or wavy, such material often producing an attractive fiddle-back figure on quarter-sawn surfaces, while the texture is open. Growth-rings are not always distinct, and gum veins are sometimes very prominent. The wood weighs between 448 kg/m³ and 768 kg/m³ with an average weight of 630 kg/m³ after reconditioning.

Drying
All these species are rather difficult to dry, particularly in thick sizes. The timber is prone to surface checking during the early stages of drying unless care is taken and there is a definite tendency for internal checking and collapse to develop. Air drying prior to kilning is said to give the best results, while high temperature reconditioning treatment is usually satisfactory in removing collapse.

Strength
Variable in general strength properties, but by comparison with true oak (*Quercus* spp.) they are much tougher, stiffer and rather stronger in bending.

Durability
Moderately durable.

Working qualities
The general run of material saws and machines quite well, and is similar to European ash in most operations although a little less hard. Resawing by deep-cutting thick material is not always satisfactory, and the use of thicknesses as originally sawn is generally preferable. The wood takes a smooth finish, can be glued, stained and polished satisfactorily. It takes and holds screws well, but tends to split in nailing.

Uses
Furniture, joinery, panelling, weatherboards, agricultural implements, boxes, crates, flooring (light to moderate traffic), handles, cooperage, building, general construction and plywood.

TAUN

Pometia pinnata   Family : Sapindaceae

Other names
kasai, awa, ako (Solomons) ; tava (Western Samoa) ; ohabu (Papua New Guinea) ; malugai (Philippines).

Distribution
A common species (with others) of the Pacific Islands.

The tree
The trees attain a height of 36m to 45m with a diameter above the buttressed base of 1.0m. Some specimens may be of poor form or slightly twisted, while butt rot is often found in over-mature trees.

The timber
The sapwood is whitish in colour, up to 50mm wide, while the heartwood is a pale pinkish-brown, turning a dull reddish-brown with age. The grain is usually straight, but may be inter-locked or wavy, and the texture is coarse and uneven. The wood weighs about 750 kg/m^3 when dried.

Drying
The timber needs care in drying in order to avoid warping and splitting tendencies. Shrinkage is 3.3 per cent radially, and 5.6 per cent tangentially.

Strength
The timber has similar strength properties to those of European beech.

Durability
Moderately durable.

Working qualities
Works and machines reasonably well, with a moderate dulling effect on cutting edges. With care, a good finish can be obtained in planing and moulding. It is said to take glue and the normal finishing treatments without difficulty.

Uses
A versatile timber, suited not only to structural work, but for peeling for veneer, turnery, boat planking and framing, pianos, wharf decking, flooring, bobbins, mouldings, joinery, door and window frames, panelling, and in some cases furniture and cabinets.

TAWA

Beilschmiedia tawa B et H. f.   Family: Lauraceae

Distribution
New Zealand.

General characteristics
A whitish to yellowish-coloured wood, with a straight grain, and fine texture, not unlike sycamore in appearance. It weighs about 750 kg/m^3 when dried. The rays produce a fine fleck figure on quarter-sawn surfaces.

Uses
Interior finish, panelling, furniture, joinery, veneer and flooring, for which purpose it has a high resistance to wear.

A further species of *Beilschmiedia* occurs in New Zealand, *B. taraire*, producing commercial taraire timber. This is similar in general appearance to tawa, but is lighter in weight, about 680 kg/m^3 and is reddish-brown in colour. It has similar uses to tawa.

Both species are non-durable and both are included in New Zealand grading rules under Clears (specially selected boards), Dressing A (natural finish boards, one face and edge) and Building A (1st class framing grade), but whereas at one time, long lengths and wide boards were readily obtainable, present day supplies are more restricted.

Three further species of *Beilschmiedia* occur in Australia, as follows, *B. bancroftii* (F. M. Bail.) C. T. White. produces yellow walnut, otherwise known as yellow nut and canary ash.

B. obtusifolia (F. Muell. ex Meissn.) F. Muell. produces blush walnut, otherwise known as hard bollygum or tormenta.

B. elliptica C. T. White et W. D. Francis produces grey walnut. The timber varies according to species from yellowish to light grey to light brown in colour, generally with straight to inter-locking grain, and with a typical fleck figure. The uses are similar to those of tawa and taraire. None of these species is related to the true walnuts (Juglandaceae).

TEA TREE

Melaleuca spp.   Family : Myrtaceae

At least sixteen species of *Melaleuca* occur in Australia and Papua New Guinea. The following is a brief description of *M. leucadendron* (L.) L. known as the New Guinea tea tree or broad-leaved tea tree of Australia.

General characteristics

The sapwood is light pinkish-brown in colour, and the heart-wood is a shade darker. The grain is straight or slightly inter-locked, and the texture is fine and even. The wood weighs about 750 kg/m³ when dried, and shrinkage is 3.3 per cent radially, and 4.5 per cent tangentially when drying from the green to 12 per cent moisture content.

The wood is strong, and similar to karri in general strength properties. It is classified as durable.

Uses

Structural and engineering ; sawn construction timber, cross arms, sleepers, heavy decking, piles, poles and posts. Non-structural ; fences and packing cases.

TERMINALIA SPECIES

The Combretaceae includes a number of species of the genus *Terminalia* found in Papua New Guinea, the Solomon Islands and Australia, as follows.

T. brassii, *T. kaernbachii*, *T. faveolata*, and *T. rubiginosa*, pro-duce brown terminalia from Papua New Guinea, while *T. brassii* is the principal species producing dafo from the Solo-mons, also known as homba, peo, maranuri and kopika. This species is another of those selected for extended provenance trials in the Solomons.

T. sepicana, *T. catappa*, *T. microcarpa* and *T. canaliculata*, produce red-brown terminalia of Papua New Guinea.

T. calamansanai, *T. copelandii*, *T. complanata*, *T. longespicata*, *T. solomonensis* and *T. hypargyrea*, produce yellow terminalia of Papua New Guinea.

T. sericocarpa, produces damson or sovereign wood of Australia, found in Queensland and the Northern Territories.

The tree
In the main these are all fast-growing trees, often reaching a height of 45m and a diameter above the buttresses of 1.5m or more.

The timber
The heartwood of the various species varies in colour, from pale yellow to light to dark brown, depending on species, while the grain, usually shallowly interlocked, is sometimes wavy or slightly crossed. The texture varies from medium to coarse.

The separation into the Papua New Guinea trade descriptions is not entirely due to colour differences, but rather that the grouping separates the timbers on the basis of physical and mechanical properties, as follows,

Brown terminalia; weight, 460 kg/m^3 when dried, shrinkage in drying from the green to 12 per cent moisture content, 1.8 per cent radially, 4.2 per cent tangentially. A relatively weak wood, unsuited to constructional work. Classified as being non-durable.

Red-brown terminalia; weight 540 kg/m^3 when dried, shrinkage said to be low. Strength properties similar to those of celtis. Durability variable, from non-durable to moderately durable.

Yellow terminalia; weight, 460 kg/m^3 when dried, shrinkage 1.9 per cent radially, 3.8 per cent tangentially. Strength properties about 10 per cent below those of red-brown terminalia in most categories, but about 15 per cent lower in modulus of elasticity.

Working qualities
Generally, all types are rather difficult to work and machine; there is a moderate to fairly severe dulling effect on cutting edges, and grain irregularities make planing and moulding to a smooth surface rather difficult. Selected logs are said to convert well to veneer, but some doubt must be expressed as to the economics of this. End use recommendations from Papua New Guinea also suggest the wood of all types can be stained, polished and glued satisfactorily.

Uses
Brown terminalia; light framing, flooring and decking, furniture,

mouldings, veneer, interior trim, joinery, panelling, plywood and doors.

Red-brown terminalia; as above, but in addition sawn construction timber. Veneer is given as both peeled and sliced, but plywood is omitted.

Yellow terminalia; as brown terminalia.

TURPENTINE

Syncarpia glomulifera (Sm.)   Family : Myrtaceae
Niedenzu

Other names
lustre, red lustre.

Distribution
Queensland and the Blue Mountains and coastal area of New South Wales.

The timber
A reddish-brown to brown timber, with an interlocked grain, and fine to medium uniform texture, weighing about 950 kg/m^3 when dried. The wood closely resembles brush box in appearance, and since turpentine has certain advantages when used in marine situations it may be advisable to know of simple methods for separating the two species. A drop of ferric chloride solution placed on the surface of turpentine turns black, while on brush box it turns green. Alternatively, a small splinter of dry heartwood of turpentine when burned as a match, leaves a black charcoal ,whereas with brush box a thick white or brownish ash is left.

Drying
Difficult to dry, with a marked tendency for plain-sawn material to check badly unless dried very carefully. Collapse can occur both in air drying and in the kiln. Controlled air drying prior to kilning and reconditioning is recommended.

Strength
A hard, dense timber with high strength properties. In most strength categories it is stronger than European oak, about 60 per cent superior to that timber in bending, stiffness, and com-

pressive strength along the grain when dry, and some 30 per cent harder. In resistance to impact it is about equal to oak.

Durability
Extremely durable.

Working qualities
Hard to work with hand tools, but machines with moderate ease. The wood turns well, and usually planes well, although a reduction of cutting angle to 20° is needed when curly or wavy grain is present. It is rather hard to nail, but holds screws well.

Uses
Marine piling, poles, fence posts, sleepers, underwater planking and sheathing, wharf decking, and constructional purposes. For piling, the bark is usually left on when used in the round, as this is said to increase the timber's resistance to marine borer attack.

VITEX
Vitex spp.   Family: Verbenaceae

The following species of *Vitex* have some commercial significance in the Pacific area.
V. cofassus occurs in Papua New Guinea and the Solomon Islands, and is known as vitex, with a prefix denoting origin. The Solomons wood also being known under the vernacular names of vasa, vata, asang bitum and hasara.
Two further species, *V. glabra* and *V. quinata*, occur in Irian Jaya and their timber is known as West Irian vitex.

The tree
Under favourable conditions the trees attain a height of 30m with a clear bole of some 15m and a diameter of 1.0m above the buttressed base. but often the tree is badly shaped and fluted.

The timber
The sapwood is usually about 50mm wide, pale yellowish-

brown in colour, while the heartwood is a darker yellowish-brown or walnut brown. The grain is straight to interlocked, and the texture is medium fine. The Papua New Guinea and Solomons wood is hard, and fairly heavy, weighing from 720 to 880 kg/m^3 when dried, but the Irian timber is much lighter, about 570 kg/m^3.

Drying
All types are said to dry quite well with only minor degrade. Shrinkage values for Irian vitex are recorded as low (3.5 to 5.0 per cent tangentially, 2.0 to 3.0 per cent radially), while New Guinea vitex, (and presumably Solomons vitex) is recorded as 4.1 per cent tangentially, and 1.8 per cent radially.

Strength
The strength of *V. cafassus* compares favourably with that of 'silver beech' (*Nothofagus*), while that of *V. glabra* and *V. quinata* is from 10 to 15 per cent inferior in general terms.

Durability
All types are durable.

Working qualities
Works and machines quite well, and gives a good, smooth finish in planing and moulding with straight-grained material, but a reduction of cutting angle to 15° is generally necessary in order to avoid the grain picking up. The timber is said to take the normal finishing treatments without difficulty, and to accept glue, screws and nails satisfactorily.

Uses
The heavier timber is used for sawn construction timber, sleepers, heavy decking for bridges and wharves, and for posts, poles and piles. Otherwise, the wood of all types is used in boat building for planking, ribs, stringers, keelsons and for joinery, sills, stair treads, linings, light framing, furniture and cabinet work. It has been suggested for plywood, but there is some doubt as to whether this is economically feasible.

WANDOO

Eucalyptus wandoo Blakely. syn.   Family : Myrtaceae
E. redunca Schau. var. *elata* Benth.

Other names
white gum.

Distribution
Western Australia.

The tree
Generally 18m to 24m tall with a diameter of 0.75m.

The timber
The wood is brownish-red in colour, very hard and dense, weighing about 1110 kg/m^3 when dried.

Uses
Classified as very durable, wandoo is used for short piles, railway sleepers, boat-building (ribs, bends and knees), waggon building, bridge and wharf planking and decking, fencing and for mining timbers. It is said to be highly resistant to chemical reaction when used in conjunction with iron or steel eg when bolted down.
Two further species occur in western Australia and produce wandoo. *E. accedens* W. V. Fitzg. produces powderbark wandoo, while *E. lane-poolei* Maid. produces salmonbark wandoo or white salmon gum.

WATER GUM

Eugenia spp. and *Syzygium* spp.   Family : Myrtaceae

Other names
kelat (Malaysia) ; satinash (Australia).

General characteristics
Various species of the above genera occur in Papua New Guinea, and as certain are grouped to produce Malaysian kelat, so selected species are grouped to produce commercial PNG

water gum. Accordingly, there is some variation in the appearance of the wood. It ranges in colour from greyish-brown and reddish-brown to dark brown, sometimes with a purple cast, and without lustre or figure. The grain is interlocked or wavy, and the texture is moderately fine to fine. The weight of the wood varies according to species from 650-770 kg/m^3 when dry.

The wood is fairly easy to work, although with a tendency for the grain to pick up in planing. It can be finished smoothly and can be stained and polished. The wood is moderately durable and is suitable for general construction and joinery.

'WAU BEECH'

Elmerrillia papuana   Family : Magnoliaceae

General characteristics
This is not a true beech (*Fagus*), but a medium weight timber found in moderate supply in Papua New Guinea, of a pale brown to golden brown colour, sometimes with a slight greenish cast. The wood is quite attractive, with a natural lustre and a straight to interlocked grain, usually with a shallow ribbon figure on quarter-sawn surfaces and a flame figure on plain-sawn surfaces due to the growth rings. The wood weighs about 470 kg/m^3 when dry, dries easily with little degrade, has good machining and finishing qualities, glues satisfactorily and is suitable for furniture, joinery, plywood and when selected for decorative veneer.

The wood is durable and is difficult to impregnate with preservatives.

'WHITE ASH, AUSTRALIAN'

Eucalyptus fraxinoides   Family : Myrtaceae
Dean et Maiden

Distribution
New South Wales.

General characteristics
White ash is very similar in appearance to Tasmanian oak, the wood being white to pale brown in colour, sometimes with a

pinkish tint. It has a straight grain, is fissile, and the texture is moderately open. The wood weighs 690 kg/m³ when dried. Like Tasmanian oak, the growth rings are mostly well-defined, commonly marked by a zone free of pores.

Some light-weight specimens of *Eucalyptus globulus*, one of the species making up blue gum, are very similar in appearance to 'white ash'. They may be separated by the burning splinter test, white ash giving a charcoal, blue gum producing an ash.

Uses

'Australian white ash' is a durable timber used for purposes to which lightness, strength, toughness and bending qualities, are requirements, eg cooperage, vehicle bodies, joinery and constructional work.

'WHITE BEECH'

Gmelina spp.   Family: Verbenaceae

Gmelina dalrympleana (F. Muell.) H. J. Lam. syn. *G. macrophylla* Benth. *G. fasciculiflora* Benth. and *G. leichhardtii* F. Muell. ex Benth. occurs in Australia, and produces 'white beech' (Australian standard name). The timber is unrelated to true beech (*Fagus*), but related to teak (*Tectona*), and this is reflected in the alternative Australian name of grey teak.

G. moluccana. syn. *G. salomonensis* occurs in Papua New Guinea, where it is also called 'white beech', and in the Solomon Islands, where it is known as arakoko, koko, buti, kangali or oarawaraha.

General characteristics

There is no distinction between sapwood and heartwood by colour, the wood being whitish, with a yellow or grey tinge. The wood has a slight lustre and a somewhat greasy feel. The grain is generally straight, and the texture is medium fine. The wood weighs on average, 460 kg/m³ when dried. It is said to dry easily and well, and to work and machine quite readily. Non-durable to moderately durable.

Uses

Furniture, cabinets, cooperage, panelling, boat planking and oars, toys, boxes, musical instruments, door and window frames, louvres, turnery and veneer.

'WHITE BIRCH'

Schizomeria ovata D. Don. and   Family: Cunoniaceae
S. whitei J. Mattf.

Other names
crabapple, humbug, squeaker (Australia) ; schizomeria (Papua New Guinea) ; bea bea, malafelo, hambia (Solomons).

Distribution
New South Wales and Queensland. A further, and similar species, *S. serrata* occurs in the Solomon Islands and Papua New Guinea.

The tree
Attains a height of 30m and a diameter of 0.75m above the buttressed base.

The timber
The sapwood is wide, said to be 100mm to 150mm wide in the Australian species, and 75mm to 100mm wide in the Solomon Islands wood. The heartwood is pale brown in colour, not very well defined from the whitish-brown sapwood. The grain is straight or interlocked, and the texture fine and uniform. The wood weighs from 560 kg/m^3 to 672 kg/m^3 when dried.

Drying
No data are available, but the wood is said to have a medium shrinkage, values given for Papua New Guinea timber, 4.8 per cent tangentially, 2.5 per cent radially.

Strength
Similar to those of 'silver beech' (*Nothofagus*).

Durability
Non-durable.

Working qualities
Reputed to work and machine without undue difficulty, and to finish cleanly and smoothly in planing and moulding, although where interlocked grain is present, some picking up could be expected, particularly on quarter-sawn surfaces. End

uses suggest that staining, polishing, gluing, nailing and screwing can be carried out without undue difficulty.

Uses
Coffin-boards, turnery, match splints, shelving and interior trim, plywood. Papua New Guinea sources also include light framing, lining, furniture and cabinet-making as further suggested uses.

PNG WHITE CHEESEWOOD

Alstonia spp.   Family : Apocynaceae

Other names
dita (Philippines) ; milky pine (Australia) ; pulai (Malaysia).

General characteristics
Malaysian pulai is the product of two principal species of *Alstonia*, ie *A. angustiloba* and *A. spathulata*, but a third species, *A. scholaris* may be included in commercial parcels.

This latter species occurs singly in Papua New Guinea producing a similar timber known as white cheesewood.

Sapwood and heartwood are not differentiated, the wood being a uniform creamy-white or light yellowish-brown. Latex traces may appear on tangential faces as lens-shaped scars. The grain is usually straight but may be interlocked, and the texture is moderately fine to moderately coarse. It weighs about 340 kg/m^3 when dry. The timber dries easily, with little degrade, machines and finishes quite well and has good gluing properties. The wood is sometimes marred by the latex traces, but in general, and with some selection, it is a useful wood for pattern making, turnery, carving, mouldings and core stock for plywood.

YELLOW GUM

Eucalyptus leucoxylon F. Muell.   Family : Myrtaceae

Other names
blue gum, white ironbark.

Distribution
South Australia, New South Wales and Victoria.

General characteristics

The sapwood, which is about 25mm wide is a shade lighter in colour than the heartwood, which is yellowish, pinkish or light brown. The grain is interlocked and the texture somewhat fine and uniform. The wood is hard, non-fissile and heavy, weighing about 850 kg/m³ when dried.

Yellow gum is used for piles and poles, mining timbers, sleepers, bridge and general construction, felloes, posts.

A further species, *E. johnstonii* Maid. including *E. subcrenulata* Maid. et Blakely. occurs in Tasmania. Formerly known as brown gum or Johnston's gum, this is now classified under the Australian standard name of Tasmanian yellow gum. It has similar uses to *E. leucoxylon*.

PART II SOFTWOODS

ARAUCARIA SPECIES

The Araucariaceae family includes several species of the genus *Araucaria* found in Australasia. The following are the principal species.

Araucaria bidwillii Hook. produces 'bunya pine', otherwise known as bunya or 'Queensland pine'. This is found in Queensland.

A. cunninghamii Sweet. produces 'hoop pine', also called 'Queensland pine'. This occurs in Queensland, New South Wales and Papua New Guinea.

A. heterophylla (Salisb.) Franco. syn. *A. excelsa* (Lamb.) R. Br. produces 'Norfolk Island pine', found in New South Wales and South Australia.

A. klinkii syn. *A. hunsteinii*. produces 'klinki pine' of Papua New Guinea.

General characteristics

All the above species are similar in appearance to 'Parana pine' (*A. angustifolia*) except they lack the pinkish streaks often common in that timber. They differ from 'kauri pine' in that they are mostly whitish or light-coloured, whereas kauri forms a brownish heartwood.

The following is a guide to the general characteristics of the main species.

'BUNYA PINE'

A straight-grained timber, light brown in colour, with little distinction between sapwood and heartwood, except where sap-stain occurs in the former, when this will be seen to be 75mm or more wide. The wood has a fine texture, and weighs about 510 kg/m^3 when dried. It is classified as being moderately durable.

'HOOP PINE'

The sapwood is wide, from 75mm to 150mm, light brown in colour, and sometimes flecked with blue-stain. The heartwood is a slightly darker brown, or yellowish brown, sometimes with a pinkish tinge. The grain is straight, the texture fine to very fine, and the wood is generally marked by leaf-traces, in some cases producing an attractive bird's eye figure. The wood weighs about 560 kg/m^3 when dried. Classified as non-durable.

'KLINKI PINE'

The sapwood is straw-coloured, not always distinct from the light yellow or very pale brown heartwood. The grain is straight, and the texture close and uniform. The wood has a natural lustre, and weighs about 448 kg/m^3 when dried. It is a non-durable timber.

Uses

All species mentioned have similar uses, including flooring, light construction, pattern-making, plywood, joinery, linings, furniture, cabinet-making, turnery, dowels, pulp, mouldings, matchboxes, broom handles, battery separators.

'CELERY-TOP PINE'

Phyllocladus spp.   Family : Podocarpaceae

Distribution

P.asplenifolius (Labill.) Hook. f. syn. *P. rhomboidalis* L. C. and A. Rich. occurs in Tasmania, while a further species, *P. hypophyllus*, is found in Papua New Guinea.

General characteristics

A yellow-coloured wood with clearly defined growth rings, straight grain and fine texture, weighing about 640 kg/m³ for *P. asplenifolius*, and 540 kg/m³ for *P. hypophyllus* when dried. Durability varies from moderately durable to durable, and the timber is used for agricultural implements, fencing, carpentry and small trees in the round for masts for small vessels.

KAURI

Agathis spp.   Family : Araucariaceae

A number of species of *Agathis* are found in the Pacific area as described below.

NEW ZEALAND KAURI

Other name
'kauri pine' (UK).

The tree
Agathis australis Salisb. occurs in New Zealand, and attains a height of 30m and a diameter of about 1.0m although it can reach a much greater size.

The timber
Kauri somewhat resembles the botanically associated 'Parana pine', but is generally darker in colour, and coarser in texture.
The colour of the wood varies from a pale greyish-brown colour to dark reddish-brown or yellowish-brown, the darker-coloured wood containing the most resin. It should be noted that neither resin cells nor resin canals occur in kauri, but resin is usually abundant in the ray cells and in vertical tracheids, usually near the rays, where it takes the form of resin plugs. This is a hard resin which contains little or no essential oil, and therefore is not fluid in dried timber, and accordingly, does not affect the painting properties of the wood.
The timber is characterized by its regular growth, for even when growth rings are apparent, there is generally little difference between early-wood and late-wood. The wood is lustrous, has a straight grain, and weighs about 580 kg/m³ when dried.

Drying
The timber dries at a moderate rate, with a tendency to warp, although this is usually more noticeable in low-grade stock. Checking is usually small, but the timber is said to shrink appreciably in a longitudinal direction.

Strength
New Zealand kauri is similar to pitch pine in general strength properties, but is some 25 per cent weaker in compression along the grain.

Durability
Moderately durable.

Working qualities
The timber is easy to work with both hand and machine tools; the dulling effect on cutting edges is very slight, and a clean, smooth finish can be obtained in planing and moulding, although stock with a mottled surface caused by grain irregularities, may require a reduced cutting angle of about 20° to avoid slight grain pick-up. It takes nails and screws well, stains, paints and polishes excellently and can be glued satisfactorily.

Uses
According to grade quality, the timber is used for vats, boatbuilding and for building construction. The timber is graded in New Zealand as Clears; specially selected boards. Dressing A; natural finish boards, one face and edge. Dressing B; board grade, suitable painting. Building A; 1st class framing grade. Building B; 2nd class framing grade. Common; rough and temporary work.

QUEENSLAND KAURI
This is the product of the following,
Agathis microstachya Bail. f. and White. otherwise known as bull kauri or North Queensland kauri.
A. palmerstonii F. Muell. knowh as North Queensland kauri.
A. robusta Masters. known as South Queensland kauri.
Various other species of *Agathis* produce blue, and black kauri, which are usually included in commercial North Queensland kauri.

The tree
The trees can grow to a height of 45m and a diameter of 1.5m or very much more, but they have been severely exploited in the past, and apart from a few plantations of A. *palmerstonii*, supplies of naturally-grown kauri are rather limited, especially of South Queensland stock.

The timber
Queensland kauri varies in colour from pale cream to light brown or medium pinkish-brown. It has a straight grain, fine, uniform texture, and is appreciably lighter in weight than New Zealand kauri, weighing about 480 kg/m^3 when dried.

Drying
Dries fairly rapidly, without undue degrade.

Strength
By comparison with New Zealand kauri, the Queensland timber is lighter in weight, and inferior in bending strength and stiffness.

Durability
Non-durable.

Working qualities
Easily worked and finished.

Uses
High-class joinery, cabinets, pattern making, butter boxes and churns, battery separators, cheap plywood.
Fijian kauri is the product of *Agathis vitiensis* Benth. & Hook. locally known as dakua. This is a similar wood to New Zealand kauri, and weighs about 550 kg/m^3 when dried. It is non-durable, and is used locally for building and joinery, carpentry, boxes and crates.

PODOCARPUS SPECIES

The Podocarpaceae family includes several species of *Podocarpus* found in Australasia. The following are the principal species.

Podocarpus dacrydioides A. Rich. produces 'New Zealand white pine', also known as kahikatea.

P. spicatus R. Br. produces New Zealand matai, also known as 'black pine'.

P. totara D. Don. and *P. hallii* T. Kirk. produces totara, found in New Zealand.

P. amarus Bl. produces 'Australian black pine', found in Queensland and also in Papua New Guinea.

P. elatus R. Br. ex Endl. produces 'Australian brown pine', or 'she pine', found in New South Wales and Queensland.

Timbers of the *Podocarpus* genera are unlike the softwoods of the Northern Hemisphere; generally, there is little difference between early-wood and late-wood, and the growth rings are not distinct, neither do resin ducts appear, and the wood of the various species accordingly have more the appearance of a hardwood. The following is a description of the principal species.

MATAI

The tree
The tree attains a height of 18m to 40m but with a merchantable bole of 5m to 20m and a diameter of 0.5m or more, up to about 1.5m.

The timber
The wood varies in colour, from yellow to brown, generally being a warm yellowish-brown. It has a straight grain, fine, even texture, and weighs about 630 kg/m^3 when dried. It is the only one of the Podocarps mentioned here which often shows a dimpled grain, due to indentations of the cambium.

Drying
Dries fairly rapidly without undue degrade.

Strength
Similar to European redwood in general strength properties, but is some 40 per cent harder.

Durability
Moderately durable.

Working qualities

Works readily by hand or machine tools and has little dulling effect on their cutting edges. It planes and moulds to a smooth finish, and turns cleanly. Can be stained, polished and painted effectively, and takes glue well but tends to split in nailing and screwing.

Uses

Flooring, bridge decking, furniture, joinery, and for building purposes, where it is classified in New Zealand as a Group 1 timber and graded as Clears, Dressing A, Dressing B, Building A, Building B, and Commons (see kauri for grade uses).

TOTARA

The tree

The tree attains a height of 39m but merchantable boles are generally from 9m to 24m in length in *P. totara*, and from 7m to 18m in *P. hallii*. The diameter varies from 0.5m to 1.5m.

The timber

The wood is medium reddish-brown in colour, with a straight grain, and a fairly fine, even texture. It weighs about 480 kg/m³ when dried.

Drying

Dries rapidly and well, and holds its place well after drying.

Strength

Compared with European redwood, totara is some 25 to 30 per cent weaker in bending and stiffness, and about 15 per cent weaker in compression along the grain. It is therefore more suited for use as columns and posts than as beams or joists.

Durability

Durable.

Working qualities

Works easily and well, but needs sharp cutters to produce a good, clean finish. The wood holds nails and screws well and gives fair results with paint, stain and polish.

Uses

Its high resistance to decay, and also to marine borers, renders totara a very desirable wood for exacting uses, but owing to its present-day limited production, it finds most use as building piles or as window joinery. Like matai, it is classed as a Group 1 timber in New Zealand. It was the traditional timber for Maori carvings and canoes, and is suitable for flooring, and veneer, especially from selected logs of *P. hallii*, which tend to a more interlocked and wavy grain development. Veneer of this type used to be exported to Europe for use in piano and cabinet work.

'WHITE PINE'

General characteristics

'New Zealand white pine', or kahikatea has a creamy white sapwood, and a light, to bright yellow heartwood, with a straight grain, and fine, even texture. It weighs about 470 kg/m³ when dried, and is moderately durable. It is easily dried and worked, and is used for flooring, framing, joinery, veneer, kitchen furniture, weatherboards (treated), boat planking, casks and boxes. It is classified in New Zealand as a Group 1 timber for building purposes.

'BLACK PINE'

General characteristics

'Black pine' of Australia and Papua New Guinea (the timber from this area includes *P. nerifolius* as well as *P. amarus*), is a light-yellowish-brown coloured wood, weighing about 430 kg/m³ when dried. It is said to dry rapidly and well, and to hold well after drying. In drying from the green to 12 per cent moisture content, shrinkage is 3.4 per cent tangentially, and 1.3 per cent radially.

It is classified as being non-durable, and is used for light framing, lining, flooring, joinery, mouldings, veneer, furniture, turnery and shelving.

A further species, *P. ferrugineus*, occurs in New Zealand, and produces miro, a light to dark brown-coloured wood, weighing about 640 kg/m³ when dried. It is moderately durable, and is used for joinery, turnery and building purposes.

313

RIMU

Dacrydium cupressinum Soland   Family: Podocarpaceae

Other names
'red pine'.

Distribution
New Zealand.

The tree
Attains a height of 18m to 36m and a diameter of 0.5m to 1.2m on average, but may reach 2.5m.

The timber
The sapwood is a pale yellowish colour, gradually darkening through an intermediate zone to the heartwood (truewood), which is a pale brownish-straw colour when freshly cut, often streaked with greyish-brown, and turning a light brown colour after exposure. The intermediate zone is said to have the same properties as heartwood. It has a straight grain and a fine, even texture, and the wood weighs about 610 kg/m^3 when dried.

Drying
Dries readily with a slight tendency to surface checking.

Strength
About 40 per cent harder than European redwood, and about 15 per cent weaker in compression along the grain. In other strength categories it is about equal to redwood.

Durability
Moderately durable.

Working qualities
Works easily by hand and machine tools, and has only a small dulling effect on cutting edges. It planes and moulds cleanly, and can be stained and polished. It glues fairly well, holds screws reasonably well, but tends to split in nailing.

Uses
One of the most important present day softwoods of New

Zealand, it is used for cladding, flooring, furniture, interior trim, and for plywood, decorative veneer and panelling.

The Tasmanian species, *D. franklinii* Hook. produces 'huon pine'. This is cream to light pinkish-brown in colour, with an extremely fine texture, and very distinct growth rings. It weighs about 530 kg/m^3 when dried, and is used for joinery, boat planking and furniture.

USE GUIDE FOR AUSTRALASIAN TIMBERS

AGRICULTURAL IMPLEMENTS

gum, blue
ironbark
jarrah
karri

kwila
malas
pine, celery top
turpentine

BOAT AND SHIP CONSTRUCTION

Decking
Calophyllum spp
gum, saligna
hopea, heavy
ironbark, grey
jarrah

karri
kamarere
kwila
padauk
terminalia, red-brown

Framing
gum, blue
gum, saligna
jarrah
karri

Meliaceae (knees)
padauk
taun
vitex
wandoo

Keels and Stems
gum, blue
gum, red river
gum, saligna
hopea, heavy

ironbark
jarrah
rata, northern
vitex

Masts
'cedar, Australian'

'pine, celery top'

Oars and Paddles
'beech, white' (*Gmelina*)
'cedar, Australian'

Flindersia spp
Meliaceae (paddles)

Planking
'cedar, Australian'
karri
Meliaceae
padauk

'pine, huon'
'pine, white'
taun
vitex

Superstructures
'cedar, Australian'
Flindersia spp

karri
Meliaceae
padauk

BOXES AND CRATES

'beech, red'
'beech, silver'
'beech, white (*Gmelina*)
Campnosperma spp
'cedar, Australian'
erima
gum, rose

kauri
'oak, Tasmanian'
'pine, bunya'
'pine, hoop'
'pine, klinki'
tea tree

CONSTRUCTION

Heavy
blackbutt
brushbox
celtis (hard)
gum, blue
gum, red river
gum, saligna
gum, spotted
gum, yellow
hopea, heavy
ironbark

jarrah
kamarere
karri
kwila
'oak, Tasmanian'
Palaquium spp.
planchonella (heavy)
stringybark
tallowwood
tea tree
turpentine

Light
ash, white
birch, white
celtis
Endospermum spp.
erima
Flindersia spp.
gum, rose
kauri
hopea, light
matai
Meliaceae
'oak, Tasmanian'

peppermint
'pine, black'
'pine, bunya'
'pine, hoop'
'pine, huon'
'pine, klinki'
'pine, white'
planchonella (light)
rimu
stringybark
totara
'walnut, Papua New Guinea'
'walnut, Queensland'

DOORS

'cedar, Australian'
Flindersia spp.
karri
Meliaceae
Palaquium spp.

'pine, black'
'pine, white'
taun
terminalia

317

FANCY GOODS

coconut palm
'oak, she'

oak, silky

FLOORING

beech, myrtle
beech, New Guinea
beech, silver
blackbutt
brushbox
Calophyllum spp.
celtis
coachwood
Endospermum spp.
gum, red river
gum, saligna
gum, spotted
heavy hopea
ironbark, red
jarrah
kamarere
karri
kwila

matai
'oak, PNG'
'oak, Tasmanian'
padauk
Palaquium spp.
'pine, black'
'pine, bunya'
'pine, hoop'
'pine, klinki'
'pine, white'
planchonella
rimu
tallowwood
taun
tawa
terminalia
'walnut, PNG'
'walnut, Queensland'

FURNITURE AND CABINETS

'beech, myrtle'
'beech, PNG'
'beech, silver'
'beech, white' (*Gmelina*)
black bean
blackwood
Calophyllum spp.
'cedar, Australian'
celtis
coachwood
Endospermum spp.
Flindersia spp.
jarrah
kamarere
karri

hopea, light
Meliaceae
'oak, PNG'
'oak, she'
oak, silky
'oak, Tasmanian'
padauk
Palaquium spp.
'pine, white' (kitchen)
rimu
taraire
taun
terminalia
'walnut, PNG'
'walnut, Queensland'

GUN STOCKS

blackwood
coachwood

Flindersia spp.
padauk

JOINERY

High-class
black bean
blackwood
Flindersia spp.
jarrah
karri
Meliaceae
'oak, PNG'
oak, silky

padauk
Palaquium spp.
rimu
tawa
taun
taraire
'walnut, PNG'
'walnut, Queensland'

Utility
beech, myrtle
beech, red
beech, silver
beech, white
Calophyllum spp.
Campnosperma spp.
'cedar, Australian'
celtis
coachwood
Endospermum spp.
Flindersia spp.
kamarere
hopea, light
matai
Meliaceae

'oak, Tasmanian'
Palaquium spp.
peppermint
'pine, bunya'
'pine, black'
'pine, hoop'
'pine, huon'
'pine, klinki'
'pine, white'
planchonella
rimu
taun
terminalia
totara
water gum

MARINE PILING AND CONSTRUCTION

Under water

(a) Teredo infested waters

gum, blue

gum, red river

ironbark

jarrah

turpentine

(b) Non-Teredo waters, in addition to above

Calophyllum spp.

coconut palm

gum, yellow

kamarere

malas

planchonella (heavy)

stringybark

tallowwood

tea tree

totara

vitex (heavy)

wandoo

Above water

(a) docks, wharves, bridges, etc.

blackbutt

brush box

Calophyllum spp.

gum, blue

gum, saligna

gum, spotted

gum, yellow

ironbark

jarrah

kamarere

karri

malas

rata, northern

stringybark

tallowwood

tea tree

turpentine

(b) decking

beech, myrtle

blackbutt

brush box

Calophyllum spp.

gum, blue

gum, red river

ironbark, grey

jarrah

kamarere

karri

matai

planchonella (heavy)

tallowwood

taun

tea tree

terminalia, red-brown

turpentine

vitex (heavy)

wandoo

MUSICAL INSTRUMENTS

beech, white (*Gmelina*)
birch, white

taun

PATTERN MAKING

kauri
'pine, bunya'
'pine, hoop'

'pine, klinki'
white cheesewood, PNG

SPORTS GOODS

blackwood
coachwood

ironbark, red
northern rata

TURNERY

beech, myrtle
beech, red
beech, silver
beech, white
birch, white
brush box
Calophyllum spp.
coachwood
Endospermum spp.
'oak, she'

padauk
Palaquium spp.
'pine, black'
'pine, bunya'
'pine, hoop'
'pine, klinki'
planchonella
taun
'walnut, PNG'
white cheesewood PNG

VATS (CHEMICAL)

jarrah

kauri, NZ

VEHICLE BODIES

ash, white
beech, silver
Flindersia spp.
gum, blue
gum, saligna

gum, spotted
ironbark
northern rata
peppermint
wandoo

VENEER AND PLYWOOD

Corestock

amberoi	erima
Campnosperma spp.	gum, saligna
celtis	planchonella
coachwood	spondias

Decorative

black bean	padauk/amboyna
blackwood	*Palaquium* spp. (selected)
Calophyllum spp.	planchonella, red
Flindersia spp.	rimu
jarrah	taun (selected)
'oak, PNG'	terminalia
'oak, she' (selected)	'walnut, PNG' (selected)
oak, silky	'walnut, Queensland'

Utility (plywood, chip baskets, small laminated items, etc.)

amberoi	'oak, PNG'
beech, myrtle	'oak, Tasmanian'
birch, white	*Palaquium* spp.
Calophyllum spp.	'pine, black'
Campnosperma spp.	'pine, bunya'
celtis	'pine, hoop'
coachwood	'pine, klinki'
Endospermum spp.	'pine, white'
erima	rimu
Flindersia spp.	tawa
gum, saligna	taraire
kamarere	taun
karri	terminalia
kauri	

AMENABILITY OF HEARTWOOD TO PRESERVATIVE TREATMENT

Extremely resistant

beech, silver
beech, wau
beech, white, (*Gmelina*)
blackbutt
blackwood
brush box
cheesewood, white
gum, rose
gum, saligna
gum, spotted
gum, water
gum, yellow
hopea, heavy
ironbark
jarrah
kamarere
karri
kwila

malas
Meliaceae
  (*Aglaia* spp. *Amoora* spp.)
'oak', PNG
oak, she
padauk
Palaquium spp.
stringybark
tallowwood
taun
terminalia, brown,
  red-brown
totara
turpentine
vitex
'walnut, PNG'
wandoo

Resistant

beech, myrtle
birch, white
Calophyllum spp.
Flindersia spp.
gum, blue
gum, red river
hopea, light
kauri, NZ
matai

'oak, Tasmanian'
'pine, black'
'pine, bunya'
'pine, white'
planchonella, red
rimu
tawa
terminalia, yellow

Moderately resistant

Campnosperma spp.
'cedar, Australian'
celtis
labula

'pine, celery top'
'pine, hoop'
'pine, klinki'
planchonella, white

Permeable

amberoi
coachwood

Endospermum spp.
erima

The above classification refers to the ease with which a timber absorbs preservatives under both open-tank (non-pressure) and pressure treatments. Sapwood, although nearly always perishable, is usually much more permeable than heartwood, accordingly, the above classification refers to the relative resistance of heartwood to penetration.

Extremely resistant
Timbers that absorb only a small amount of preservative even under long pressure treatments. They cannot be penetrated to an appreciable depth laterally, and only to a very small extent longitudinally.

Resistant
Timbers difficult to impregnate under pressure and require a long period of treatment. It is often difficult to penetrate them laterally more than about 3mm to 6mm.
Incising is often used to obtain better treatment.

Moderately resistant
Timbers that are fairly easy to treat, and it is usually possible to obtain a lateral penetration of the order of 6mm to 18mm in about 2–3 hours under pressure, or a penetration of a large proportion of the vessels.

Permeable
Timbers that can be penetrated completely under pressure without difficulty, and can usually be heavily impregnated by the open-tank process.

TERMITE RESISTANCE

Termite activity represents a serious hazard to buildings in Australasia, particularly to house foundations. The chief food of termites is cellulose, which they obtain from living and dying vegetation and from wood and wood-based products.

Building legislation prescribes various forms of physical barrier systems to be incorporated into the construction of buildings, such as termite caps, against the attack by subterranean termites. However these will not necessarily prevent a colony of termites gaining access to a building structure, although their installation does serve as an early warning system when frequent and adequate inspection of a building is carried out, since the visual bridge created by the termite tubes, or free-standing access tunnels, passing over the caps, can be readily detected. Appropriate protective measures can then be applied, such as chemical treatment of the foundation soil.

Concrete, brick or steel piers that may support buildings do not offer any better protection from termites than do wood supports, as they may either construct internal tunnels through cavities or completely by-pass the foundation by tubes or access tunnels constructed on the face of seemingly impervious materials.

The use of timbers like jarrah and karri, red river gum, and other indigenous and imported timbers which offer some natural resistance to termite attack, minimises the generally disastrous effect of termites, but chemical soil treatments at the time of building, and preservative and insecticidal pressure treatment of building timber, not only widens the range of suitable timber species, but offers greater protection to termite attack. Termite caps, to be reasonably effective, must be in the form of a continuous physical barrier, free from perforation, but as mentioned they cannot be entirely relied upon to offer suitable safeguards against termite attack.

5

CENTRAL AMERICA AND THE CARIBBEAN

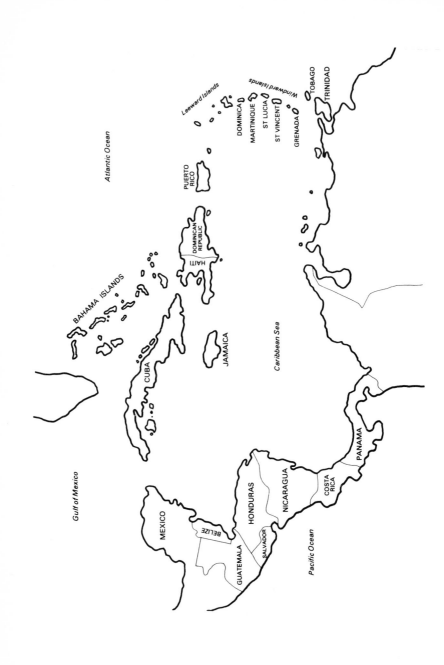

INTRODUCTION

This chapter is concerned with the present and potential commercial timber species which grow in Central America and the Caribbean islands which comprise the Greater and Lesser Antilles, that is, the comparatively narrow isthmus connecting the continents of North and South America, bounded on the north by Mexico, and on the South by Colombia, and lying between the Pacific Ocean and the Caribbean Sea, and the many West Indian islands which separate the Atlantic Ocean from the Caribbean Sea.

Central America, which includes Guatemala, Honduras, Salvador, Nicaragua, Costa Rica, Panama and Belize, is only about 1600 kilometres in length, with a width which varies from over 800 kilometres in the north to less than 80 kilometres in the south. The whole of this area can be roughly divided into three types of terrain, the mountainous core or tierras frias, the lower slopes and moderately elevated areas known as the tierras templadas, more suited to agriculture and cattle raising, and the coastal areas, the tierras calientes, which are covered by jungle-type forests which yield valuable timbers.

The various islands of the Greater Antilles, Cuba, Haiti, Jamaica and Puerto Rico also contain mountainous cores, whilst in the Lesser Antilles, Dominica, St Lucia and St Vincent are young volcanic islands.

Thus, by comparison with South America the forest resources of Central America and the Caribbean are relatively small. Nevertheless, they represent an important economic factor in the life of the area, both in terms of supporting local industry and in the export of wooden goods to different parts of the area and overseas, particularly to North America. For several decades now changes have been taking place in the forestry outlook of many of the islands in particular, and new planting programmes have been instituted involving the introduction of timber species from elsewhere in the tropics; teak is an example described in these pages.

Many of the timbers indigenous to the area have been known on the world's timber markets for centuries, especially mahogany, cedar, satinwood and pitch pine, but there are other species of great commercial interest. Reference should also be made to Timbers of the

World, Volume 1, Chapter 2, 'South America' to obtain as complete a picture as possible of the commercial timber species of these areas, with a description of their properties and uses, and thus to enable all who work with timber to assess the value of what in some cases are obscure species, for any immediate use.

PART I HARDWOODS

ALMACIGO

Bursera simaruba (L) Sarg.   Family : Burseraceae

Other names
red gombo, gumbo-limbo, chaca (Belize) ; West Indian birch
(Caribbean area generally).
The trade name 'birch' is confusing and should be discontinued,
since the true birches belong to the Betulaceae family of the
botanical group of Fagales, whereas *Bursera* species belong to
the Geraniales group.

Distribution
Southern Florida, throughout the West Indies, and on the
continent from southern Mexico, Central America and into
northern South America.

The tree
Generally a slender, unbuttressed tree of short to medium
height. It reaches its best development in the lowland forests,
where it attains a height of 18.0m and a diameter of about
0.5m, although in Belize the tree is a little taller and often 0.75m
in diameter.

The timber
There is no clear distinction between sapwood and heartwood,
the wood being whitish, yellowish, or light brown in colour.
The growth rings are usually much lighter in colour in their inner
portion, contrasting with the more brownish outer portion of
the rings, and this produces a ribbon type of figure on longitudinal surfaces similar to that found in pine and spruce. The
grain is fairly straight, the texture varies from fine to medium,
and the wood which is fairly soft, weighs about 320 to 480
kg/m³ when dried.

Drying
The wood dries very well with only slight checking and warping.
It usually contains a very high moisture content when green, and
both sapwood and heartwood are very susceptible to dis-

coloration due to staining fungi. The timber should therefore be chemically treated immediately after conversion.

Strength
Limited tests carried out at Madison showed almacigo to be considerably below the pines, firs and spruces in all mechanical properties tested except in resistance to splitting or cleavage, in which it compared favourably with these woods.

Durability
Non-durable.

Working qualities
Works easily and well with all hand and machine tools. It turns well, planes to a smooth finish, takes all stains well and polishes satisfactorily, and holds nails firmly without splitting. Logs peel well without preliminary steaming or bark removal, and produce good rotary cut veneer, but the tendency for fungal staining, and the sometimes crooked shape of the logs pose some difficulty. A large producer of veneer and plywood in Mexico has estimated the yield of acceptable face veneer to be of the order of 30 to 40 per cent. The quality of the veneer varies from a small proportion of woolly-surface stock to that containing a bird's-eye figure reminiscent of maple, but the average run of veneer contains numerous pin knots and the occasional mineral streak, and when made up into plywood has the appearance of yellow birch (*Betula alleghaniensis*).

Uses
Almacigo is used in the countries of origin for flooring, match sticks, boxes and crates, house construction and general carpentry. The wood is greatly favoured in Mexico for plywood manufacture, and the trade name of 'Mexican white birch' is well-known in the Caribbean. As lumber, the wood has similar uses to the soft pines and spruces, but lacks the strength of these woods, which would suggest that the local use of almacigo for flooring is probably too ambitious, except in rather thicker dimensions than is usual. Any large-scale use of this wood demands immediate chemical treatment to avoid fungal staining; logs are susceptible to attack by sapstain fungi as soon as they are felled, and discoloration can penetrate 300mm or so into both ends of a log within a week of felling. Spraying the logs with fungicide immediately after felling is however, a good control measure.

ANDIROBA

Carapa guianensis Aubl.   Family : Meliaceae

Other names
crabwood (Guyana) ; figueroa, tangare (Ecuador) ; krappa (Surinam) ; carapote (Guadeloupe).
The description 'Para mahogany', 'Brazilian mahogany', 'Surinam mahogany', etc, is misleading and should not be used.

Distribution
Andiroba occurs in the West Indies from Cuba to Trinidad, and on the continent from Honduras south through Central America, Guyana, Surinam, and into Brazil, Colombia, Peru and Venezuela.

The tree
The tree is very abundant in the Amazon flood plains in the State of Para and Amazonas, and in Guyana, often growing in nearly pure stands. The trees are evergreen, straight, and of good form, commonly 24.0m to 30.0m in height and 0.6m to 1.0m in diameter. Boles are clear of branches for 10.0m to 27.0m.
The trees grow rapidly and reach felling size in 20 to 25 years in the marsh forests of Guyana, around 30 to 35 years in the Mora forests, and about 40 to 60 years in the hill forests.

The timber
Andiroba resembles a plain mahogany, and some grades of 'cedar' (*Cedrela*) in colour, general appearance and technical properties, but lacks the high lustre and attractive figure present in the better grades of mahogany. The sapwood is pinkish to pale greyish-brown, not sharply defined from the heartwood, and is generally 25mm to 50mm wide. The heartwood is light salmon to reddish-brown when freshly sawn, becoming reddish-brown to brown when dry. The colour is somewhat darker than mahogany because of the amount of dark-coloured gum in the vessels.
The texture varies from coarse to fine, but is mostly medium, the grain is usually straight, but may be interlocked. Ripple marks occur sporadically in the denser tissue. The wood is generally harder and denser than mahogany, and weighs about 640 kg/m^3 when dried.

Drying
Air dries and kiln dries rather slowly with a tendency to split, check and collapse during the early stages of drying, but without serious bowing or cupping. A low temperature high humidity schedule is recommended for kiln drying.

Strength
The mechanical properties of andiroba vary according to the density of the wood, but in general they are superior to those of Central American mahogany, being approximately equal to those of black walnut (*Juglans nigra*).

Durability
Moderately durable.

Working qualities
Andiroba is more difficult to machine than American mahogany, but it can be worked with moderate ease with both hand and machine tools. In planing and moulding, straight-grained material finishes smoothly, but quarter-sawn material is apt to pluck out, and a cutting angle of 15° is recommended, but considerable sanding is often required to obtain a smooth finish. The wood holds nails well, but tends to split when nailed. It glues well and takes all kinds of finishes, but requires the use of filler on the softer variety. It peels well for veneer, although end splitting of logs causes a certain amount of loss.

Uses
Andiroba has been on the world timber market for many years, but often with unfavourable results due to poor conversion and drying practices. In more recent years, better milling and drying practices, and increased knowledge of the wood's properties has improved its marketable qualities and therefore its scope of use.

It is used in Central and South America for furniture, turnery shingles, joinery, flooring, masts, house construction, boxes and crates. In Guyana, it is one of the local woods designated for louvres for shutters, weather strips, sash frames, and siding in the better class wooden housing. Andiroba has also been used successfully in the Netherlands as a substitute for oak in veneer manufacture.

ANGELIN

Andira inermis H.B. & K. and
Andira spp.

Family : Leguminosae

Other names
kuraru, koraro, (Guyana) ; rode kabbes, (Surinam) ; yaba
(Cuba) ; angelim (Brazil) ; and variously throughout the
Caribbean as pheasant wood, corn wood, almendro, chaperno,
cuja, quira, quinillo, macaya and almendro colorado.

Note
This timber has been known in the UK and Europe as partridge
wood, and the name has also been applied to species of
Vouacapoua, but it is more correctly applied to the timber of
Caesalpinia spp.

Distribution
Angelin occurs throughout the West Indies and on the continent
from southern Mexico through Central America to northern
South America and Brazil.

The tree
The trees are evergreen, unbuttressed with flat crowns, and
often with adventitious shoots. In Guyana under good conditions, it generally reaches its best development, attaining a
diameter of 1.5m but diameters of 0.75m and heights of 27.0m
to 36.0m are not uncommon. In Trinidad, angelin grows to a
diameter of 1.0m but the form is not good as a rule.

The timber
The narrow sapwood is a pale brown to greyish-yellow, and is
usually clearly demarcated from the yellowish-brown to dark
reddish-brown heartwood which is not unlike the darker type
of Honduras mahogany. A distinct feature of the wood is the
light coloured, wavy bands of soft, parenchyma tissue, which,
alternating with darker bands of fibre gives a palm-like pattern
on flat surfaces, similar in appearance to partridge wood. The
pores are large, and sometimes contain gummy deposits.
The texture is coarse, and the grain generally straight. The
weight of *A. inermis* is about 800 kg/m^3 when dried.

Drying
Angelin air dries at a moderate rate and with normal care develops only slight degrade.

Strength
No strength data are available, but the wood is reported to be strong, comparing favourably with mora, wallaba, and other woods of similar density.

Durability
Very durable.

Working qualities
Saws and works reasonably well, but it is difficult to plane because of the alternating bands of hard and soft tissue. Even with sharp tools and cutters, a fine ridged surface results, but this can usually be eliminated in final sanding. The wood glues satisfactorily, but despite the smooth finish that can usually be obtained, it is rather difficult to polish, the soft bands absorbing polish more readily than the harder fibre tissue.

Uses
Angelin is used locally for heavy construction, bridge building, house framing and sheathing; its high figure and attractive colouring render it suitable for turned items, billiard cue butts, furniture and cabinet work. It is reported to be without resonance and therefore suited to the production of radio and television cabinets. It has been used in the UK for umbrella handles, walking sticks, police truncheons and other turned products. It is suitable for piling in non-*Teredo* waters and has been recommended for plywood and veneer because of its attractive and unusual appearance.

AROMATA

Clathrotropis macrocarpa Ducke., and   Family: Leguminosae
C. brachypetala (Tul) Kleinh.

Other names
blackheart, mayaro poui (Trinidad); cabory, timbó pau (Brazil).

Distribution
Both species are native to Guyana, with *C. brachypetala* extending into Trinidad, Grenada, Surinam and Venezuela, and *C. macrocarpa* having extensive distribution in Brazil and reaching Colombia.

The tree
The trees are without buttresses but are generally swollen at the base; they attain a height of about 30.0m and a diameter of 0.5m in Guyana. The main stem is usually clear for 12.0m to 15.0m.

The timber
The sapwood is wide, and yellowish to brownish-white in colour. The heartwood is pinkish-brown to dark brown with lighter streaks due to prominent vessel lines. It is straight grained and coarse textured, with a harsh feel but waxy appearance. It is hard, heavy, tough and strong, but is not very attractive in comparison to many other tropical American woods. It weighs from 993 to 1200 kg/m^3 when dried.

Drying
No information, but probably difficult because of its high density.

Strength
No detailed information, but reputed to be very strong and tough, and difficult to split under vertical compression.

Durability
Moderately durable.

Working qualities
The wood is considered only moderately difficult to work; it finishes smoothly, and takes a high polish.

Uses
In Trinidad the wood is preferred for oil-derrick sub-structures because of its high density, hardness and resistance to splitting. It should be suitable for heavy construction, piling in non-*Teredo* waters, bridge timbers and boat building.

BALATA

Mimusops bidentata A.DC., syn   Family : Sapotaceae
Manilkara bidentata (A.DC.) Chev.

Other names
ausubo (Puerto Rico); nispero (Panama); bulletwood (St Lucia).

Distribution
Balata is native to the West Indies, Central America and northern South America (ie massaranduba of Brazil). It is widely distributed in Trinidad, Dominica, the Dominican Republic, Puerto Rico, Guadeloupe, Martinique, St Vincent and most of the small islands of the Caribbean.

The tree
It is a large dominant tree of the rain forests, attaining a height of 36.0m and a diameter of 1.0m or more. The stem is straight, clean and cylindrical, sometimes reaching a timber height of 18.0m. The trees are basally swollen, and buttresses develop on the larger trees.

The timber
The sapwood is whitish or pale brown, distinct, but not sharply differentiated from the heartwood, which is deep red in colour with a smooth oily feel. It is very hard and dense, weighing about 1120 kg/m^3 when dried. The wood has a fine uniform texture, and the grain is usually straight but sometimes inter-locked.

Drying
It is difficult to dry, tending to develop severe checking, warp and casehardening. Drying methods should therefore aim at a slow removal of moisture.

Strength
An extremely strong wood with strength characteristics similar to those of greenheart.

Durability
Very durable.

Working qualities
Moderately easy to work despite its high density. It machines and finishes to a very smooth surface and takes a fine polish. It is difficult to glue.

Uses
Heavy constructional work, textile items, including shuttles; turnery, marine and bridge construction, stair treads, flooring, bench tops and because of its excellent steam-bending properties, for boat frames.

BASRALOCUS

Dicorynia guianensis Amsh. syn   Family : Leguminosae
D. paraensis Benth

Other names
angélique, teck de la Guyane, (French Guiana).

Distribution
Basralocus is one of the most common trees within its range in French Guiana and Surinam. It is said not to extend into other parts of the Guianas and lower Amazon Basin. It is particularly abundant in eastern Surinam and western French Guiana.

Note
Two distinct types of angélique wood are recognised, angélique rouge and angélique gris. The former wood is darker in colour than the latter, although the physical and mechanical properties are approximately the same for each. Angélique gris is of fairly rare occurrence and of minor commercial importance. The description which follows is of angélique rouge, or basralocus.

The tree
A large, well-formed, heavily buttressed tree, reaching a maximum height of 45.0m and a diameter up to 1.5m on the best sites. Piling 12.0m to 18.0m long, and timbers 9.0m in length and up to 0.6m square are usually commonly available.

The timber
The sapwood has a reddish cast and is sharply demarcated from

339

the heartwood, which is a russet colour when freshly cut, turning on exposure to a lustrous brown, often with a distinct reddish cast. A parenchyma pattern, resembling that of walnut, is distinct on flat-sawn surfaces. The wood weighs about 720 kg/m³ when dried.

Drying
The timber dries rapidly, but requires care. It has some tendency to split and check and to warp slightly. Thick stock often develops severe casehardening. Low temperature kiln schedules are suggested as a possible means of correcting this difficulty.

Strength
In the green condition basralocus is similar to teak in most strength properties.

Durability
Durable to very durable.

Working qualities
The working qualities vary according to the density and silica content, but generally are rated satisfactory. The wood finishes smoothly, glues well or moderately well and splits easily. It holds its place well under atmospheric changes.

Uses
Its high resistance to decay, moderate resistance to marine borers, and good strength properties make basralocus highly acceptable in marine construction, for piling, poles, posts, and other similar uses where *Teredo* are not a major factor. The wood is commonly used for construction purposes, bridge decking, boat framing, vehicle body work and sleepers. To a limited extent it is also used for furniture, flooring and barrel staves.

Its small radial shrinkage of 4.6 per cent (from green to oven-dry), makes it suitable for quarter-sawn flooring and boat decking, and it is also suitable for boat frames and planking, general building construction and agricultural implements.

BOIS BANDE

Richeria grandis Vahl.　　　　　　　　Family: Euphorbiaceae

Other names
zabricot grandes feuilles (Grenada).

Distribution
Fairly common in the rain forests at the higher elevations in Dominica and Grenada where it is found in association with *Oxythece* and *Licania* rather than with *Dacryodes* and *Sloanea*.

The tree
A medium-sized tree reaching a height of 27.0m and a diameter of 0.6m with a straight, clean bole.

The timber
The heartwood is reddish-brown when freshly cut, turning yellowish-brown with darker bands when dried. It weighs about 608 kg/m^3 when dried, and is reputed to be a tough, strong wood.

Drying
Dries easily without undue warping and checking. 25mm boards are air dry in 4 months.

Durability
Moderately durable.

Working qualities
Works easily and has only a slight blunting effect on cutting edges.

Uses
A useful structural timber used locally for house building and for planking in boats for which purpose it is regarded as one of the best local timbers.

BOIS GRIS

Licania ternatensis Hook f.   Family: Rosaceae

Other names
bois diable (Dominica) ; bois de masse (St Lucia).

Distribution
One of the commonest dominant trees of the rain forest in Dominica, St Lucia, St Vincent and Grenada.

The tree
The tree is large, up to 30.0m high and a diameter of 0.75m. The stem is straight and clean without buttresses.

The timber
The heartwood is dark reddish-brown in colour; dense, straight-grained and with a fine texture. The sapwood is white, and equally hard and tough as the heartwood. It contains a high silica content, and weighs about 1040 kg/m^3 when dried.

Drying
Moderately difficult to dry, with a tendency to warping, checking and casehardening.

Strength
Compares closely with greenheart.

Working qualities
Machining characteristics of bois gris are poor because of the wood's great density and high silica content. It is hard to drill, but bores cleanly.

Uses
Owing to its hardness the timber is not in demand locally, but its strength and toughness render it suitable for heavy constructional work, particularly for marine piling. In this latter respect, a closely related species, *Licania densiflora*, the marishballi of Guyana showed a considerable resistance to marine borer attack in Hawaiian waters, while another related species, *Licania buxiflora* also showed extremely high resistance to *Teredo* attack in tests at Wrightsville, USA. The probable but unproved high marine borer resistance of untreated bois gris suggests it should serve for piling and other marine construction.

BOIS LAIT

Sapium caribaeum Urb.   Family: Euphorbiaceae

Other names
la glu (Dominica and St Lucia).

342

Distribution
The tree occurs in secondary rain forests, being one of the commonest pioneer species where the forest has been cleared, and is found occasionally in high forest where there is a gap in the canopy.

The tree
It is a medium to large-sized tree, attaining a height of up to 30.0m and a diameter of 0.75m with a straight, clean stem.

The timber
The wood is light grey in colour, with a uniform smooth and fine texture. It is very light in weight, being about 448 kg/m^3 when dried.

Drying
Easy to dry, and does not warp, split or check excessively.

Strength
Moderately strong.

Durability
Perishable, but readily absorbs wood preservatives.

Working qualities
The timber is easy to work. It saws cleanly across end grain and planes easily to a smooth finish. It takes nails without splitting and has good nail-holding properties.

Uses
Owing to its light weight and ease of working and nailing properties, it is particularly suitable for boxes and crates, but it is also suitable for interior work where a soft hardwood is required.

BULLHOOF

Drypetes brownii Standl.   Family : Euphorbiaceae

Other names
male bullhoof or bullhoof macho.

Distribution
Yucatan area of Mexico to southern Belize and Guatemala.

The tree
Bullhoof is a medium sized tree attaining a height of 36.0m and a diameter of 0.75m. The boles are straight, cylindrical, and generally clear of branches for 15.0m to 18.0m above the low buttresses.

The timber
The heartwood is pale yellowish-brown when freshly cut, turning a light reddish-brown on exposure. A dark brown core up to 250mm in diameter is often present in the heart of old trees. Brown streaks caused by darker coloured growth-ring tissue show on longitudinal surfaces. The grain is usually straight, and the texture fine and uniform. The wood weighs about 736 kg/m^3 when dried.

Drying
Dries without excessive splitting, checking and distortion.

Strength
Hard, heavy, tough and strong, the strength properties compare favourably with English oak.

Durability
Moderately durable.

Working qualities
Bullhoof is only moderately difficult to work with hand and machine tools, and is similar to English oak. A smooth finish is obtained in planing without any tendency to roughened grain. It turns easily, but needs to be pre-bored before nailing to prevent splitting and bending of nails.

Uses
Shafts for agricultural equipment, general construction, sleepers; its light colour, close texture, and good turning qualities could possibly indicate its suitability for plywood manufacture.

Note
Two unrelated species (Ulmaceae), occur in Belize; they are *Celtis schippii* and *Ampelocera hottlei* (female bullhoof); together with *Drypetes brownii* they often comprise 30 trees per acre, and may be mixed in parcels of bullhoof. *C. schippii* is soft and light, and more suited for boxes and utility plywood rather than as a constructional timber.

BUSTIC

Dipholis spp., principally *D. salicifolia* (L). A.DC.   Family: Sapotaceae

Other names
almendro, jubilla, (Cuba); chachiga (Belize); bulletwood (Jamaica); nispero amarillo (Costa Rica).

Distribution
The various species of *Dipholis* have a combined range including southern Florida, West Indies, southern Mexico and Central America.

The tree
The trees vary in size according to species and geographical location, but are generally small, averaging 15.0m tall and about 0.5m in diameter.

The timber
The heartwood of all the species is brownish to reddish-brown, with little distinction from the sapwood. The grain is fairly straight and the texture is medium fine. It is a very hard and heavy wood, weighing about 960 kg/m^3 when dried.

Drying
No information is available. It is reported to have a tendency to 'crack badly', suggesting the wood is not stable in response to atmospheric changes.

Strength
A strong, tough timber, superior to oak in all strength properties except work to proportional limit and shock in impact bending.

Durability
Moderately durable.

Working qualities
Bustic is not difficult to work and finishes smoothly.

Uses
It is used extensively in the Caribbean area for heavy construction, flooring, bridge runners, telephone poles, sleepers, fence posts, cart and waggon parts.

CACONNIER ROUGE

Ormosia monosperma (Sw.) Urb. syn.   Family: Leguminosae
Ormosia dasycarpa Jacks.

Other names
l'angelin (Grenada); jumbie bead, sarinette (St Vincent); dedefouden (St Lucia).

Distribution
This is a dominent tree of the rain forest. It is common in St Vincent, frequent in Dominica and St Lucia, and rare in Grenada.

The tree.
It is a large tree, reaching 30.0m in height and a diameter of 0.75m. The stem is straight and clean.
It should not be confused with the true angelin (*Andira inermis*).

The timber
The timber is light golden yellow sometimes tinged with red; the texture is coarse, with a harsh feel and the grain is usually irregular. It is moderately heavy, weighing about 720 kg/m^3 when dried.

Drying
It dries rapidly and well, without warping and splitting.

Durability
Non-durable.

Working qualities
Fairly easy to work, and planes to smooth, lustrous finish. Tends to split when nailed.

Uses
Flooring, furniture, interior joinery and construction. It is commonly used for split shingles in Dominica.

CARAPITE

Amanoa caribaea Krug & Urb.   Family : Euphorbiaceae

Other names
None.

Distribution
Dominica and Guadeloupe; it is a rain forest species which occurs only on water-logged soils overlying a hard-pan. In such situations it is a dominant tree, and may form over 30 per cent of the crop.

The tree
Carapite is a tall tree with a straight, clean bole above the buttresses, and aerial shoots which sometimes develop. It attains a height of 30.0m and a diameter of 0.6m.

The timber
The heartwood is deep red-brown when freshly cut, becoming duller on exposure to a dark chocolate brown. It is a dense wood weighing about 1040 kg/m^3 when dried, and has a fine texture interspersed with large, prominent vessels containing a white deposit giving a streaky appearance to the wood. The sapwood is white, and clearly defined from the heartwood.

Drying
Reported to dry slowly but is not liable to warp or split.

Working qualities
Although hard, the wood is not unduly difficult to plane. It saws cleanly across the grain and drills easily. Owing to its density it is hard to nail, but does not split readily.

Uses
A hard, heavy, strong wood, with good natural durability, it is used locally for bridge building and is highly regarded for bridge decking. It is reported to make admirable flooring where hard wearing qualities are required.

CATIVO

Prioria copaifera Griseb.   Family: Leguminosae

Other names
cautivo (Panama).

Distribution
West Indies and Central America.

The timber
The heartwood is medium to light brown in colour, often streaked with occasional gum streaks. Although it is a rather dull looking wood it possesses an attractive golden lustre. The sapwood is pinkish; the wood is fine textured and has a straight grain. It weighs about 470 kg/m^3 when dried.

Drying
Rather difficult to dry, particularly in thick sizes which are liable to collapse, especially in wood containing dark streaks.

Durability
Non-durable.

Working qualities
Easy to work and finishes fairly well, with a slight tendency to woolliness in planing. The presence of gum is sometimes a problem.

Uses
Interior joinery, furniture, doors, vehicle body parts and boxes.

'CENTRAL AMERICAN CEDAR'

Cedrela odorata L.   Family : Meliaceae

Other names
'Cedar', qualified by country of origin, eg Honduras, Belize, Nicaraguan, Tabasco, Trinidad, West Indian, Spanish, etc. Commonly called acajou, or acajou rouge in Dominica, Trinidad, Guadeloupe and Martinique, this name is confusing since it is the French for mahogany. The wood is also commonly known in Latin America as cedro, in English speaking areas as 'cigar box cedar', but the preferred trade name is 'Central American cedar'.

Distribution
Three species of *Cedrela* are of primary importance in Central America and the Caribbean : *Cedrela mexicana* M. J. Roem, *C. guianensis* A. Juss., and *C. odorata* L., the first two species being considered synonymous with *C. odorata* since any variations in their properties can be attributed to the age and condition of individual trees rather than to botanical differences. Other species, but principally *Cedrela fissilis* Vell. produce 'South American cedar'.

The tree
The trees make their best growth on well-drained humid sites and in favourable conditions attain a height of 27.0m to 40.0m and a diameter of 0.6m to 1.2m. Large trees are occasionally found with diameters of 2.0m or a little more. The trees are buttressed from 1.5m to 3.5m up the tree, but clear boles 15.0m to 24.0m are common.

The timber
The wood of young trees, especially those of very rapid growth, is lighter in colour, softer, but somewhat tougher than that of older trees. The more slowly grown, dense, pungent-odoured timber is preferred and commands a higher price on local markets.

The heartwood is pinkish to reddish-brown when freshly cut, becoming red or dark reddish-brown, occasionally with a purplish tinge, after exposure. The sapwood is greyish-white or pinkish. The wood has a medium to high lustre; the grain is usually straight but is sometimes interlocked, and the wood is sometimes highly figured in buttresses and butts. The texture is generally medium but the darker-coloured wood may have a coarser texture than the lighter-coloured wood. In general, 'Central American cedar' resembles the lighter types of Central American mahogany. It weighs about 480 kg/m^3 when dried.

Most wood has a characteristic odour similar to that of coniferous cedar (*Cedrus*). It is semi-ring porous or ring porous, and therefore has a visible growth pattern on tangential surfaces. It has very desirable properties, the one exception being a tendency for some material to exude a gum that mars the wood surface.

Drying
Generally an easy wood to dry, either in the open air or in a kiln. It dries at a rapid rate with only very minor warping, and only slight checking and end splitting, but it has a tendency under some conditions for knots to split rather badly. In Dominica, Puerto Rico and Trinidad, 25mm boards are reported to air dry in 3 to 6 months. There is a tendency for individual pieces to distort or collapse during kiln drying, but this may be controlled by using a low temperature schedule.

Strength
'Central American cedar' is roughly comparable to Honduras mahogany in all strength properties except hardness, resistance to shear, and compression and tension across the grain, in which it is a little inferior to mahogany.

Durability
Durable.

Working qualities
Works easily with both hand and machine tools, with very little dulling of cutting edges. It planes to a clean surface and normally finishes smoothly, but knives and saws must be kept sharpened in order to avoid the slight tendency to woolliness.

The presence of gum in some logs gives a little trouble in planing and polishing but, in general, the wood stains and polishes well after suitable filling. It takes nails and screws well and can be glued satisfactorily. It can be peeled cold for veneer and plywood.

Uses
Furniture, panelling, cabinet-making, high-class joinery, cigar boxes, boat-parts, light construction and plywood. In the tropics it is used for flooring and for general house construction, for venetian blinds, musical instruments, doors, pattern-making, drawing boards and for sliced and rotary cut veneer for decorative use.

COCOBOLO

Dalbergia retusa Hems. and   Family: Leguminosae
allied species

Other names
granadillo (Mexico).

Distribution
Occurs along the west coast of Central America.

The tree
A medium sized tree with a fluted trunk, attaining a height of 20.0m to 30.0m and a diameter of 1.0m.

The timber
The sapwood is light cream to dingy white in colour, sharply demarcated from the heartwood, which varies from light yellow to rich red with many other coloured streaks and zones. After exposure these colours darken superficially to deep red. The wood has a fine uniform texture, with a very variable grain. A hard, heavy wood, it weighs from 990 to 1200 kg/m^3.

Drying
Dries slowly with a tendency to split and check.

Durability
Very durable.

Working qualities
Easy to work provided saws and cutting edges are kept sharp. When planed or turned the smooth surface is cold to the touch like marble. It takes stain and polish readily, but is unsuitable for gluing.

Uses
Its chief use is for cutlery handles, brush backs, inlaying, and it is sometimes used for truncheons, small tool handles, turnery and small decorative items.

COCUSWOOD

Brya ebenus DC.   Family : Leguminosae

Other names
cocus (UK); 'brown', 'green' or 'Jamaica ebony' (USA); granadillo (General).

Distribution
West Indies, principally from Jamaica and Cuba.

The timber
The sapwood is very light yellow, and the heartwood is brownish-yellow to dark chocolate-brown, and sometimes almost black. The wood is usually beautifully veined, with a fine, uniform texture, and of an oily nature. It is hard and heavy, and weighs about 1200 kg/m³ when dried.

Uses
Usually produced in the form of small logs from 1.2m to 2.4m long and 75mm to 150mm in diameter, the wood is used for small fancy articles, musical instruments, principally flutes and clarinets, turnery, inlays, handles of knives and tools, policemen's truncheons, brush backs and cabinet work.

CORDIA, AMERICAN LIGHT

Cordia alliodora Cham.   Family : Boraginaceae

Other names
cordia; salmwood (Belize); Ecuador laurel.

Distribution
West Indies and Tropical America.

General characteristics
A moderately light weight wood, weighing about 550 kg/m^3 when dried, it is a dull golden-brown colour, with an attractive ray-fleck figure on quarter-sawn surfaces. It is generally straight-grained, with a rather coarse texture.
It is said to dry without excessive degrade, and to work easily with little dulling effect on cutting edges, and to plane to a very smooth finish. It takes stain and polish satisfactorily.

Uses
Boat decking, furniture, joinery, vehicle bodies, light construction. It is recorded as being moderately durable.

COURBARIL

Hymenaea courbaril L.   Family : Leguminosae

Other names
locus, rode locus (Surinam) ; jutaby, jatoba (Brazil) ; algarrobo (Puerto Rico).

Distribution
Hymenaea courbaril is found from southern Mexico, through Central America and the West Indies, and into northern South America to northern Brazil, Bolivia and Peru.

The tree
Courbaril is a large, nearly evergreen tree, growing to a height of 45.0m and a diameter of 1.5m but normally it is less than 30.0m with a diameter of about 1.0m. The trunk is usually basally swollen or buttressed.

The timber
When freshly cut, the heartwood is salmon red to orange brown, becoming russet to reddish brown when dried. The sapwood is usually wide, sharply demarcated from the heartwood and greyish white or pinkish in colour. The heartwood frequently is marked with dark streaks and may at times have a golden lustre.

The grain is usually interlocked and the texture is medium to coarse. The wood weighs about 910 kg/m³ when dried.

Drying
Rather difficult to dry; it tends to dry at a fast to moderate rate with moderate surface checking and warping, but slow drying will reduce this tendency and also casehardening which is also liable.

Strength
Courbaril is a very strong, hard, tough wood. It compares favourably with American white oak in all strength properties except compression perpendicular to the grain, where it is slightly inferior to oak.

Durability
Non-durable to moderately durable according to amount of sapwood present.

Working qualities
Moderately difficult to work, due largely to its high density. It nails badly but has good screw holding properties. It glues well, turns satisfactorily and finishes smoothly, but does not take a high polish.

Uses
Furniture, cabinet-making, joinery and turnery. Its high shock resistance renders it suitable for sports goods and tool handles as a substitute for ash. Very resistant to wear as flooring and stair treads for which purpose it takes a fairly good polish. It is used locally for ship planking, tree-nails, gear cogs, wheel rims, looms, general building construction and for lock gates in areas free from marine borers.

DEGAME

Calycophyllum candidissimum D.C.   Family: Rubiaceae

Other names
degame lancewood' (UK) ; lemonwood (USA).

Distribution
Cuba, Central America, Tropical South America.

The timber
The wood is generally exported in the form of small round logs, with the bark on, produced from trees ranging from 200mm to 450mm in diameter. The thick sapwood is white to light brown in colour with a small light olive-brown heartwood. The wood has an exceedingly fine and uniform texture, and is generally straight-grained. It is hard, heavy, tough, resilient, bending well without breaking, and weighs about 820 kg/m³ when dried.

Working qualities
Not difficult to work, fairly easy to carve, polishes well and holds its place well when manufactured. Not easy to split.

Uses
Used as a substitute for true lancewood (*Oxandra lanceolata*), and is used for turnery, tool handles, fishing rods, cabinet-work, shuttles, pulleys and archery bows.

ENCENS

Protium attenuatum (Rose) Urban   Family: Burseraceae

Other names
bois encens.

Distribution
The tree appears to be restricted to the southern part of the Lesser Antilles in Guadeloupe, Dominica, Martinique, St Lucia and St Vincent.

The tree
It is a straight, almost unbuttressed tree of the rain forests, attaining a height of 24.0m or 27.0m and a diameter of 0.6m or more.

The timber
The wood resembles mahogany in superficial appearance due to the relatively soft, fine-textured, pink-coloured heartwood.

The sapwood is white, and the grain uniform and fine. It weighs about 512 kg/m³ when dried.

Drying
Dries without appreciable degrade and remains stable after manufacture.

Strength
Detailed information is lacking, but limited tests suggest the wood is fairly elastic but fissile.

Durability
Non-durable.

Working qualities
Works easily and well and planes to a smooth lustrous surface. It takes nails well and polishes satisfactorily. When well finished has a very attractive mahogany-like appearance.

Uses
Furniture, cabinet-making, panelling, interior trim.

FUSTIC

Chlorophora tinctoria Gaud.   Family : Moraceae

Other names
moral, moral fino (Ecuador) ; tatajuba (Brazil).

Distribution
West Indies and Tropical America.

The timber
Originally an important source of dye, fustic is the source of natural yellows, browns and olives, but the wood is also used commercially. The heartwood is golden yellow, darkening on exposure to brownish-red, sharply demarcated from the whitish sapwood. The wood is hard, heavy, and strong, and weighs about 880 to 960 kg/m³ when dried. It is usually straight-grained and the texture varies from medium to coarse.

Working qualities
Rather difficult to work and dulls cutting edges fairly quickly. It polishes well and is highly resistant to decay.

Uses
It is used for carpentry and wheelwright's work, and is also used in naval construction. The colouring matter is soluble in water and it is doubtful if the wood could be used for purposes where it is liable to become wet.

GOMMIER

Dacryodes excelsa Vahl.   Family: Burseraceae
D. hexandra (Hamilt.) Griseb

Other names
gommier blanc, gommier montagne (Guadeloupe and Martinique); tabonuco (Puerto Rico).

Distribution
Gommier occurs in Puerto Rico and the Lesser Antilles, generally in small groups along ridge-tops and upper slopes of the rain forests in Dominica, St Lucia, St Vincent, Grenada, Guadeloupe and St Kitts.

The tree
Gommier is a large to very large evergreen tree reaching a height of 36.0m and a diameter of 1.0m to 1.5m although mature trees are more commonly 18.0m to 24.0m tall and 0.5m to 0.75m in diameter. They are deep rooted, without buttresses, and able to stand up well to the numerous hurricanes of the Caribbean. The boles are straight and well formed.

The timber
Gommier is variously reported to resemble birch (*Betula*), mahogany, and sometimes yellow poplar (*Liriodendron*). It is perhaps closer in appearance to the botanically associated gaboon or okoumé (*Aucoumea*), but harder, heavier, and much finer textured.
The sapwood is narrow, greyish in colour, and not clearly demarcated from the heartwood which is uniform pale brown

with a purplish cast when freshly cut, turning a pinkish brown when dried, and a lustrous brown on exposure. The grain is more or less roey and sometimes interlocked, producing an attractive ribbon stripe. The lustre is high and often satiny in appearance. The texture is fine to medium and uniform, and in general is somewhat finer textured than mahogany.
The wood weighs about 640 kg/m^3 when dried.

Drying
It dries easily with no appreciable distortion or other defects. Its volumetric shrinkage from green to oven dry is 10.5 per cent; tangentially it is 6.4 per cent, and radially 4.1 per cent, which is superior in terms of drying to those values for African and Honduras mahogany.

Strength
Moderately hard, tough and strong, it compares favourably with mahogany.

Durability
Moderately durable.

Working qualities
The timber is easy to work but with a tendency to dull cutting edges due to the high silica content of the wood. When sharp cutting edges are maintained, the wood finishes smoothly and takes glue and all finishes effectively. It is a good wood for turning and for holding nails.

Uses
Gommier is used extensively in the Caribbean area for furniture and cabinet-making, and in Puerto Rico is often stained and sold as 'mahogany'. It is also used for boat-building, shingles and crates. In the Caribbean, it is considered very susceptible to termite attack, and for exacting purposes not as good as mahogany with its known resistance to termites.
Gommier also produces very good veneer. Tests made at the Centre Technique du Bois indicate that gommier is suitable for plywood, with selected stock suitable for decorative veneer. This was substantiated by other tests carried out in Canada with the recommendation that eccentric peeling produced better quality veneer.

GUAYACAN

Tabebuia guayacan Hemsl.   Family : Bignoniaceae

Other names
lapacho.

Distribution
Central America.

The timber
The timber is very similar to ipê and others of the Lapacho group (see white tabebuia) being olive-brown to blackish, frequently with light and dark stripes, and occasionally oily looking. The sapwood is white to yellow, sometimes with a pinkish cast, and sharply demarcated from the heartwood. It is hard, heavy, tough and strong, fine to medium textured, with interlocked grain, and weighs about 929 kg/m³ when dried.
Guayacan differs slightly from ipê (*Tabebuia serratifolia*) in that it is not considered as being so durable, and ripple marks are more prominent in guayacan, otherwise there is little difference in drying, working properties, and uses to which both timbers are applied.

Uses
Guayacan is used for constructional purposes, flooring and decking, posts, sills and sleepers.

HURA

Hura crepitans L.   Family : Euphorbiaceae

Other names
assacu, acacu (Brazil); possentrie (Surinam); sand box (General).

Distribution
Hura occurs naturally in moist to wet sites through the West Indies and from Central America to northern Brazil and Bolivia.

It reaches its best development along the narrow reefs of the coastal plain near Paramaribo, Surinam in nearly pure stands. It is very common in Trinidad, and is present in commercial quantities in Guyana and French Guiana.

The tree
Hura is commonly a large, straight, well-formed tree, which in favourable locations attains diameters of 1.0m to 1.5m and a height of 27.0m to 40.0m with clear boles of something like 12.0m to 22.0m long. The trees are often swollen basally or have small buttresses.

The timber
The sapwood is yellowish-white, often indistinct from the heartwood, but sometimes sharply demarcated. The heartwood is cream to light buff when freshly sawn, turning pale yellowish-brown, pale olive grey, or dark brown on exposure, or sometimes retaining its original cream colour. The innermost heartwood of large logs is often darker than the exterior portion.
Hura superficially resembles simaruba but lacks the bitter taste. It is light in weight and has a soft, warm feel, but the surface is sometimes woolly. It weighs between 370 and 430 kg/m^3 when dried. The grain is straight to interlocked, the texture is fine and the wood has a high lustre. Indistinct purplish or greenish streaks and a slight ribbon stripe on radial surfaces often give hura an attractive figure.

Drying
It is moderately difficult to air dry. It dries fairly rapidly, which tends to prevent blue stain, but this often results in warping, at times severe. A low temperature – high humidity kiln schedule, designed for slow, careful drying is recommended.

Strength
No detailed information available.

Durability
Moderately durable.

Working qualities
Can be readily machined when air dry, but chipped and torn grain are frequently encountered with wood that has extreme

interlocked grain. Takes stain well, nails satisfactorily and glues easily.

Uses
Hura is used locally for general carpentry, interior construction, boxes, crates and furniture, joinery, plywood and veneer.

LANCEWOOD

Oxandra lanceolata Baill.   Family : Anonaceae

Other names
asta (USA) ; yaya (Cuba) ; bois de lance (France).

Distribution
Cuba and Jamaica mainly, with a rather restricted occurrence in Guyana.

The tree
The tree is small, growing to a height of about 9.0m and a diameter of 0.5m.

The timber
The wood is pale yellow in colour with little or no distinction between sapwood and heartwood. It is fine textured and straight-grained, and is noted for its strength and resilience. It weighs about 990 kg/m^3 when dried.

Durability
Moderately durable.

Working qualities
Fairly easy to work without undue blunting of cutting edges. It is however, inclined to chatter in sawing and to ride on cutters, and tools should therefore be kept sharp, and the wood held firmly. It is capable of a high, smooth finish, and turns admirably. It splits very easily.

Uses
Archery bows, fishing rods, billiard cues, turnery, small parts for organs and the textile industry.

LAURIER PETITES FEUILLES

Ocotea floribunda (Sw.) Mez. syn.   Family : Lauraceae
Strychnodaphne floribunda Griseb.

Other names
laurier ti feuilles (St Lucia).

Distribution
Fairly common in St Lucia, less so in Grenada, and infrequent in Dominica and St Vincent.

The tree
A medium sized tree of the rain forest, attaining a height of about 27.0m and a diameter of 0.6m with a straight clean stem.

The timber
The wood is light yellowish-grey in colour; lustrous, with an interlocking grain and a smooth, fine texture; fairly light in weight, about 576 kg/m^3 when dried.

Drying
Reported to dry readily without splitting or warping.

Strength
No information is available, but the timber is reported to be moderately strong.

Durability
Moderately durable and resistant to preservatives.

Working qualities
Works with moderate ease. It tends to pick up in planing due to the interlocked grain, but a smooth lustrous finish is obtained if the knives are kept well sharpened. Drills easily and takes nails without splitting.

Uses
Its good appearance and light weight renders the wood suitable for furniture, joinery and interior trim.

LAURIER POIVRE

Hieronyma caribaea Urb. syn.   Family : Euphorbiaceae
H. alchorneoides Rolfe.

Other names
tapana (Grenada) ; horseflesh mahogany (St Vincent) ; bois d'amande (St Lucia).

This is the equivalent of suradan (*H. alchorneoides* and *H. laxiflora*), which grows in Central and South America.

Distribution
Of fairly common occurrence in Dominica and St Lucia, but also found in each of the Windward Islands.

The tree
A large dominant tree with a straight, clean stem, attaining a height of about 36.0m and a diameter of 0.75m.

The timber
The wood is dark reddish-brown in colour, and the texture is medium to coarse. It is hard and rather heavy, weighing about 720 kg/m³ when dried.

Drying
Dries slowly with an inclination to warp.

Working qualities
The timber is hard to plane but with sanding works up to a smooth finish. It saws and mortises cleanly across the grain ; drills easily and takes nails without splitting.

Uses
Its strength and durability make it a good structural timber and it is also suitable for boat-building. It takes an excellent polish and with its dark red-brown colour, makes an attractive furniture wood.

LIGNUM VITAE

Guaiacum spp.   Family : Zygophyllaceae

Guaiacum officinale L. produces thin-sap lignum vitae.
Guaiacum sanctum L. produces thick-sap lignum vitae.
Guaiacum guatemalense Planch. occurs in Nicaragua and is synonymous with *G. sanctum*, although occasionally reported as a separate species. *G. officinale* is sometimes referred to as 'genuine' lignum vitae, as opposed to *G. sanctum* which is often called 'bastard' lignum vitae. Logs of either species may be identified by their bark ; *G. officinale* has thin, smooth bark, with irregular-shaped glossy flakes of varying size and depth, similar to sycamore, while the bark of *G. sanctum* is rough.

Other names
G. officinale; guayacan (Spanish) ; bois de gaiac (France) ; guayacan negro, palo santo, (Cuba) ; ironwood (USA).
G. sanctum; guayacan blanco, gaiac femelle, guayacancillo.

Distribution
The combined range of the two main species is from southern Florida and the Bahamas through Jamaica, Cuba, Hispaniola, Puerto Rico and the Lesser Antilles to Martinique, and on the continent from Mexico southward through Central America to Colombia and Venezuela.

The tree
Lignum vitae is a small, slow-growing tree, normally 6.0m to 9.0m high and about 0.3m in diameter, although some trees grow to 0.75m. Clear boles in excess of 3.0m to 3.5m are uncommon. Bolts or logs 0.6m to 3.0m long and from 75mm to 450mm or 500mm in diameter are marketed. Logs of *G. officinale* are reported to be larger generally, and to have a greater proportion of heartwood than those of *G. sanctum*.

The timber
Extremely hard and heavy, lignum vitae is one of the heaviest woods in the trade, and weighs on average 1250 kg/m³ at 15 per cent moisture content. The heartwood is a dark greenish-brown to almost black and readily distinguished from the narrow pale yellow or cream-coloured sapwood. The wood is very fine and uniform in texture with a heavily interlocked grain. It

has a characteristic oily feel due to the resin (guaiac content) that constitutes about one-fourth of the air-dry weight. Heating the wood to a temperature of 100°C causes the resin to ooze out and reduces its self-lubricating properties.

Drying
Because of its refractory tendencies, considerable care is required to avoid shakes and splitting during drying. End coating logs with a bituminous or proprietory compound helps to reduce this form of degrade.

Strength
Compared with English oak, lignum vitae is 3 to 4 times harder. Straight grained material has a resistance to splitting in a radial plane about double that of oak, but splits very easily on the tangential plane at loads of about 30 to 40 per cent of those for oak. However, most material has severely interlocked and irregular grain and to split it would require much greater loads than those needed for straight-grained material.

Durability
Very durable.

Working qualities
It is a very difficult timber to work with hand tools and difficult to saw and machine with power tools, tending to ride over the cutters in planing. A short tooth pitch and limited hook are needed in sawing in order to reduce vibration, and a cutting angle of 15° will help prevent raised or chipped grain when planing quarter-sawn faces. Increased pressure is also needed to hold the wood firmly during planing. In most other operations a good finish is possible; the wood turns and shapes very well and takes a high polish. Owing to its oily nature special surface treatment is required for satisfactory gluing.

Uses
Its principal use is in bearings and bushing blocks for propellor shafts of ships, pulley sheaves, dead-eyes, and as a replacement for metal bearings in steel and tube works. It is reported to last 3 to 7 years as unlubricated bearings in ships and from 50 to 70 years as pulley sheaves. It is also used for tinsmith's mallet heads and for 'wood's' in the game of bowls.

MAGNOLIA

Talauma dodecapetala (Lam) Urb.   Family : Magnoliaceae
syn. *Annona dodecapetala* Lam.

Other names
bois pin (Dominica) ; bois pain marron (St Lucia) ; wild bread-fruit (St Vincent).

Distribution
This is a large dominant tree of the rain forests. It is fairly common in St Vincent, St Lucia and Dominica, but is absent from Grenada.

The tree
The tree is known locally as magnolia because of the resemblance of its leaves, flowers and wood to those of the closely related genus *Magnolia*. The tree attains a height of 30.0m or more, and is straight, erect and well formed ; long buttresses are common, and boles clear of branches usually are 12.0m to 18.0m long, with a diameter of 1.0m or more.

The timber
There is a marked contrast between sapwood and heartwood ; the sapwood, which may be very wide in medium sized trees, is light yellow in colour, and the heartwood varies from dark brown to deep olive-green in which purplish streaks sometimes appear. The rays are irregular and long, giving rise to 'pith flecks' on tangential surfaces. The texture is smooth and uniform, and the grain is straight ; the wood weighs about 640 kg/m^3 when dried.

Drying
It dries without serious degrade. 25mm boards air dry in six months on St Lucia.

Strength
It is reported to be strong, and resistant to shock, bending and compression stresses, and is difficult to split.

Durability
Heartwood moderately durable ; sapwood (which may be wide), non-durable, but it readily absorbs preservative.

366

Working qualities
Works very easily and planes to a smooth finish. The heartwood does not take nails or screws well.

Uses
Furniture, joinery, flooring, vehicle bodies, boat-building, etc. Local recommendations suggest separation of the heartwood and sapwood because of their marked difference of character, the sapwood only being used as a non-durable soft wood.

MAHOE

Hibiscus elatus Sw. Family: Malvaceae

Other names
blue mahoe, mountain mahoe (Jamaica); majugua, majagua azul (Cuba).

Distribution
Mahoe occurs throughout Jamaica and Cuba, and has been widely planted and naturalized from Florida to Trinidad and Tobago, and on the continent from Mexico to Peru and Brazil. Heavy cutting in the past has reduced the volume of merchantable timber for the time being.

The tree
Mahoe commonly grows to a height of 18.0m to 21.0m and a diameter of 0.3m to 0.5m although on favourable sites 0.9m diameters occur. The boles are straight and of fairly good length.

The timber
The sapwood is narrow and nearly white, and the heartwood, basically greyish-brown or olive in colour, is often richly variegated with streaks of purple, metallic blue or olive, or separated by plain olive patches. The grain is fairly straight and the texture medium. It is a moderately heavy wood, weighing about 752 kg/m^3 when dried.

Drying
No information available.

Strength
Although test data are not available, mahoe is considered a hard, tough and elastic wood of overall good quality.

Durability
Durable to very durable.

Working qualities
Works easily but needs particular care to attain a good polish.

Uses
The timber is highly prized in Jamaica and Cuba for high-grade furniture and cabinet-making, inlay work, interior trim, flooring, sills, door and window frames. Freshly polished wood has the appearance of marble, but unless well finished rapidly assumes a very dull colour.

MAHOGANY

Swietenia spp.   Family : Meliaceae

The mahoganies of Central America and the West Indies (*Swietenia* spp), differ among themselves to a much greater extent than do the related mahoganies of Africa (*Khaya* spp). These differences are attributable to geological areas of growth and whether the trees are forest-grown or plantation-grown.

Nearly 400 years has elapsed since Spanish mahogany (*Swietenia mahagoni*) was first shipped to the UK and Europe, and later to America and elsewhere, to become the most cherished cabinet wood in the world.

Despite its value for cabinet-making, enormous quantities of small diameter mahogany were used annually to fire the boilers of Caribbean sugar mills and locomotives, and larger trees were felled for use as railway sleepers, fence posts and other utilitarian purposes.

This indiscriminate wastage of Spanish mahogany finally resulted (1946) in the governments of Cuba, Haiti, and the Dominican Republic banning the export of mahogany logs and lumber, and today, other Caribbean sources can only supply small quantities at intermittent intervals.

Spanish mahogany has now become of more historical than commercial significance.

Fortunately, another species, *Swietenia macrophylla* King., has filled the position formerly held by *Swietenia mahagoni* Jacq., but world demand has led to felling at smaller diameters, and to the establishment of plantations, where growth is often very rapid, and the wood less dense.

368

CENTRAL AMERICAN MAHOGANY (*Swietenia macrophylla* King.)

Other names
According to country of origin, Honduras, Mexican, Tabasco, Guatemalan, Nicaraguan, Costa Rica, Panama, Brazilian, Peruvian and Colombian mahogany; araputanga, mara, mogno (Brazil); zopilote gateado (Mexico); acajou (France); caoba and caoba hondureña are the most commonly used names in Spanish-speaking areas.

Distribution
S. macrophylla occurs from southern Mexico southward along the Atlantic slope of Central America from Belize to Panama, and in Colombia, Venezuela, and parts of the upper reaches of the Amazon and its tributaries in Peru, Bolivia and Brazil.
The tree makes its best development on well-drained soils, but it does fairly well on many sites from sea level to 900.0m in altitude.

Note
Swietenia humilis Zucc. (*S. cirrhata* Blake.) occurs in dry locations along the Pacific coast from Western Mexico to Costa Rica. The wood is indistinguishable from that of *S. macrophylla*.
Swietenia belizensis Lundell. occurs in Belize and may be mixed with *S. macrophylla*.
Swietenia candollei Pittier.
Swietenia tessmannii Harms.
Swietenia krukovii Gleason and Panshin.
These three species are found in South America, but are generally considered to be synonymous with *S. macrophylla*.

The tree
Forest-grown trees are often very large, sometimes 45.0m high, with a diameter of 2.0m or more above a heavy buttress.
Plantation-grown trees often make very rapid growth, frequently reaching small saw-log size in 20 years on good sites, and under average conditions, 300mm to 355mm saw-logs (diameter inside bark) are grown in about 40 years.

The timber

The sapwood is generally 25mm to 50mm wide, yellowish-white in colour, sharply demarcated from the heartwood, which is pinkish or salmon coloured when freshly sawn, later becoming light reddish-brown with a golden lustre. The grain which is pinkish or salmon coloured when freshly sawn, later becoming light reddish-brown with a golden lustre. The grain is commonly interlocked, producing a wide attractive striped figure on radial surfaces. The texture is rather fine to medium, and is uniform.

Deposits of dark-coloured gum in the pores are common, and white deposits are sometimes present. Ripple marks on the tangential longitudinal surfaces can usually be observed.

Plantation-grown wood is generally somewhat less dense than forest-grown wood, the latter weighing about 560 kg/m^3 and the former about 496 kg/m^3 when dried. There appears to be no appreciable difference in density and technical properties of wood from the different countries.

Drying

Central American mahogany can be air dried and kiln dried rapidly and easily, without appreciable warping or checking. The presence of tension wood and gelatinous fibres is not uncommon in *S. macrophylla* and such wood can result in a high rate of longitudinal shrinkage during kiln drying.

Strength

The strength properties are extremely good for a timber of its weight. For this reason it was at one time used almost exclusively for aeroplane propellers. Plantation-grown wood is slightly below forest-grown wood in bending strength and work to maximum load in static bending in proportion to its slightly lower density. On the other hand, plantation-grown wood is generally superior in hardness, compression across the grain and shear. In the air dry condition, plantation-grown material is very much lower in modulus of elasticity, although both types are about equal in shock resistance.

Durability
Durable.

Working qualities
One of the most satisfactory and easiest of woods to work, either with hand or machine tools. The sometimes frequent presence of tension wood gives rise to fuzzy surfaces in machining, which necessitates heavy sanding, but the use of sharp cutting edges where woolliness is encountered is generally sufficient, along with sanding, to produce an excellent finish. The wood is easy to glue, takes nails and screws well and will take an excellent polish.

It is one of the easier woods to slice or rotary cut into veneer, although flitches will frequently develop cracks when not properly boiled.

Uses
High-class furniture and cabinet-making, panelling, planking for boats, pianos, burial caskets, moulds and dies, pattern-making, veneer and plywood.

MANNI

Symphonia globulifera L. f.   Family: Guttiferae

Other names
matakkie (Surinam); waika chewstick (Belize); manniballi, brick-wax tree, (Guyana); mangle blanc (Dominica); vanahi (Brazil); bois cochon (French Guiana).

Note
Another, botanically unrelated timber is also marketed in Guyana as manniballi (*Inga alba* Willd. Leguminosae family).

Distribution
Manni occurs in the West Indies in Cuba, Dominica, St Lucia, etc, and on the continent from Mexico through Central America to northern South America.

The tree
The trees are generally 30.0m in height with long, straight boles which average 21.0m to 24.0m long, and around 0.75m in diameter, although taller and larger diameter trees are found in Belize and Guyana. The trees are commonly supported by stilt-like roots, and sometimes have elbow buttresses up to 1.2m in height.

371

The timber

The colour of the heartwood may be variegated yellowish, greyish, or greenish-brown; several shades of these colours may occur as stripes on the face of a single board. A distinct, but unattractive silver-grain figure is visible on quarter-sawn faces; there is a medium to high lustre. The sapwood is whitish and clearly defined. The wood weighs about 705 kg/m^3 when dried, and has a harsh feel due to the coarse texture; the grain is straight to irregular.

Drying

The wood tends to dry fairly rapidly with an inclination to warp and surface check. A slow rate of drying should be promoted, and in air drying the boards should be protected from hot sun.

Strength

Similar to American white oak in most strength categories.

Durability

Durable.

Working qualities

An easy wood to work, it hardly dulls cutting edges, although harsh and splintery. The abundant parenchyma soft tissue combined with irregular grain tends to roughen on planing. The wood polishes well and takes glue satisfactorily.

Uses

General construction, piling in fresh water, sleepers, tight cooperage.

MAURICIF

Byrsonima martinicensis Kr. & Urb.   Family: Malpighiaceae

Other names

bois tan rouge (St Lucia); laurier deux pointes (Dominica).

Distribution

Common in Dominica, less frequent in the other islands.

The tree

Mauricif is sub-dominant in the rain forest of Dominica, where it attains a height of 21.0m and a diameter of about 0.45m. The stem is straight and clean.

The timber
The wood is light reddish in colour, with grey streaks. It is dense with a fine, uniform texture and moderate weight of about 688 kg/m³ when dried. The timber behaves well in drying, and is naturally durable.

Working qualities
The timber works easily with all tools. It saws cleanly and planes to a smooth finish. It drills easily and takes nails without splitting.

Uses
It is a most useful timber for a variety of purposes. With its strength and durability it is suitable for structural work, and it can also be used for door and window frames, furniture and all interior work.

NARGUSTA

Terminalia amazonia (J. F. Gmel.)   Family : Combretaceae
Exell.

Other names
fukadi, coffee mortar (Guyana) ; almendro (Belize) ; cochun (Mexico) ; white oliver (Trinidad) ; guayabo (Venezuela).

Distribution
Nargusta is common on the moist slopes and flat lands within the rain forests of Mexico, southward through Central America and into northern South America to Brazil and Peru, and on the island of Trinidad.

The tree
A large, virtually evergreen tree with a long, clear, symmetrical bole above the large buttresses. It reaches heights of 21.0m to 42.0m with diameters of 1.2m to 1.5m. However, trees with diameters larger than 0.75m are often hollow. Boles are commonly 18.0m to 21.0m long on good sites.

The timber
The sapwood is yellowish, not clearly separated from the heartwood which is varied in colour ; it may be brownish-

yellow, light yellowish-brown or yellowish-olive. Sometimes the wood has distinct and prominent reddish streaks or stripes at widely spaced intervals. The lustre is medium to high, the texture is medium, and the grain shows marked irregularity; it is usually interlocked showing a distinct stripe or roe figure on quarter sawn surfaces. It is a rather heavy wood and weighs about 800 kg/m^3 when dried.

Drying
Moderately difficult to air and kiln dry, tending to split and check. It is also difficult to remove moisture from the centre of thick stock.

Strength
A hard strong wood, it is superior in most strength properties to American white oak, but inferior to that wood in cleavage.

Durability
Durable.

Working qualities
Somewhat difficult to work; comparable to beech generally but some raised and torn grain is liable in planing. Glues, stains and polishes easily. Should be pre-bored before nailing to prevent splitting.

Uses
Furniture, cabinet-making, flooring; framing, planking and decking in boat-building, turnery, plywood, and as a general substitute for oak.

PETIT CITRON

Ilex spp.   Family: Aquifoliaceae

Other names
ti-citron.

Distribution
West Indies.

General characteristics

Ilex cuneifolia and *Ilex sideroxylon* var. *typica* are small evergreen holly-type trees occurring in the Windward and Leeward Islands. The timber is generally darker in colour than European holly, of medium weight, fine texture, and generally produced from small logs about 3.0m long and 0.5m in diameter. The wood is used locally for house-building for sills, posts and rafters, and for cart wheel felloes. It also makes excellent oars.

PIPIRIE

Pithecellobium jupunba (Willd.) Urb.   Family: Leguminosae

Other names

savonette, dalmare (Grenada); wild tamarind (St Vincent); dalmare (St Lucia).

Distribution

Occurs in gaps with secondary growth, and is common in Dominica, St Lucia, Grenada and St Vincent.

The tree

A medium-sized tree up to 27.0m in height, with a diameter of 0.5m or slightly more; it has a straight, clean, cylindrical bole.

The timber

The heartwood is light yellow with reddish streaks, and is coarse in texture, with straight grain, although cross-grain is sometimes evident. It weighs about 480 kg/m^3 when dried.

Drying

Dries rapidly with a tendency to split.

Working qualities

Pipirie is fairly soft, and is easy to work, It tends to pick up in planing when cross-grain is present, but it is capable of a smooth lustrous finish. It takes nails and screws well. It takes stain and polish satisfactorily, but is rather absorbent.

Uses

It is a non-durable wood, suitable for all types of work where lightness and appearance are required, eg panelling, furniture, interior joinery and trim. As it is generally straight grained and easily split, it is used locally for shingles; it has a high absorbency for preservatives.

PRIMA VERA

Tabebuia donnell-smithii Rosa.　　　Family: Bignoniaceae
syn *Cybistax donnell-smithii* Rose

Other names
durango, palo blanco (Mexico); San Juan (Honduras).

Distribution
Central America.

The timber
There is little distinction between sapwood and heartwood, the timber in general being yellowish-white to light yellowish-rose in colour. It was a popular timber in America for furniture, panelling, and general decorative work, under the name 'white mahogany', since it resembles mahogany in most aspects except colour. It generally shows a mottled or roey grain, often strongly marked, which is usually more reminiscent of satinwood than of mahogany. The texture is medium to coarse, and the grain straight to interlocking. It is moderately light in weight, about 450 kg/m³ when dried.

Drying
Reported to be easy to dry.

Working qualities
Works easily and finishes smoothly. Pin-worm hole may be troublesome and require filling.

Uses
Furniture, panelling, high-class joinery and veneer.

QUARUBA

Vochysia hondurensis Sprague.   Family : Vochysiaceae

Other names
yemeri, emery, emory, yemoke (Belize) ; San Juan (Honduras) ;
palo de chancho (Costa Rica).

Distribution
V. hondurensis is one of the few species of the genus occurring
outside South America. It is distributed in the tropical zone
from southern Mexico and Belize to Costa Rica. It is found
throughout Belize both on silt soils along river banks and on
sandy soils. It attains its best development on the coastal plain
where it grows in almost pure stands. It occurs extensively in
second growth situations, on abandoned farmlands on soils
of the poorer type.

The tree
Medium to large unbuttressed, canopy trees growing to heights
of 40.0m or more and a diameter of about 1.0m. The boles are
straight, clear and cylindrical, and usually 15.0m to 18.0m long.

The timber
Quaruba is similar in some respects to 'Central American cedar
(*Cedrela*), mainly in appearance. The heartwood dull pinkish-
brown or uniform pink in colour, and the sapwood is greyish
white to buff, usually 100mm to 150mm wide, merging into
the heartwood. Typically straight-grained, it is sometimes
shallowly interlocked ; the texture is coarse to medium and
rather fibrous. Vertical traumatic gum ducts, filled with orange-
brown gum, are sometimes present, and may be large enough to
be considered an objectionable defect. The wood weighs about
480 kg/m^3 when dried.

Drying
Dries fairly rapidly with moderate twist and slight checking,
but kiln drying must be carried out with care, particularly when
drying thick stock in order to reduce the marked tendency to
collapse in stock 32mm thick or more. Good sticking practices
are important and piles should be weighted down to reduce
distortion tendencies.

Strength
Compares favourably with European redwood (*Pinus sylvestris*), but is 40 to 50 per cent harder, and 40 per cent superior in resistance to splitting.

Durability
Non-durable.

Working qualities
Quaruba has relatively poor machining properties due to its coarse, fibrous, hard, and tough nature. It resembles a coarse grade of mahogany in machining properties, but unlike mahogany, has a tendency to blunt cutting edges. Sawing along the grain is satisfactory, but woolly surfaces are common on end grain in cross-cutting. A fairly wide tooth pitch is necessary for best results. Raised grain is a common defect in planing and moulding operations, and cutters must be kept sharp.

The open texture requires a considerable amount of filling before polishing. It takes glue, nails, and paint well, and polishes to a good finish, but water stains should not be used as they cause considerable raised grain. The wood is considered to be suitable for plywood manufacture.

Uses
Joinery, boxes and crates, inexpensive furniture and painted articles. It is suitable for utility plywood.

RESOLU

Chimarrhis cymosa Jacq.   Family: Rubiaceae

Other names
bois riviere (Dominica and St Lucia) ; waterwood (St Vincent) ; penda (Cuba).

Distribution
A rain forest species, it is a pioneer of secondary forest and occurs frequently along stream banks and on well-drained river flats. It is recorded from Cuba, Jamaica, Guadeloupe, Martinique, Dominica, St Lucia, Trinidad, Colombia, Venezuela and Guyana.

The tree
Resolu is a medium-sized, evergreen tree, up to 24.0m or more in height and a diameter of about 1.5m. The stem is straight with shallow buttresses, and is sometimes slightly fluted.

The timber
The wood is light orange-yellow colour with a rather coarse texture, and is medium hard. It weighs on average 750 kg/m^3 when dried.

Drying
The timber is reported to air dry in Dominica in 4 to 5 months, but with a tendency to split readily.

Strength
No information is available, but the wood is reported to be brittle.

Durability
Probably durable.

Working qualities
The wood is not difficult to work. It saws cleanly across the grain and planes to a smooth finish. It tends to split when nailed and should be pre-bored.

Uses
Used locally for sheathing, flooring and framing. In St Vincent it is used extensively in the flumes for water-wheels, and in the construction of water channels and troughs in the arrowroot factories.

ROBLE

Tabebuia spp.   Family: Bignoniaceae

Roble, the Spanish name for oak (*Quercus*), is applied to several groups of trees in tropical America, including a few species of *Tabebuia*. The wood of these species is superficially like oak but lacks the characteristic large rays of the oak group.

Distribution
Tabebuia rosea (Bertol) D.C., formerly known as *T. pentaphylla*, extends from Mexico through Central America to Colombia and Venezuela. The wood is commonly exported as roble, apamate or amapa, and also occasionally from Belize as mayflower.

Tabebuia heterophylla (D.C.) Britton, is generally considered synonymous with *T. pentaphylla* and *T. pallida* (Lindl) Miers. This tree is native from Hispaniola, Puerto Rica and the Virgin Islands through the Lesser Antilles to Grenada and Barbados. Common names are roble, roble blanco (Puerto Rico); poirier rouge and poirier blanc (Guadeloupe); poirier (Dominica); apamate and pink poui (Grenada). The name 'white cedar' is also used in the Caribbean, but is confusing and should be discontinued.

The tree
Both species attain large sizes under favourable conditions; a height of 30.0m and a diameter of 0.75m but owing to local demand for the timber, trees are now generally smaller in accessible situations and heights of 18.0m or less are more common. Boles grow clear for 6.0m to 8.0m and occasionally 15.0m above the buttresses, which often extend 2.0m or 3.0m above the ground. Diameters of 0.5m are common, yet sometimes reaching 0.9m.

The timber
The wood of both species is similar in appearance and properties. The sapwood is narrow, white to yellowish, turning light brown on drying, and generally not very distinct from the heartwood, which is light brown with a golden, or sometimes greyish hue. Fine brown lines of parenchyma give the wood a distinctive figure on quarter-sawn surfaces and an attractive feather pattern on plain-sawn surfaces. The grain is straight to interlocked and the texture is medium to somewhat coarse. The wood is comparatively heavy and varies somewhat in weight according to the species and origin; *T. rosea* from Panama weighs on average 592 kg/m³ and that from Venezuela 560 kg/m³, while *T. heterophylla* from Puerto Rico averages 672 kg/m³ when dried.

Drying
Roble dries in the open air at a fast rate with a nominal amount of surface checking and slight warping; 25mm stock has been air dried in 3 to 4 months in Dominica and Puerto Rico without appreciable degrade. The wood also kiln dries with little degrade.

Strength
Tough and strong for its weight, roble is similar or superior to American black walnut (*Juglans nigra*).

Durability
Durable.

Working qualities
Except in planing, roble has excellent working properties. It can be sawn, shaped, turned and bored with excellent results and holds its place after manufacture. Some care is required in planing to prevent torn and chipped grain, but the wood can be planed to a glossy smoothness. It tends to split when nailed or screwed, and should therefore be pre-bored with sufficiently large lead holes. It takes mahogany and oak stains well, and can be finished naturally with excellent results. It takes a high polish under all conditions of finishing, and is also considered easy to glue. Roble produces good sliced veneer but requires careful boiling.

Uses
Its stability, ease of working, pleasing appearance and good strength render it ideal for furniture, cabinet-making, flooring, handles for sports equipment and agriculture, boat decking and other boat parts, paddles, shingles and general construction.

It is prized as a face veneer in Mexico, particularly when quarter-sliced, when its mottle figure gives a very attractive appearance.

ROSEWOOD, HONDURAS

Dalbergia stevensonii Standl.   Family: Leguminosae

Other names
nogaed (USA).

381

Distribution
Confined entirely to Belize.

The tree
Attains a height of 15.0m to 30.0m and is commonly forked at about 7.0m from the ground. The trunk is fluted, and about 1.0m in diameter.

The timber
The sapwood is yellowish in colour, 25mm to 50mm wide, and sharply delineated from the heartwood which is pinkish-brown to purple with irregular black zones or markings, which are independent of the growth rings. These alternate dark and light bands give the wood an unusual and very attractive appearance. The wood is very hard and heavy; it weighs about 960 kg/m^3 when dried. The texture is medium, and the grain straight to slightly roey. Fresh heartwood has a rose-like odour which generally dissipates with age.

Drying
The wood dries slowly with a tendency to split.

Strength
No information.

Durability
Very durable.

Working qualities
Hardness makes this timber somewhat difficult to work; it dulls cutting edges more readily than many other woods. It planes well, but must be held firmly, and a cutting angle of 20° is recommended, particularly where interlocked or wavy grain is present. It turns excellently and finishes well, except for some trouble with very oily specimens, but does not take a high natural polish.

Uses
Musical instruments eg finger boards for banjos, guitars and mandolins, percussion bars for xylophones; harp bodies, piano legs, veneered piano cases. Some of the best figured wood is made into veneer for furniture, cabinets, billiard tables, bank and store fittings. Mouldings, picture frames, and novelties.

SABICU

Lysiloma latisiliqua (L) Benth.   Family : Leguminosae

Other names
jigue (Cuba).

Distribution
The West Indies.

The timber
The wood is a dull brown colour with a coppery tinge and a bright lustre. It is medium textured, roey grained and moderately hard and heavy, weighing about 768 kg/m^3 when dried.

Durability
Very durable.

Working qualities
Sabicu is easy to work with both hand and machine tools, finishing smoothly with a high natural polish.

Uses
Formerly it was much employed in ship-building, where its good qualities gained for it a high reputation. It was also used extensively by Sheraton and the brothers Adam for cabinet-making. At the present time it is used locally for wheelwright work, mill rollers and sleepers.

SAMAN

Pithecellobium saman (Jacq) Benth.   Family : Leguminosae
syn *Samanea saman*

Other names
algarrobo (Mexico) ; rain-tree (Haiti).

Distribution
Native to Mexico, Central America and northern South America, it has also been widely planted throughout the West Indies and in tropical regions elsewhere.

The tree
Saman attains heights of 30.0m to 38.0m and diameters of 1.0m to 1.25m in the forest, but when grown in the open it develops massive wide-spreading crowns and short, very thick trunks, in some cases with a girth of 6.0m.

The timber
Saman resembles black walnut (*Juglans nigra*) in technical properties, structure, and general appearance. The narrow sapwood is white to yellow or light cinnamon, clearly demarcated from the heartwood, which is dark chocolate-brown when freshly cut, turning a light brown when dried. The wood is often marked with darker streaks resembling those of European walnut. The grain may be straight or irregular, and cross-grain may be present; the texture is medium, and the wood has a medium lustre. Young trees are reported to produce lighter, softer, and more easily worked timber, but later growth is slower, the wood is comparatively heavy, tough, and rather refractory. It weighs about 560 kg/m^3 when dried.

Drying
Requires careful drying if distortion is to be avoided; surface checking is generally considered to be minimal. Shrinkage values are reported to be exceptionally low for a wood of this density.

Strength
Medium hardness and strength; comparable to mahogany in most strength categories, but lower in modulus of rupture and elasticity.

Durability
Durable.

Working qualities
Easy to work and takes a beautiful finish. Material containing irregular grain works to a fairly good finish, but care is needed to obtain clean boring and mortising.

Uses
Furniture, cabinet-making, pattern-making, decorative veneer.

SATINWOOD, WEST INDIAN

Fagara flava Krug and Urb. syn   Family : Rutaceae
Zanthoxylum flavum Vahl. and
possibly allied species.

Other names
Jamaica satinwood (UK) ; San Domingan satinwood (USA) ;
yellow sanders (West Indies) ; aceitillo (Cuba).
Not to be confused with Sri Lanka satinwood(*Chloroxylon
swietenia*).

Distribution
The tree grows in Bermuda, the Bahamas and southern Florida,
but it attains its best development in Jamaica, where it reaches
a height of 12.0m and a diameter of 0.5m.

The timber
A golden yellow to cream coloured wood having an odour of
coconuts when freshly sawn. It has a fine texture, with straight
to irregular grain, often with a roe or mottle figure. It weighs
about 900 kg/m^3 when dried.

Durability
Non-durable.

Working qualities
Works well with most tools with only a moderate dulling effect
on cutting edges. Where irregular grain is encountered, a cutting
angle of 20° helps to improve the finish. Turns excellently and
takes a fine polish.

Uses
Furniture, high-class cabinet-making, turnery, small textile
bobbins, marquetry and fancy articles.

SIMARUBA

Simaruba amara Aublet.   Family : Simarubiaceae

Other names
maruba, marupa, bois blanc (Dominica and St Lucia).

Distribution
Rare in the heavy rain forests but a common constituent of secondary rain forest in gaps and clearings. Found in all the Windward Islands.

The tree
It is a large tree, without buttresses, reaching a height of 36.0m and a diameter of 0.75m. The stem is long, straight and clean.

The timber
The sapwood is white, with little distinction from the heartwood which although light yellow when freshly cut, becomes whiter when dry. It is soft, smooth in texture and light in weight, about 450 kg/m^3 when dried.

Drying
Rather difficult to air dry from the green state. It dries rapidly with an inclination to split, but this tendency has been reduced by restricting the width of boards to 200mm.

Strength
It compares favourably with American yellow poplar (*Liriodendron*) in most strength properties, but is about 50 per cent weaker in tension perpendicular to the grain.

Durability
Non-durable but permeable.

Working qualities
Simaruba is very easy to work. It saws easily across the grain and gives a clean cut. It planes readily to a smooth finish, drills easily and cleanly and takes nails well without splitting. It accepts paint and varnish satisfactorily.

Uses
Owing to its strength, lightness, easily worked qualities, and smooth finish, this timber is highly suitable for furniture and all kinds of interior work, especially as a substitute for softwood.

STERCULIA

Sterculia caribaea R.Br.   Family : Sterculiaceae

Other names
mahot cochon, mahoe (West Indies generally) ; anacaguita (Cuba and Puerto Rico) ; castano (Central America generally).

Distribution
The West Indies from Jamaica, Guadeloupe, Dominica, Martinique and Trinidad, to Venezuela and Guyana. It is common in Dominica and fairly common in St Lucia.

The tree
A large unbuttressed tree, with a heavy, rounded crown, reaching a height of 40.0m and a diameter of 1.0m on the best sites, but more commonly 30.0m high and about 0.6m diameter. The boles are about 18.0m to 21.0m long, cylindrical and with a low taper.

The timber
The sapwood is about 50mm wide, not very distinct from the heartwood, and is subject to discoloration by sap-staining fungi. The heartwood is light greyish-brown, sometimes with reddish streaks, while numerous brown ray flecks appear on quarter-sawn surfaces. The grain is usually straight, and the texture is medium to coarse. Soft, and light in weight, the wood weighs about 512 kg/m^3 when dried.

Drying
Moderately difficult to dry. It air dries fairly rapidly but tends to warp and twist. The schedule for kiln drying should aim at retarding the drying rate when degrade should not be severe.

Strength
About normal for wood of this density, but it does not possess high strength properties and should not be used where exceptional strength is required.

Durability
Non-durable.

Working qualities
Easy to work but the finish is somewhat fibrous, and sharp cutting edges are required to obtain good results. Nails well, stains and polishes satisfactorily if a fair amount of filler is used.

Uses
Light construction, concrete forms, boxes and crates, interior joinery. It is said to produce good pulp for paper making.

TABEBUIA, WHITE

Tabebuia stenocalyx Sprague & Stapf.   Family : Bignoniaceae

Other names
Within the genus *Tabebuia* are two distinct groups of timbers, one, the Lapacho group, characterized by the presence of an abundance of a yellow powder (lapachol compound) in the vessels, and noted for their great strength and durability; *Tabebuia serratifolia* belongs to this group and produces ipê of South America. The second group is the 'white cedar' group, so-called because the bark of the tree resembles that of *Cedrela* spp. The wood of *Tabebuia* however, in no way re-resembles that of *Cedrela*, and although commonly called 'white cedar' or 'cedre blanc' throughout the Caribbean and Central America, the name is confusing and should be discontinued. White tabebuia would appear to be a better description.

Distribution
This is a common tree of the seasonal and dry evergreen forest at low elevations, but it sometimes extends to the lower fringes of the rain forest. It is very common in all the Windward Islands and regenerates profusely on poor soils in the dry areas. It also occurs in Trinidad, Guyana and French Guiana.

The tree
Normally a large tree attaining a height of over 30.0m and a diameter of 0.75m but owing to demand, trees of this size are rare in accessible areas, and more usually they are about 27.0m high with a diameter of 0.5m above low buttresses. Old trees growing in the open often have short, thick, deeply fluted boles, with the ridges extending to the buttresses.

388

The timber
The heartwood varies in colour from creamy, yellowish or greyish-brown to brownish, often with dark flecks showing on the surface. The sapwood is lighter in colour and not clearly differentiated from the heartwood. The grain is fairly straight, the texture is medium and the wood has a moderately high lustre. It is a moderately hard, firm wood without the yellow deposits found in timbers of the Lapachol group. The wood weighs about 640 kg/m^3 when dried.

Drying
It does not warp or split, but dries slowly.

Strength
White tabebuia possesses good strength properties for a wood of its density, and is only slightly inferior to oak.

Durability
Moderately durable.

Working qualities
Although logs are reported to spring badly during conversion, the dried wood saws, planes, shapes, mortises, bores and sands easily with smooth clean edges in all operations. It finishes and polishes very smoothly with a glossy finish, resembling yellow birch in some respects.

Uses
Owing to its strength, reasonable durability, and attractive appearance, the wood is in great demand for a wide variety of purposes. It is used for boat decking, and boat parts where a high resistance to decay is not essential. The natural bends in old, open-grown trees is much sought after for ribs and knees of schooners and the timber has long been in demand for boat-building in the Caribbean. It is used for furniture, flooring, paddles, interior house trim, carpentry, building construction, and for boxes and crates. Its use has been suggested for sports goods and agricultural implements as a substitute for ash, and as decorative veneer. Owing to the growth characteristics of many of the accessible trees, boards over 3.0m in length are difficult to obtain.

TEAK

Tectona grandis L.f.   Family : Verbenaceae

Teak is not indigenous to tropical America, but it has been widely
planted in continental tropical America and the West Indies, and
since it represents a future source of exportable surplus material,
it is included in this booklet.

Other names
It is marketed locally as plantation-grown teak, or as teak, teck
(French) or teca (Spanish).

Distribution
Teak is planted extensively in Guyana, Puerto Rico, Cuba,
Haiti, Jamaica, and in other islands of the West Indies and
countries in the Caribbean area, but it is best known from
Trinidad, Honduras and Belize. It has been grown most successfully in Trinidad and other areas on deep, well-drained soil
with rainfall of 1200mm to 3000mm, but it is also reported to do
well on a variety of soils and geographical formations provided
that there is a good sub-soil drainage. Plantations are thriving
in Trinidad on areas formerly occupied by semi-deciduous
forests and rain forests.
Teak is also well established on lands carrying second-growth
brush, on former cocoa estate lands, and on other areas of
heavy clay soil with good drainage, but it is interesting to note
that H E Castens, in 'An investigation of soil conditions in
compartment 1, Bivet Reserve, Prome Division, with reference
to dying off of *Tectona grandis*'., Burma Forest Dept., Bulletin
18, Rangoon, 1927, states that teak should only be planted in
the alluvial valley soil and on areas of deep loamy sand and
loam on the lower ridges. He further concluded that teak
planted on clay soils in Burma does not do well, a factor which
may account for the differences in characteristics between
forest-grown Burma teak and teak grown in some plantations.

The tree
Teak is a very large deciduous tree in its native habitat and a
height of 30.0m and a diameter of 1.0m is not unusual. In dry
forests the growth rate is slow; 5 to 8 years are required to

grow 25mm in diameter. In moist forests, and in cultivated plantations under very favourable conditions in the Caribbean area, teak may grow as much as 25mm or more in 2 years, and the trees may attain diameters of 0.75m or more in 60 years, as opposed to 100 to 200 years for similar sized trees growing naturally in Burma.

Saw-log sized trees have been produced in Honduras in 20 years under extremely favourable conditions, while plantations in other tropical areas have shown similar results, but in general, plantation-grown trees require up to twice this time to reach economic maturity.

The timber

The heartwood of plantation-grown teak is olive green when freshly cut, becoming golden brown, and eventually very dark brown upon exposure. The sapwood is yellowish to white coloured, and 25mm to 50mm wide, sharply demarcated from the heartwood. It is usually straight-grained and of uniform fine texture, and the wood has the traditional oily feel. Growth rings are distinct and appear on side grain as narrow brown lines darker than the rest of the wood.

There is a belief that plantation-grown teak is always lower in density than forest-grown wood; comparisons however, have shown that teak from Burma and Indonesia weighed on average 640 kg/m^3 when dried, and that from Honduras weighed the same, while teak grown in Trinidad was a little heavier at 688 kg/m^3.

Drying

Teak from all sources dries with a minimum of degrade. In tests carried out at Yale University, plantation-grown stock from Honduras air dried rapidly and well, but material from green logs required more initial protection against rapid drying, than is the case with material from ring-girdled trees normally felled in Burma and Thailand, and it was found that there was liable to be considerable variation in the drying rate of individual boards, because differences between the initial and final moisture contents are occasionally great.

Strength

Tests of the mechanical properties of plantation-grown teak from Trinidad showed it equal or superior to forest-grown

Burma teak in static bending, compression parallel to the grain, tension parallel to the grain, and hardness and toughness properties. In similar tests, teak from Honduras was slightly superior to Burma teak in compression across the grain, shear, cleavage and toughness; slightly lower in stiffness, crushing strength and tension across the grain, and similar in other properties. Studies at Dehra Dun, India, also showed no essential difference in strength properties between forest-grown and plantation-grown Indian teak.

Durability

Teak grown in its natural habitat has long been recognised as a very durable timber when used in conditions inducive to decay, and of excellent resistance to marine borers and termites. However, controlled tests of untreated, 10 year old teak from plantations in Trinidad indicated the wood is only moderately durable to fungus attack and definitely susceptible to attack by subterranean termites. Pure culture tests with 20 year old, plantation-grown teak from Honduras showed the wood to be somewhat variable but generally very durable to damage by both white-rot and brown-rot fungus.

Plantation-grown teak possesses excellent weathering characteristics. Unpainted wood is almost entirely free from warp and checking when exposed to the weather.

Although teak heartwood is highly resistant to preservative treatment, it is common practice in Trinidad to treat plantation-grown teak posts by the open tank process. This treatment adds considerable life to the thick sapwood content of small posts.

Working qualities

Plantation-grown teak is easily worked with both hand and machine tools. Its dulling effect on cutting edges (teak contains up to 1.4 per cent silica by weight) can be overcome by using carbide or other high-quality steel. Reduced spindle speeds are recommended when using ordinary, good-quality, high-speed steel knives and cutters. It takes nails and screws fairly well, glues moderately well despite its oily nature, and gives good results with polish and varnish.

Uses

Thinnings from plantations in Trinidad are split and used in wire fencing, or are squared and used for house framing, but plantation-grown teak is used as lumber for the same purposes as forest-grown material, including veneer, boat and ship-building, furniture and chemical resisting items.

TONKA

Dipteryx odorata (Aubl) Willd.   Family : Leguminosae

Other names
koemaroe (Surinam) ; kumaru (Guyana).

Distribution
Naturally distributed throughout northern South America and Central America, the tree has been widely cultivated in Mexico and the West Indies, particularly in Jamaica.

Although the primary aim of cultivation has been vested in the collection of the tonka beans produced by the tree, commercially valuable as a substitute for vanilla for cocoa production and for flavouring snuff and tobacco, nevertheless the timber is also an excellent material.

The tree
A fairly large, unbuttressed tree, 24.0m to 36.0m high, with a diameter of 0.5m to 0.75m but are often larger on the best sites. The boles are clean and cylindrical, and generally 18.0m to 24.0m long.

The timber
The heartwood is reddish-brown or purplish-brown, with light yellowish-brown or purplish streaks when freshly cut, turning to a variegated reddish and yellowish-brown after drying, but on exposure to light, assuming a uniform yellowish-brown or light brown colour. The sapwood is about 50mm wide, distinct from the heartwood and yellowish-brown in colour. The wood has a waxy or oily feel, a fine texture, and irregular and often interlocked grain. It is an extremely hard and heavy wood, weighing about 1070 kg/m³ when air dry.

Drying
Considering its density, the wood is relatively easy to dry. It tends to surface check if dried rapidly, but moderate to slow drying rates should reduce the tendency.

Strength

The strength of the green wood closely resembles that of greenheart, except in tension across the grain and side hardness in which tonka is superior. Air dry wood is much stronger than green wood except for an appreciable reduction in cleavage resistance and tensile strength across the grain. In general it is superior to white oak in all properties except cleavage resistance.

Working qualities

Tonka is a heavy, hard, and tough wood which makes it rather difficult to work, but with sharp tools it saws and bores cleanly, and when severely interlocked grain is absent, planes and finishes to a smooth surface. It takes a high polish, but glues poorly.

Uses

Tonka is very resistant to decay in contact with the ground, and a life of 10 to 22 years has been reported for untreated railway sleepers, which is considered superior to sleepers produced from creosoted white oak. The wood is also used extensively for fishing rods, cogs and shafts, paving blocks, barge and dock fenders, flooring, tool handles, agricultural implements, sporting goods, and other uses calling for good shock resistance and high bending strength. Its hardness and oily nature also allows its use for bearings, cogs, etc, in place of lignum vitae, where friction wear is a problem. High-grade face veneer has also been produced from the wood in the USA.

VIROLA, LIGHT

Virola spp., principally   Family : Myristicaceae
Virola koschnyi Warb.

Light virola includes banak which is very similar in appearance and properties to baboen (*V. surinamensis*) which occurs both in Central America and in South America.

Other names

V. koschnyi; banak (Belize) ; sangre (Guatemala and Nicaragua) ; fruta colorado (Costa Rica) ; bogabani (Panama).

V. surinamensis; baboen (Central America generally) ; muscadier a grive (Fr. West Indies).

Distribution
V. koschnyi ranges from Belize and Guatemala to Panama.
V. surinamensis grows in some of the southern West Indies from Guadeloupe to Grenada, Trinidad and Tobago, and on the continent of South America.

The tree
Both banak and baboen are moisture-loving trees, attaining a height of 42.0m and a diameter of 1.5m under favourable conditions, but usually they are shorter, with cylindrical boles clear of branches to about 18.0m to 24.0m and a diameter of about 1.0m.

The timber
Light virola is cream or tan colour when freshly sawn, the heartwood becoming pinkish, golden brown, or deep reddish-brown on exposure and distinguishable from the lighter-coloured sapwood. The wood has straight grain, medium to coarse texture, and low lustre. It weighs about 528 kg/m^3 when dried.

Drying
Requires care. There is a tendency for material over 50mm thick to retain its moisture despite rapid surface drying, and this, coupled with a high shrinkage ratio and a strong tendency to split radially, can lead to excessive distortion, deep checking and splitting. Thinner sizes can be dried without excessive degrade provided the rapid drying properties are recognised and catered for by suitable drying treatment.
In drying from the green to 12 per cent moisture content, light virola shrinks 3 per cent radially, and 9 per cent tangentially, while from green to oven-dry, the values are 4.8 per cent and 13.4 per cent respectively.

Strength
Light virola is superior to Honduras mahogany in stiffness, shock resistance and shear, but below that timber in other strength properties.

Durability
Non-durable.

Working qualities
Banak and baboen work easily and very satisfactorily. Nails and screws can be driven without the wood splitting; it glues well, and can be stained without difficulty to resemble mahogany fairly well, and gives satisfactory results in polishing and varnishing. Despite its difficult drying properties, it holds its place well when manufactured, with practically no tendency to warp or check.

Uses
Banak and baboen are mostly used for plywood, but are suitable in lumber form for many uses requiring a light, easily worked, non-durable timber. In many areas of the Caribbean and in Central America, both woods are replacing mahogany plywood in the manufacture of furniture and cabinets, and for panelling.

YOKEWOOD

Catalpa longissima (Jacq) Sims   Family: Bignoniaceae
Syn *Macrocatalpa longissima* (Jacq) Britton

Other names
Although unrelated to the true oaks (*Quercus*), the alternative common names in the Caribbean area are 'French oak', 'Haitian oak', 'Jamaica oak', bois chêne, and chêne de Amérique.

Distribution
It is common to Jamaica, Haiti, Cuba and the Dominican Republic, and the tree has been introduced into Guadeloupe and Grenada.

The tree
It is a large tree, attaining a height of 24.0m and a diameter of 1.0m. It has a high degree of tolerance to unfavourable site conditions and grows well on rocky and degraded sites and on arid, dry coastal plains.

The timber

The heartwood is greyish to light brown in colour, contrasting with the lighter coloured sapwood. The wood has a fairly high lustre, is generally straight-grained, and the texture is medium to coarse. The wood has a faint odour, reminiscent of paraffin, and weighs about 592 to 800 kg/m³ when dried.

No data are available in respect of drying, and strength properties.

Durability

Durable.

Working qualities

No information except that the wood is reported to saw easily.

Uses

Used in Jamaica for boat-building and house construction for sills, shingles, framing and flooring. It is used for similar purposes in Haiti, and also for furniture.

PART II   SOFTWOODS

PITCH PINE, CARIBBEAN

Pinus caribaea Morelet and   Family : Pinaceae
Pinus oocarpa Schiede

Other names

Pinus caribaea; Honduras, Bahamas, Nicaraguan, etc, pitch pine, Caribbean longleaf pitch pine. (UK).
Pinus oocarpa; ocote pine (Central America) ; west coast Nicaraguan pitch pine, Caribbean longleaf pitch pine (UK).

Note

Pinus caribaea is the principal coniferous species found in the Caribbean area ; Formerly considered the same as slash pine of the south-eastern USA, it was discovered that minor morphological differences necessitated separation of the species and United States slash pine has now been given the distinctive name *Pinus elliottii* Engelm.

Distribution
Pinus caribaea grows in the Bahamas, western Cuba, the Isle of Pines, and in Central America from Belize to eastern Guatemala, northern Honduras and north-eastern Nicaragua.

The tree
The size of the trees vary somewhat according to location, but usually they grow to a height of about 30.0m with a diameter of 1.0m and are free from branches for about 15.0m to 21.0m.

The timber
The wood closely resembles American pitch pine ; the heartwood is reddish-brown, the depth of colour varying with the amount of resin present and the sapwood, which is 50mm to 75mm wide, is pale yellowish-brown. The wood is coarse in texture with a more or less pronounced resinous odour, and the grain is typically straight. Growth zones of dark tissue produce conspicuous bands on all surfaces, and while a relatively wide band of late-wood appears to terminate the annual growth, there are in addition, from one to several lines of dense wood forming secondary rings frequently present.

The average number of primary rings per 25mm varies from 5 close to the pith to about 16, 180mm to 250mm from the pith, in wood from Belize and Nicaragua, but that from the Bahamas by comparison is more slowly grown, and therefore more narrow-ringed.

The average weight of the wood is 720 kg/m³ when dried.

Drying
Pitch pine air dries rather slowly with a tendency for end splitting in thick stock to occur. It also kiln dries slowly, and care is needed to avoid checking, splitting and distortion.

Strength
Caribbean pitch pine is a hard, dense, resinous timber of high strength properties resembling those of the densest grade of American pitch pine when dried, but some 15 per cent more resistant to shock loads and to splitting, and about 45 per cent harder.

Durability
Moderately durable.

Working qualities

The wood is easy to work with either hand or machine tools, comparing closely with American pitch pine in resistance to cutting and cleanness of finish. Its dulling effect on cutting edges is not severe unless prolonged runs are made with cutters or teeth clogged with resin. Resin also adheres to machine tables and fences causing difficulty in ease and steadiness of feeding if the resin is not occasionally removed, and is particularly troublesome when the timber is only partially dried. The use of a fairly long tooth pitch offers some relief during sawing operations.

There is a slight tendency for grain pick-up and tearing around knots during planing and moulding; this can be minimized by careful setting and jointing of knives to assure that each knife shares equally in the cutting. The timber takes screws and nails satisfactorily with only a slight tendency to splitting, and can be successfully stained and varnished, although pitch pickets may cause difficulty in painting. It can also be glued satisfactorily.

Uses

Caribbean pitch pine is used for the same purposes as American pitch pine, for marine piling and structures, bridges, vat-making, decking, masts and spars, and temporary bulk heads in boat-building, interior joinery, particularly for schools and churches, and for carpentry and flooring.

YELLOWWOOD

Podocarpus guatemalensis Standl.   Family: Podocarpaceae

Other names

The wood is also known as 'cypress' in Belize. This name is confusing and should be discontinued.

Distribution

The tree occurs in Belize, Guatemala and southern Mexico.

The tree

A small to medium-height tree, between 9.0m and 18.0m tall, and a diameter of about 0.5m.

The timber
The timber is very similar to other *Podocarpus* species, being non-resinous, light yellowish-brown in colour throughout, although some logs may show a darker coloured core. Generally straight-grained, with a fine, uniform texture, it weighs about 510 kg/m^3 when dried.

Drying
Dries at a moderate rate with some tendency to split and check.

Strength
Equal or superior to European redwood (*Pinus sylvestris*) in all properties except stiffness in bending, in which yellowwood is slightly inferior.

Durability
Moderately durable.

Working qualities
Works easily. Nails without splitting, and takes stain, paint and varnish satisfactorily.

Uses
Joinery, boxes and crates, concrete forms, and general utility, Would probably be acceptable for utility plywood.

USE GUIDE FOR CENTRAL AMERICAN AND CARIBBEAN TIMBERS

AGRICULTURAL IMPLEMENTS

balata
basralocus
bullhoof
courbaril
manni
nargusta

pitch pine
roble
tabebuia, white
tonka
yokewood

BOAT AND SHIP CONSTRUCTION

Decking
andiroba
basralocus
cordia
courbaril
laurier poivre
nargusta

pitch pine
roble
tabebuia, white
teak
yokewood

Framing
angelin
balata
basralocus
courbaril
manni
nargusta

pitch pine
roble
tabebuia, white
teak
tonka
yokewood

Keels and stems
basralocus
bois gris
courbaril
pitch pine

tabebuia, white
teak
tonka
yokewood

Oars
petit citron

Paddles
roble

Planking
bois bande
'cedar'

courbaril
mahogany

Boat and Ship Construction (cont.)
Planking (cont.)

nargusta
pitch pine
roble

saman
tabebuia, white
teak

Superstructures

andiroba
'cedar'
courbaril
gommier

laurier poivre
mahogany
teak

BOXES AND CRATES

almacigo
andiroba
bois lait
cativo
'cedar'
encens
gommier
hura

manni
maruba
pitch pine
roble
sterculia
virola, light
yellowwood
yemeri

CONSTRUCTION

Heavy

angelin
aromata
balata
bois gris
bustic
carapite
guayacan

laurier poivre
manni
mauricif
pitch pine
resolu
yokewood

Light

andiroba
bois bande
bois lait
bullhoof
cativo
'cedar'
cordia
encens
gommier

hura
laurier petites feuilles
magnolia
maruba
pipirie
sterculia
virola, light
yellowwood
yemeri

DOORS

bois bande
cativo
'cedar'
cordia
encens

gommier
laurier petites feuilles
mahogany
pipirie
virola, light

FANCY GOODS

cocobolo
cocuswood

rosewood
satinwood

FLOORING

andiroba
balata
basralocus
bustic
caconnier rouge
carapite
cordia
courbaril
guayacan
hura
magnolia

mahoe
mahogany
manni
nargusta
pitch pine
resolu
roble
tabebuia, white
teak
tonka
yokewood

FURNITURE

andiroba
angelin
caconnier rouge
cativo
'cedar'
cordia
courbaril
degame
encens
gommier
hura
laurier petites feuilles
laurier poivre
magnolia
mahoe

mahogany
manni
mauricif
nargusta
prima vera
roble
rosewood
sabicu
saman
satinwood
simaruba
tabebuia, white
teak
virola, light
yokewood

JOINERY

High-class
andiroba
bois bande
caconnier rouge
cativo
'cedar'
cordia
courbaril
encens
fustic (dry interior
    situations only)

gommier
laurier poivre
mahoe
mahogany
mauricif
pitch pine
prima vera
teak
virola, light

Utility
almacigo
bois lait
bullhoof
hura
laurier petites feuilles
magnolia

pipirie
simaruba
sterculia
yellowwood
yemeri

MARINE PILING AND CONSTRUCTION

Under water
(a) *Teredo* infested waters
basralocus
bois gris

bustic
pitch pine (treated with
    preservative)

(b) Non-*Teredo* waters
In addition to above,
aromata
angelin
bullhoof

courbaril
manni
teak
tonka
yokewood

Above water
(a) Docks, wharves, bridges,
etc.
angelin
aromata
balata
basralocus

bois gris
bustic
carapite
guayacan
tonka
pitch pine

(b) Decking
basralocus
carapite
guayacan
pitch pine
yokewood

MUSICAL INSTRUMENTS

'cedar'
cocuswood
lancewood
mahogany
rosewood

PATTERNMAKING

almacigo
'cedar'
mahogany
simaruba
saman

SPORTS GOODS

courbaril (sub. for ash)
degame
lancewood
lignum vitae
rosewood
tabebuia, white (sub. for ash)
tonka

STAIR TREADS

balata
bois bande
cordia
courbaril
laurier poivre
mahogany
yokewood

TERMITE RESISTANCE (HEARTWOOD) *

Very resistant
balata
courbaril
mahogany (*Swietenia
mahagoni*)

Resistant
angelin
bois gris
'cedar'
nargusta
pitch pine
resolu
saman
teak

Moderately resistant

angelin
bullhoof
mahogany (*Swietenia macrophylla*)

manni
yokewood

Very susceptible

almacigo
andiroba
encens
gommier
hura
roble

simaruba
sterculia
tabebuia, white
virola, light
yemeri

* The above classification is based on results of tests carried out in Puerto Rico and Trinidad and refers to resistance to attack by both subterranean and dry-wood termites. Where the resistance to either type of pest differs, the lower rating is given.

TURNERY

andiroba
angelin
balata
bullhoof
cocobolo

cocuswood
degame
lancewood
nargusta
satinwood

VEHICLE BODIES

basralocus
bustic
cativo

cordia
magnolia

VENEER AND PLYWOOD

Corestock

almacigo
andiroba
'cedar'
gommier
hura

simaruba
virola, light
yellowwood
yemeri

Decorative

almacigo	nargusta
andiroba	prima vera
angelin	roble
'cedar'	rosewood
courbaril	saman
gommier	tabebuia, white
hura	teak
mahogany	tonka
manni	virola, light

Utility (Plywood, chip-baskets, small laminated items, etc.)

almacigo	pitch pine
bullhoof	simaruba
gommier	yellowwood
hura	yemeri

AMENABILITY OF HEARTWOOD TO PRESERVATIVE TREATMENT

Extremely resistant

angelin	cocobolo
aromata	encens
basralocus	guayacan
bois gris	laurier petites feuilles
bullhoof	mahogany
bustic	manni
carapite	nargusta
cedar	teak

Resistant

andiroba	bois bande

Moderately resistant

caconnier rouge	mauricif
cativo	resolu
gommier	pitch pine

Permeable

almacigo	quaruba
bois lait	simaruba
hura	virola, light
pipirie	yellowwood

The above classification refers to the ease with which a timber absorbs preservative under both open-tank (non-pressure) and pressure treatments. Sapwood, although nearly always perishable, is usually more permeable than heartwood, accordingly, the above classification refers to the relative resistance of heartwood to penetration.

Extremely resistant
Timbers that absorb only a small amount of preservative even under long pressure treatments. They cannot be penetrated to an appreciable depth laterally, and only to a very small extent longitudinally.

Resistant
Timbers difficult to impregnate under pressure and require a long period of treatment. It is often difficult to penetrate them laterally more than about 3mm to 6mm.
Incising is often used to obtain better treatment.

Moderately resistant
Timbers that are fairly easy to treat, and it is usually possible to obtain a lateral penetration of the order of 6mm to 18mm in about 2-3 hours under pressure, or a penetration of a large proportion of the vessels.

Permeable
Timbers that can be penetrated completely under pressure without difficulty, and can usually be heavily impregnated by the open-tank process.

REFERENCES

BOLZA, E. Properties and uses of 175 timber species from Papua New Guinea and West Irian. Australia. Division of Building Research, Report 34, Highett, CSIRO. 1975.

BOZA, E. and KLOOT, N. H. The mechanical properties of 174 Australian timbers. Australia. Division of Forest Products, Technological Paper 25. Melbourne, CSIRO. 1963.

BRITISH STANDARDS INSTITUTION. Nomenclature of commercial timbers, including sources of supply. British Standards BS 881 and 589. London, BSI. 1974.

BUILDING RESEARCH ESTABLISHMENT. A handbook of softwoods. BRE Report. London, HMSO 2nd ed. 1977.

BUILDING RESEARCH ESTABLISHMENT. PRINCES RIS—BOROUGH LABORATORY. Handbook of hardwoods, revised by R. H. Farmer. 2nd ed. London, HMSO. 1972.

FRASER, H. The principal timber trees of the Windward Islands. Kingston, Jamaica, Conservator of Forests. 1957.

GRAY, V. R. Timber in New Zealand. Journal of the Institute of Wood Science, June 1974, 6(5) No. 35, 13-17.

HAIR, D. and SPADA, B. Hardwood timber resources of the United States. Paper presented to Conference on Tropical Hardwoods, Syracuse University, August 1969. New York, Syracuse University. 1969.

HOWARD, Alexander L. Trees in Britain and their timbers. London Country Life Ltd. 1947.

HOWARD, Alexander L. A Manual of timbers of the world. London, Macmillan & Co. Ltd. 3rd ed. 1948.

JANE, F. W. The structure of wood, revised by K. Wilson and D. J. B. White. London, Adam & Charles Black. 2nd ed. 1970.

KLOOT, N. H. and BOLZA, E. Properties of timbers imported into

Australia. Australia. Division of Forest Products, Technological Paper No. 12. Melbourne, CSIRO, 1961.

LONGWOOD, F. R. Present and potential commercial timbers of the Caribbean with special reference to the West Indies, the Guianas and British Honduras. US. Department of Agriculture, Agriculture Handbook 207. Washington, USDA. 1962 (1971).

McELHANNEY and associates. Canadian woods: Their properties and uses. Ottawa, Forest Products Laboratories of Canada. 1935.

PHILIPPINES. FOREST PRODUCTS RESEARCH AND IND-USTRIES DEVELOPMENT COMMISSION. Philippine Timber Series Nos. 1-14, Laguna, FPRIDC. nd.

PLEYDELL, G. J. Timbers of the British Solomon Islands. London, United Africa Co (Timber) Ltd. for Levers Pacific Timbers Ltd. 1970.

RECORD, S. J. and HESS, R. W. Timbers of the New World. New Haven, Yale University Press; London, Oxford University Press. 1943.

STANDARDS ASSOCIATION OF AUSTRALIA. Nomenclature of Australian timbers. Australian Standard AS 02. Sydney, SAA. 1970.

STOKOE, W. J. The Observer's book of trees and shrubs of the British Isles. London and New York, Frederick Warne and Co. Ltd. nd.

TRADA 'Timbers of the World' Volume 1 Africa, South America, Southern Asia and South East Asia. Lancaster, The Construction Press. 1979.

INDEX

ANDAMAN PADAUK 1—305
Andaman pyinma 1—315
Andaman redwood 1—305
Andira inermis 2—335
ANDIROBA 1—143; 2—333
ANGELIN 2—335
angelim 2—335
angelim do Para 1—146
ANGELIM PEDRA 1—147
angélique 1—152; 2—339
angélique gris 1—153; 2—339
angélique rouge 1—153; 2—339
angouran 1—87
ANINGERIA 1—15
Aningeria adolfi-friderici 1—15
Aningeria altissima 1—15
Aningeria pseudo-racemosa 1—15
Aningeria robusta 1—15
Anisoptera cochinchinensis 1—394
Anisoptera costata 1—393
Anisoptera curtisii 1—393, 394
Anisoptera glabra 1—394
Anisoptera laevis 1—393
Anisoptera marginata 1—393
Anisoptera megistocarpa 1—393
Anisoptera oblonga 1—393, 394
Anisoptera scaphula 1—393
Anisoptera thurifera 2—58
ANJAN 1—262
anjili 1—258
Anogeissus acuminata 1—265
Anogeissus latifolia 1—263
anokye 1—99
anoniwana 1—228
Annona dodecapetala 2—366
'Antarctic beech' 2—366
Anthocephalus chinensis 2—270
Anthocephalus cadamba 2—270
ANTIARIS 1—16
Antiaris toxicaria 1—16
Antiaris welwitschii 1—16
anyan 1—19
anyanran 1—19
anyaran 1—19
apa 1—8, 237
apamate 2—380
apaya 1—17
apeya 1—17
APITONG 2—12
Apodytes dimidiata 1—77
apopo 1—115
appayia 1—17
APPLE WOOD 2—188
appurz 1—336
aprono 1—71
Apuleia leiocarpa 1—207
Apuleia praecox 1—207
arakoko 2—303
ARANGA 2—14
aranga 2—271

arangan 2—14
araputanga 1—194; 2—369
ARARIBA 1—147
arariba amarelo 1—147
arariba carijo 1—147
arariba rajado 1—147
arariba rosa 1—147
arariba tinga 1—147
arariba vermelho 1—147
ARAUCARIA SPECIES 2—306
Araucaria angustifolia 1—243
Araucaria araucana 1—241
Araucaria bidwillii 2—306
Araucaria cunninghamii 2—306
Araucaria excelsa 2—306
Araucaria heterophylla 2—306
Araucaria hunsteinii 2—306
Araucaria klinkii 2—306
arbor vitae, eastern 2—192
arbor vitae, giant 2—195
arere 1—88
arimanu 2—281
AROMATA 2—336
Artocarpus anisophyllus 1—370
Artocarpus chaplasha 1—280
Artocarpus dadah 1—370
Artocarpus elasticus 1—414
Artocarpus fulvicortex 1—370
Artocarpus heterophyllus 1—370
Artocarpus hirsuta 1—258
Artocarpus incisus 1—370
Artocarpus integer 1—370
Artocarpus kemando 1—370
Artocarpus lanceifolius 1—370
Artocarpus maingayii 1—370
Artocarpus nitidus 1—370
Artocarpus rigidus 1—370
Artocarpus scortechinii 1—414
asame-tsuge 2—22
ASH, AMERICAN 2—159
ash, alpine 2—292
ash, Bennett's 2—261
ASH, BLACK 2—160
ash, black 2—281
ash, brown 2—160
ash, bumpy 2—261
ash, Canadian 2—161
ash, canary 2—295
ash, coast 2—266
ash, Crow's 2—261
ash, English 2—87
ASH, EUROPEAN 2—87
ash, French 2—87
ASH, GREEN 2—160
ASH, JAPANESE 2—14
ash-leaved maple 2—178
ash, leopard 2—261
ash, mountain 2—292
ash, New England 2—247
ash, northern silver 2—261

ash, olive 2—87
ash, Polish 2—87
ash, Queensland silver 2—261
ash, red 2—160
ash, silvertop 2—266
ash, Slavonian 2—87
ash, southern silver 2—261
ash, Victorian 2—292
ASH, WHITE 2—161
ASH, WHITE AUSTRALIAN 2—302
ash, yellowwood 2—261
aspen 2—113, 114
aspen, big tooth 2—183
ASPEN, CANADIAN 2—182
aspen, English 2—114
aspen, European 2—114
aspen, Finnish 2—114
aspen, quaking 2—182
aspen, Swedish 2—114
Aspidosperma peroba 1—208
Aspidosperma polyneuron 1—208
assacu 1—176; 2—359
assamela 1—7
assié 1—114
asta 2—361
Astronium fraxinifolium 1—170
Astronium graveolens 1—170
ATA-ATA GROUP 2—28
ata-ata 2—28
Atlantic cedar 2—122
'Atlantic white cedar' 2—192
Atlas cedar 2—122
atom-assié 1—96
atui 1—34
Aucoumea klaineana 1—45
aune 2—86
AUSTRALIAN BLACKWOOD
    2—249
'AUSTRALIAN CEDAR' 2—255
'Australian oak' 2—291
'Australian silky oak' 2—285
'Australian walnut' 2—282
'AUSTRALIAN WHITE ASH 2—302
AUSTRIAN PINE 2—129
ausubo 2—338
Autranella congolensis 1—81
AVODIRÉ 1—17
awa 2—293
awari 1—103
awun 1—14
awuru 1—83
AXLEWOOD 1—263
ayabala 2—271
AYAN 1—19
aye lotofa 1—108
ayinre 1—12
ayous 1—88
Azadirachta integrifolia 2—26
azobé 1—41

B

ba 1—29
babbar 1—265
babli 1—265
baboen 2—395
baboen ordalli 1—235
BABUL 1—265
bacomixa 1—172
bacomixava 1—172
bacoropary 1—204
bacu 1—182
badam 1—269
badi 1—98
bagac 2—12
Bagassa guianensis 1—229
Bagassa tiliaefolia 1—229
bagasse 1—229
bagbalogo 2—18
BAGTIKAN 2—40
BAGUACU 1—148
bagulibas 2—6
bahai 1—3; 2—18
Bahia rosewood 1—215
Bahia wood 1—155
Baikiaea plurijuga 1—111
Baillonella toxisperma 1—73
baitoa 1—155
baku 1—68
Balanocarpus heimii 1—361
BALATA 2—338
balata 1—200
BALAU 1—404, 405
balau, red 1—405
balaustre 1—147
'bald cypress' 2—198
Balfourodendron riedelianum 1—206
balinghasay 2—12
balm poplar 2—183
BALSA 1—143
balsam 2—204
balsam cottonwood 2—183
BALSAM FIR 2—204
balsam poplar 2—183
BAMBOO 2—16
bamboo, spiny 2—16
Bambusa blumeana 2—16
Bambusa vulgaris 2—16
bamura 1—265
banak 1—225; 2—394
bang 1—55
BANGA WANGA 1—20
bangkal 2—23
BANGKIRAI 1—355
banglang 1—314
bangoran 2—30
baniti 2—12
bantulinau 2—28
banutan 2—29
BANUYO 2—17

banzu 1—34
baramanni 1—151
barklak 1—196
BAROMALLI 1—151
barosingsing 2—30
barré 1—19
barwood 1—100
BASRALOCUS 1—152
basralocus 2—339
Bassia ramiflora 2—12
BASSWOOD 2—161
basswood, NG 2—259
BATETE 2—18
BATICULIN 2—18
batikuling 2—18
batlatinau 2—28
BATULINAU 2—28
bea bea 2—304
beach Calophyllum 2—253
bean, Moreton Bay 2—246
bean, red 2—271
bean tree 2—246
'bean, walnut' 2—282
BC hemlock 2—209
BC soft pine 2—217
'BC pine' 2—199
BEECH, AMERICAN 2—162
'beech, Antarctic' 2—276
'beech, Chilean' 1—214
beech, Danish 2—88
beech, English 2—89
BEECH, EUROPEAN 2—88
beech, French 2—88
'beech, hard' 2—273
BEECH, JAPANESE 2—19
'beech, myrtle' 2—275
'beech, negro-head' 2—276
'beech, New Guinea' 2—276
'beech, northern silky' 2—276
'beech, red' 2—273
beech, Siebold's 2—19
'beech, silky' 2—276
'beech, silver' 2—273
beech, Slavonian 2—88
'beech, South American' 1—214
'beech, Southland' 2—273
'beech, tanglefoot' 2—276
'beech, Tasmanian' 2—275
beech, Turkish 2—90
'BEECH, WAU' 2—302
'BEECH, WHITE' 2—303
Beilschmiedia spp 1—58, 157
Beilschmiedia bancroftii 2—295
Beilschmiedia elliptica 2—295
Beilschmiedia insignis 1—377
Beilschmiedia obtusifolia 2—295
Beilschmiedia praecos 1—377
Beilschmiedia taraire 2—295
Beilschmiedia tawa 2—295
Beilschmiedia tonkinensis 1—377

bel-bel 2—63
BELIAN 1—356
Beninwood 1—64
BENGUET PINE 2—63
Bennett's ash 2—261
BENTEAK 1—266
berangan 2—278
bendang 1—416
BERLINIA 1—21
Berlinia bracteosa 1—21
Berlinia confusa 1—21
Berlinia grandiflora 1—21
bété 1—71
bethabara 1—178
Betula alleghaniensis 2—165
Betula lenta 2—165
Betula lutea 2—165
Betula maximowicziana 2—21
Betula papyrifera 2—164, 165
Betula papyrifera var *occidentalis* 2—165
Betula pendula 2—91
Betula pubescens 2—91
betula wood 2—165
bewana 1—192
biar 1—337
bicuiba branca 1—234
bicuiba becuva 1—234
bicuiba vermelha 1—234
big-tooth aspen 2—183
big tree 2—224
bija 1—429
BIJASAL 1—429
bijlhout 1—237
bikal-babui 2—16
bili-budlige 1—277
bili-devdari 1—277
bilinga 1—98
billian 1—356
bilsted 2—171
bindang 1—416
BINGGAS 2—19
BINTANGOR 1—357
BINUANG 1—358
binuang 2—260
BIRCH 2—163
birch, American 2—164, 165
birch, Canadian yellow 2—165
birch, English 2—91
BIRCH, EUROPEAN 2—91
birch, common 2—91
birch, curly 2—92
birch, Finnish 2—91
birch, flame 2—92
birch, hard 2—165
BIRCH, JAPANESE 2—21
birch, masur 2—92
BIRCH, PAPER 2—164
birch, Quebec 2—165
birch, red 2—165
birch, silver 2—91

415

'BOXWOOD, MARACAIBO' 1–154
boxwood, northern yellow 2–281
'BOXWOOD, SAN DOMINGO' 1–155
boxwood, Turkish 2–92
'boxwood, Venezuelan' 1–154
'boxwood, West Indian' 1–154
Brachylaena hutchinsii 1–80
brachystegia 1–93
Brachystegia eurycoma 1–93
Brachystegia fleuryana 1–117
Brachystegia leonensis 1–93
Brachystegia nigerica 1–93
'Brazilian mahogany' 2–333
'Brazilian pine' 1–243
BRAZILWOOD 1–155
breadfruit, wild 2–366
brick-wax tree 2–371
broad-leaved ironbark 2–265
broad-leaved leopard tree 2–261
broad-leaved peppermint 2–280
broad-leaved tea tree 2–296
Brosimum alicastrum 1–217
Brosimum paraense 1–221
Brosimum utile 1–217
brown ash 2–160
brown ebony 2–352
brown gum 2–306
brown oak 2–107
'brown pine, Australian' 2–311
brown terminalia 2–296
brown-top stringybark 2–291
bruinhart 1–142
BRUSH BOX 2–252
Brya ebenus 2–352
bucuvucu 1–234
BUBINGA 1–25
bubungu 2–278
Buchaniana arborescens 2–12
BUCKEYE 2–188
bukal 1–272
bulatinau 2–28
Bulnesia arborea 1–232
BULLET WOOD 1–272
bulletwood 2–338, 345
BULLHOOF 2–343
bullhoof, female 2–345
bullhoof macho 2–343
bullhoof, male 2–343
bull kauri 2–309
bull oak 2–285
bumpy ash 2–261
buna 2–19
buni 2–253
buntugon 2–6
'BUNYA PINE' 2–306, 307
'bunya pine' 2–306
burda 1–322
Burkea africana 1–67
BURMA BLACKWOOD 1–274
'Burma cedar' 1–276

BURMA PADAUK 1–307
Burma sal 1–318
BURMA TULIPWOOD 1–328
Burma yellowheart 1–261
'BURMESE CEDAR' 1–276
Bursera simaruba 2–331
BUSTIC 2–345
buti 2–303
butternut 2–186
buttonwood 2–181
Buxus macowani 1–23
Buxus sempervirens 2–22, 92
Buxus wallichiana 1–271
Byrsonima martinicensis 2–372

C

cabinet cherry 2–166
cabory 2–336
Cabralea cangerana 1–159
CACONNIER ROUGE 2–346
Caesalpinia echinata 1–155
Cairn's pencil cedar 2–278
CALAMANSANAY 2–23
CALANTAS 2–25
calantas, bird's eye 2–26
calantas, curly 2–26
'Californian incense cedar' 2–189
Californian redwood 2–140, 224
Californian sugar pine 2–220
Californian white pine 2–217
Calocedrus decurrens 2–289
CALOPHYLLUM SPECIES 2–253
Calophyllum alatum 2–253
Calophyllum australianum 2–253
Calophyllum brasiliense 1–220
Calophyllum costatum 2–253
Calophyllum inophyllum 1–357, 429;
  2–253
Calophyllum kajewski 2–253
Calophyllum spp. 1–357, 429
Calophyllum tomentosum 1–429; 2–253
Calophyllum vitiense 2–253
Calophyllum wightienum 1–429
Calycophyllum candidissimum 2–354
CAMAGON 2–27, 29
camphor 1–26
CAMPNOSPERMA SPECIES 2–254
Campnosperma auriculata 1–414
campnosperma brevipetiolata 2–254
Campnosperma coriacea 1–414
Campnosperma macrophylla 1–414
Campnosperma montana 1–414
Campnosperma panamensis 1–216
Campnosperma zeylanicum 1–414
Canadian ash 2–161
CANADIAN ASPEN 2–182
CANADIAN POPLAR 2–183
CANADIAN RED PINE 2–218

418

422

EUROPEAN LARCH 2–126
EUROPEAN LIME 2–103
EUROPEAN MAPLE 2–104
European Oak 2–105
EUROPEAN PLANE 2–112
European redwood 2–133
European spruce 2–138
EUROPEAN WALNUT 2–118
European white elm 2–98
European whitewood 2–135, 138
European yew 2–142
Eusideroxylon zwageri 1–356
Euxylaphora paraensis 1–205
evergreen oak 2–109, 110
eyan 1–115
eyen 1–19
eyong 1–109

F

Fagara flava 2–385
Fagara heitzii 1–107
Fagara macrophylla 1–107
Fagaropsis aneolensis 1–62
Fagraea cochinchinensis 1–412
Fagraea fragrans 1–261, 412
Fagraea gigantea 1–412
Fagraea racemosa 1–412
Fagus crenata 2–19
Fagus grandifolia 2–162
Fagus orientalis 2–90
Fagus sylvatica 2–88
Fagus sylvatica varieties 2–90
false acacia 2–115
famelona a grande feuilles 1–61
fangeri 2–271
farinheira 1–164
faro 1–91
farsha 1–188
FAVEIRO 1–168
female bullhoof 2–345
fern-leaved beech 2–90
Ferreirea spectabilis 1–226
field maple 2–105
figueroa 2–333
Fijian kauri 2–310
FIR, ALPINE 2–202
FIR, AMABILIS 2–203
FIR, BALSAM 2–204
'FIR DOUGLAS' 2–124, 199
FIR, GRAND 2–205
fir, grand 2–136
FIR, JAPANESE 2–64
fir, lowland 2–205
fir, mountain 2–202
FIR, NOBLE 2–206
fir, noble 2–137
fir, Pacific silver 2–203
fir, Rocky Mountain 2–202

FIR, SILVER 2–135
FIR, SILVER, HIMALAYAN 1–334
FIR, TRUE 2–201
fir, western balsam 2–202, 205
fir, white 2–202, 203, 205
Fistulina hepatica 2–107, 267
Fitzroya cupressoides 1–240
flambeau rouge 1–151
Flindersia acuminata 2–261
Flindersia australis 2–261
Flindersia bennettiana 2–261
Flindersia bourjotiana 2–261
Flindersia brayleyana 2–262
Flindersia collina 2–261
Flindersia laevicarpa var *heterophylla*
    2–262
Flindersia oxleyana 2–261
Flindersia pimenteliana 2–262
Flindersia pubescens 2–261
Flindersia schottiana 2–261
Flindersia schottiana var *pubescens*
    2–261
FLINDERSIA SPECIES 2–261
Flindersia xanthoxyla 2–261
flindosy 2–261
flooded gum 1–293; 2–251
'forest oak' 2–284
fou 1–87
foxglove tree 2–34
fraké 1–4
framiré 1–52
Fraxinus americana 2–161
Fraxinus excelsior 2–87
Fraxinus mandschurica 2–14
Fraxinus nigra 2–160
Fraxinus pennsylvanica 2–160
FREIJO 1–169
frei jorge 1–169
French plane 2–112
French walnut 2–118, 119
fromager 1–28
fruta colorado 2–394
fu 1–89
fukadi 2–373
fuma 1–28
FUSTIC 2–356

G

GABOON 1–45
gaiac femelle 2–364
galingasing 1–378
galing libor 1–259
gambari 1–48, 294
Gambeya africana 1–61
Gambeya lacourtiana 1–61
Gambeya madagascarensis 1–61
Gambeya subnuda 1–61
gandala 1–318

424

425

426

428

Larix leptolepis 2—65, 127
Larix occidentalis 2—211
larut 1—399
LAUAN 2—36
lauan, dark red, 2—37
lauan, light red 2—37
LAUAN, RED 2—37
LAUAN, WHITE 2—37, 38
laurela 1—187
Laurela aromatica 1—186
Laurela sempervirens 1—186
Laurela serrata 1—187
'LAUREL, CHILEAN' 1—186
laurel, Ecuador 2—352
'laurel, Indian' 1—301
laurier deux pointes 2—372
LAURIER PETITES FEUILLES
    2—362
LAURIER POIVRE 2—363
laurier ti feuilles 2—362
lausi 2—256
LAWSON'S CYPRESS 2—128, 191
Lawson's cypress 2—191
leatherwood 2—261
Lebanon cedar 2—122
lein 1—283
lemesu 1—412
lemon-scented gum 2—288
lemonwood 2—354
leopard ash 2—261
leopard tree, broad-leaved 2—261
leopardwood 2—261
letpan 1—267
letterhout 1—223
letterwood 1—223
leuri 1—333
Libocedrus decurrens 2—189
Licania buxiflora 1—187
Licania densiflora 1—187
Licania laxiflora 1—188
Licania macrophylla 1—187
Licania micrantha 1—187
Licania majuscula 1—188
Licania mollis 1—188
Licania persaudii 1—188
Licania ternatensis 2—341
Licania venosa 1—188
light celtis 2—256
light hopea 2—263
light planchonella 2—281
LIGHT VIROLA 2—394
LIGNUM VITAE 2—364
lignum vitae, bastard 2—364
lignum vitae, genuine 2—364
lignum vitae, Philippine 1—48
lignum vitae, thick-sap 2—364
lignum vitae, thin-sap 2—364
liki 2—286
lilac, Persian 1—303
limba 1—4

limba bariolé 1—5
limba blanc 1—5
limba clair 1—4
limba dark 1—4
limba, light 1—4
limba noir 1—4
LIMBALI 1—59
limbo 1—4
lime, American 2—161
lime, common 2—103
LIME, EUROPEAN 2—103
lime, large-leaved 2—103
lime, small-leaved 2—103
linden 2—103
line 1—189
linggi 2—286
LINGUE 1—189
Liquidambar styraciflua 2—171
Liriodendron tulipifera 2—182
lisak 2—23
litchi 1—189
Lithocarpus perclusa 2—278
Litsea castanea 1—378
Litsea curtisii 1—378
Litsea finestrata 1—378
Litsea ferruginea 1—378
Litsea firma 1—378
Litsea gracilipes 1—378
Litsea grandis 1—378
Litsea machilifolia 1—378
Litsea megacarpa 1—378
Litsea maingayi 1—378
Litsea medularis 1—378
Litsea petiolata 1—378
Litsea robusta 1—378
Litsea tomentosa 1—378
LIUSIN 2—45
live oak 2—181
loblolly pine 2—215
locus 2—353
locust 1—164
locust, black 2—115
LODGEPOLE PINE 2—131, 214
lolagbola 1—110
LOLIONDO 1—60
Lombardy poplar 2—114
London plane 2—112
long-jack 2—261
longleaf 2—215
long leaf pitch pine 2—215
long leaf pitch pine, Caribbean 2—397
longui noir 1—61
LONGUI ROUGE 1—61
Lophira alata 1—41
Lophopetalum javanicum 1—397
Lophopetalum maingayi 1—397
Lophopetalum pachyphyllum 1—397
Lophopetalum pallidum 1—397
Lophopetalum subovatum 1—397
Lophopetalum wighteanum 1—397

430

432

meranti, white 1—385, 386, 388
MERAWAN 1—390
merawan 2—263
MERBAU 1—391; 2—51
merbau 2—270
MERPAU 1—393
MERSAWA 1—393
messmate 2—291
messmate stringybark 2—291
MESUA 1—304
Mesua ferrea 1—304
Metrosideros queenslandica 2—272
Metrosideros robusta 2—272
'Mexican white birch' 2—332
Mezilaurus itauba 1—180
Mezzettia leptopoda 1—380
mfu 1—62
mfuari 1—40
Michelia champaca 1—279
Micropholis gardnerianum 1—172
milky pine 2—305
Millettia laurentii 1—116
Millettia stuhlmannii 1—116
Mimusops bidentata 1—200; 2—338
Mimusops djave 1—73
Mimusops elengi 1—272
Mimusops hexandra 1—273
Mimusops littoralis 1—272
Mimusops toxisperma 1—73
Mindanao white lauan 2—37
Mindoro pine 2—64
mingerhout 1—76
minzu 1—44
mirabow 1—391
miro 2—313
MISSANDA 1—72
Mitragyna ciliata 1—3
Mitragyna stipulosa 1—3
mkangazi 1—64
mkondekonde 1—75
mkora 1—8
mkufi 1—34
mlimangombe 1—104
mninga 1—82
MOABI 1—73
moboron 1—10
mockernut hickory 2—172
mofoumou 1—45
mogno 2—194, 369
mohwa 1—272
MOLAVE 2—52
monko 1—40
Monocarpia marginalis 1—380
Monopetalanthus spp. 1—113
Monterey pine 1—122
moonba 1—235
moordooke 2—278
MORA 1—202
morabukea 1—203
Mora excelsa 1—202

Mora gonggrijpii 1—203
moral 2—356
moral bobo 1—174
moral comido de mono 1—174
moral fino 2—356
moreira 1—55
Moreton bay bean 2—246
Moreton Bay chestnut 2—246
morinda 1—334, 335
moroti 1—206
Morus mesozygia 1—37
mountain ash 2—292
mountain fir 2—202
mountain mahoe 2—367
mountain spruce 2—227
MOUVENDO 1—33
movingui 1—19
mowana 1—76
mpewere 1—34
mpingo 1—22
mringaringa 1—31
MTAMBARA 1—74
muave 1—72
muchai 1—77
mudengwa 1—29
MUERI 1—75
muermo 1—232
mugaita 1—104
mugga 2—265
mugis 2—11
mugona 1—31
MUGONHA 1—76
MUGONYONE 1—77
mugunya 1—76
MUHIMBI 1—79
muhindi 1—79
muhugwe 1—80
MUHUHU 1—80
muhunya 1—83
muirapiranga 1—221
MUIRATINGA 1—203
mujiwa 1—3
mujua 1—14
mukali 1—15
mukalati 1—67
mukangu 1—15
mukarakati 1—62
mukongu 1—40
MUKULUNGU 1—81
mukumari 1—31
mukushi 1—111
mukusi 1—111
mukwa 1—82
muna 1—15, 70
munara 1—72
munganga 1—26
mungaringare 1—77
mungenge 1—43.
mungoma 1—31
MUNINGA 1—82

olonvogo 1—107
omo 1—31
OMU 1—96
onglen 1—356
OPEPE 1—98
Oregon alder 2 159
Oregon maple 2 176
'Oregon pine' 2 199
oriental plane 2 112
oriental wood 2 282
oro 1—16
Ormosia dasycarpa 2—346
Ormosia monosperma 2—346
OSAGE ORANGE 2—188
osan 1—15
osiers 2—120
Ostrya virginiana 2 174
otie 1—54
otutu 1—35
OVANGKOL 1 99
ovoga 1—102
ovoué 1—35
owewe 1—44
Oxandra lanceolata 2—361
Oxystigma oxyphyllum 1—110
OZIGO 1—32
oziya 1—91

P

Pacific hemlock 2 209
Pacific maple 2 176
Pacific silver fir 2 203
Pacific walnut 2 276
pacuru 1—204
padang 2—395
padauk 1—354
PADAUK, AFRICAN 1—100
PADAUK, ANDAMAN 1—305
PADAUK, BURMA 1—307
PADAUK, SOLOMONS 2—286
padauk, Solomons 2—54
pagoda tree 2 59
pagura bunu 2 253
Pahudia rhomboidea 2—60
pakoelle 1—204
PAKURI 1—204
pala 1—273, 308
Palaquium ahernianum 2—56
Palaquium clarkeanum 1—395
Palaquium cuneatum 2—56
Palaquium cryptocarifolium 1—395
Palaquium ellipticum 1—308
Palaquium erythrospermum 2—278
Palaquium firmum 2 278
Palaquium foxworthyi 2—56
Palaquium galactoxylum 2—278
Palaquium gigantifolium 2—56
Palaquium gutta 1 395

Palaquium herveyi 1—395
Palaquium hexandrum 1—395
Palaquium hispidum 1—395
Palaquium luzoniensis 2—56
Palaquium maingayi 1—395
Palaquium merrillii 2—56
Palaquium microphyllum 1—395
Palaquium obovatum 1—395
Palaquium philippense 2—56
Palaquium ridleyi 1—359
Palaquium rostratum 1 395
Palaquium semaram 1—395
PALAQUIUM SPECIES 2—56, 278
Palaquium stehlini 2—278
Palaquium stellatum 1—359
Palaquium tenuipetiolatum 2—56
Palaquium walsurifolium 1—395
Palaquium xanthochymum 1—395
PALDAO 2—57
PALI 1—308
palissander 1—315
palissandre du Brazil 1—315
palissandre du Congo 1—116
PALM, COCONUT 2—258
palo blanco 1—154; 2—376
palo de chancho 2—377
palo de hierro 2—48
palo de oro 1—223
palo machete 1—231
palomaria 2—18
palo muerto 1—204
palo negro 2—27, 28
palo santo 2—364
paloto 2—278
palu 1—273
paluahan 2—6
PANAKKA 1—309
panchonta 1—308
panga panga 1—116
PAPER BIRCH 2—164
papo 1—27
papri 1—271
Papua walnut 2—276
Parahancornia amapa 1—166
'Para mahogany' 2—333
'PARANA PINE' 1—243
Para rubber tree 1—174
Parashorea lucida 1—389
Parashorea malaanonan 1—415; 2—37, 40
Parashorea plicata 1—415; 2—40
Parashorea stellata 1—326
Parashorea tomentella 1—415
Paratecoma peroba 1—238
Para wood 1—155
parina 2—63
Parinarium corymbosum 2—45
Parinarium laurinum 2—46
Partocarpus bracteatus 1—414
Partocarpus venenosus 1—414

PUSSUR WOOD 1—311
Putt's pine 2—261
Pycnanthus angolensis 1—54
Pygeum africanum 1—75
pyin 1—312
PYINMA 1—314
pyinma, Andaman 1—315
PYINKADO 1—312
Pyrus communis 2—112

Q

Qualea albiflora 1—198
Qualea coerula 1—198
Qualea glaberrima 1—198
Qualea rosea 1—198
QUARUBA 1—212; 2—377
quaruba jasmirana 1—212
quatamba 1—206
Quebec birch 2—165
Quebec spruce 2—225
Quebec yellow pine 2—222
QUEENSLAND KAURI 2—309
Queensland maple 2—262
'Queensland pine' 2—306
Queensland silver ash 2—261
'QUEENSLAND WALNUT' 2—282
Quercus acuta 2—55
Quercus alba 2—178
Quercus borealis 2—178
Quercus castaneaefolia 2—111
Quercus cerris 2—109
Quercus dentata 2—55
Quercus falcata var *falcata* 2—178
Quercus falcata var *pagodaefolia* 2—178
Quercus gilva 2—55
Quercus glandulifera 2—55
Quercus ilex 2—109
Quercus lyrata 2—178
Quercus michauxii 2—178
Quercus mongolica var *grosseserrata*
   2—55
Quercus montana 2—178
Quercus myrsinaefolia 2—55
Quercus pedunculata 2—105
Quercus petraea 2—105
Quercus phillyraeoides 2—55
Quercus prinus 2—178
Quercus robur 2—105
Quercus rubra 2—178
Quercus sessiliflora 2—105
Quercus shumardii 2—178
Quercus suber 2—110
Quercus virginiana 2—181
quinillo 2—335
quira 2—335

R

RADIATA PINE 1—122
rain-tree 2—383
RAMIN 2—400
ramin telur 1—400
RAPANEA 1—104
Rapanea rhododendroides 1—104
RATA, NORTHERN 2—272
RAULI 1—214
raumuga 2—281
RED ALDER 2—159
red ash 2—160
red balau 1—405; 2—42
red bean 2—271
'red beech' 2—272
red-brown terminalia 2—296
red cedar 2—255
'red cedar' 2—195
'red cedar, eastern' 2—193
'RED CEDAR, WESTERN' 2—195
red deal 2—133
red gombo 2—331
RED GUM, AMERICAN 2—171
red gum 2—284
red hickory 2—173
red ironbark 2—264
RED LAUAN 2—37
red lustre 2—298
RED OAK 2—178
red oak 2—105, 111
red pine 2—133
'red pine' 2—314
RED PINE CANADIAN 2—218
RED PINE, JAPANESE 2—66
red planchonella 2—281
RED RIVER GUM 2—284
red selangan batu 1—404; 2—42
RED SPRUCE 2—227
red sterculia 1—108
red stringybark 2—289
red touriga 2—253
redwood, Andaman 1—305
redwood, Archangel 2—133
redwood, Baltic 2—133
redwood, Californian 2—140, 224
redwood, European 2—133
redwood, Finnish 2—133
redwood, Polish 2—133
redwood, Russian 2—133
redwood, Siberian 2—133
redwood, Swedish 2—133
RENGAS 1—402
reriang 1—412
RESAK 1—403
RESOLU 2—378
rewar 1—334
'RHODESIAN TEAK' 1—111
rian 1—273
Richeria grandis 2—340

442

443

445

white gum 2—301
white hemlock 2—207
white hickory 2—173
white ironbark 2—305
WHITE LAUAN 2—38
'white mahogany' 2—376
'white mahogany, Indian' 1—276
white mountain ash 2—292
WHITE OAK 2—179
white oak 2—108
'white oak' 2—276
white pliver 2—373
white pear 1—77
WHITE PEROBA 1—238
'WHITE PINE' 2—313
white pine 2—138, 222
white pine, Californian 2—217
white pine, eastern 2—222
white pine, Malabar 1—430
'white pine, New Zealand' 2—311, 313
white pine, northern 2—222
WHITE PINE, WESTERN 2—221
white planchonella 2—281
white poplar 2—114
white salmon gum 2—301
WHITE SERAYA 1—415
WHITE SIRIS 1—322
white sterculia 1—109
white stringybark 2—289
WHITE TABEBUIA 2—388
white tola 1—10
white-top stringybark 2—292
whitewood 2—135, 138
WHITEWOOD, AMERICAN 2—186
whitewood, Baltic 2—138
whitewood, canary 2—186
whitewood, Finnish 2—138
whitewood, Russian 2—138
whitewood, Swedish 2—138
whitewood, Yugoslavian 2—138
wild breadfruit 2—366
wild cherry 2—94
wild tamarind 2—375
wilg 2—120
Wilkinson's stringybark 2—290
WILLOW 2—61, 120
WILLOW, BLACK 2—189
willow, close-bark 2—120
willow, common 2—120
willow, crack 2—120, 122
willow, cricket-bat 2—120
willow, white 2—120
wishmore 1—84
witte mora 1—202
woollybutt 2—292
wowoli 1—290
wych elm 2—98, 99

X

Xanthostemon verdugonianus 2—48
Xylia dolabriformis 1—312
Xylia xylocarpa 1—312
Xylopia ferruginea 1—380
Xylopia fusca 1—380

Y

yaba 2—335
YACAL 2—29
yahu 1—225
yama-zakura 2—26
yamane 1—48
yang 1—295
yarri 2—247
yaya 2—361
yeddo spruce 2—66
yellow baticulin 2—18
YELLOW BIRCH 2—165
'YELLOW CEDAR' 2—196
'yellow cedar, Pacific Coast' 2—196
yellow cypress 2—197
yellow deal 2—133
YELLOW GUM 2—305
yellowheart 1—412
yellowheart, Burma 1—261
yellow northern boxwood 2—281
yellow nut 2—295
YELLOW PINE 2—222
YELLOW PINE, SIBERIAN 2—135
yellow poplar 2—186
yellow poui 1—178
yellow sanders 2—385
yellow spruce 2—227
yellow stringybark 2—290
yellow teak 2—281
yellow terminalia 2—296
yellow walnut 2—295
YELLOWWOOD 2—399
yellowwood 1—120; 2—261
yellowood ash 2—261
yemane 1—294
yemene 1—48
yemeri 2—377
yemoke 2—377
yen-ju 2—59
yepi 1—262
yerma 1—263
YEW 2—142
yew, common 2—142
yew, European 2—142
yezo matsu 2—66
yindaik 1—274
yinma 1—281
YOKEWOOD 2—396
yomhom 1—276
yon 1—265

Z